CHOOSING AND USING

paper

FOR GREAT GRAPHIC DESIGN

RotoVision

A RotoVision Book

Published and distributed by RotoVision SA
Route Suisse 9
CH-1295 Mies
Switzerland

RotoVision SA
Sales and Editorial Office
Sheridan House, 114 Western Road
Hove BN3 1DD, UK
Tel: +44 (0)1273 72 72 68
Fax: +44 (0)1273 72 72 69
www.rotovision.com

First published in hardback 2007
This edition published 2011

10 9 8 7 6 5 4 3 2 1
ISBN: 978-2-88893-164-5

Art Director: Tony Seddon
Design and artwork: Keith Stephenson and Spike at Absolute Zero°
Additional photography: Jane Waterhouse

Reprographics in Singapore by ProVision Pte.
Tel: +65 6334 7720
Fax: +65 6334 7721

Printed in China by Midas Printing International Ltd.

CHOOSING AND USING paper FOR GREAT GRAPHIC DESIGN

MARK HAMPSHIRE + KEITH STEPHENSON

contents

introduction

Notwithstanding the rise of digital media, paper and print techniques remain at the heart of many graphic-design projects. From glossy corporate brochure to gritty fanzine, paper tends to act as the default medium—often used in conjunction with electronic forms of communication. When approaching the design of a piece of printed communication, inspiration can come from the availability of a particular paper or the development of an innovative printing or finishing technique. Some designers benefit from working in consultancies with the support of a dedicated production department—materials gurus who keep abreast of the latest innovations and can offer solutions for every conceivable print project. For those who do not enjoy this resource, we hope that this book will offer inspiration for a diverse range of paper-focused design briefs.

Conceived as a comprehensive source book for any designer working with paper, the book comprises two key aspects: inspiration and information. For inspiration, there are examples of recent work in paper from designers around the world. Projects have been sourced based on the premise that the choice of a specific paper, print, or finishing technique has facilitated or enhanced the end result. Then there is information to help with the basics of planning and executing a project in paper, from fold styles to paper sizes, binding techniques to packaging nets.

Because the book is intended to focus on the practical aspects of choosing and using paper, we have focused on materials and techniques. We have purposely avoided the rich and fascinating subject of the history of paper. We could not do it justice here, and there is much source material for those who want to pursue the subject. We have, however, tried to source projects from beyond the strict discipline of graphic design. So, art, fashion, and product design all feature, demonstrating the warmth and versatility of the medium. Projects are grouped by type, technique, or theme.

PUSHING THE BOUNDARIES showcases projects that demonstrate the versatility of paper and breadth of materials and paper-finishing techniques available to today's designer.

CORPORATE LITERATURE is one of the most common applications of paper-based design. From annual report to brand building, this chapter covers diverse approaches to corporate communication.

MAILERS + PR pieces require eye-catching solutions to ensure distinctiveness. The examples here all use paper to achieve arresting results.

PAPER MANUFACTURERS' PROMOTIONS offer inspiration, not only because of the new and innovative materials they demonstrate, but also for the creative freedom with which many designers approach these communication pieces.

IDENTITY + SELF-PROMOTION explores various approaches to branding. Many of the examples are from businesses and individuals in creative fields, which is why they display a high degree of innovation.

PACKAGING + PRODUCTS are paper staples, so here we've attempted to show a selected number of exciting, sometimes unexpected, uses of paper and card.

ONE-OFF CREATIONS pays homage to craft and fine art. In this chapter we step outside the strict graphic-design arena and view some exceptional examples of high-concept creativity in paper.

LIMITED BUDGETS can sometimes govern the direction of a design brief. Here we show how paper choice can be the key to overcoming financial constraints without creative compromise.

SURFACE EFFECTS + THE POWER OF TOUCH demonstrates paper's tactile, often sensual, qualities.

3D CONCEPTS can be achieved through intricate paper engineering, by folding, perforating, and die-cutting. Here we show some of the most adventurous and successful examples.

We have grouped information in chapters where it has most relevance to the showcased examples. So you will find diagrams of pocket folders and binding styles in the chapter on corporate literature, while folding styles, though having wide-ranging applications, are most appropriate in the chapter on mailers and PR.

Standard packaging nets feature in the packaging and products chapter. Other information—paper sizes, a glossary, and information on featured designers and papers—is grouped together in the final chapter.

Icons highlight specific finishes or techniques utilized in a project, so offering a quick overview and helping you to cross-reference work. Thus, if you have a particular interest in work on recycled stock, the recycled icon will help you to pinpoint those projects of interest, however they have been categorized.

Finally, we have given measurements in both metric and avoirdupois (as per country of origin first), but paper weights are not converted, so we use lb weights for US and gsm for Europe.

A GUIDE TO THE SYMBOLS USED IN THIS BOOK

3D ELEMENTS

CUTTING TECHNIQUES

BINDING

INTERESTING SURFACE EFFECT, EITHER PRINT OR UV VARNISHING

EMBOSSING, DEBOSSING, HAMMERPRESS, OR LETTERPRESS

RECYCLED STOCK

FOLDING TECHNIQUES

HAND-FINISHING

PERFORATIONS

CHAPTER 1

pushing the boundaries

125
099
39
30°

PUSHING THE BOUNDARIES

Hyperkit

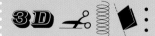

PROJECT LIFE SIZE BY HYPERKIT
DESIGNER HYPERKIT
CLIENT VICTIONARY

PAPER FACTS:
STOCK GENERAL PAPER STOCK: UNCOATED PAPER 140lb; POSTCARD, STENCIL, POP-UP DESK-TIDY: CHROMOLUX 300lb
SIZE 210 × 275mm (8¼ × 10¹³⁄₁₆in)
PRINT TECHNIQUES FOUR-COLOR OFFSET LITHO, SILKSCREEN
ADDITIONAL TECHNIQUE DIE-CUT

PRINTER PERFECT ART PRINTING CO.
BINDING SEWN BOUND

SPECIAL CONSIDERATIONS:
"Our aim was to produce a book that could be used in everyday life Throughout you will find items such as a penpot, a photo album, a stencil, and place settings. There are areas that the reader can change and adapt to suit them. *Life Size* uses a number of different paper stocks that work to help bring these ideas to life."

Tim Balaam, Hyperkit, UK

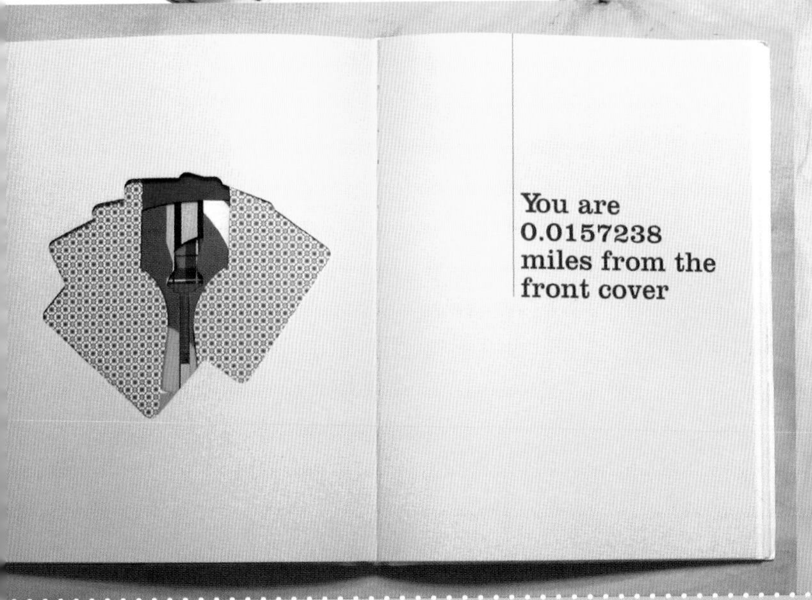
You are
0.0157238
miles from the
front cover

Created to change perceptions of how a book is used and how it behaves, *Life Size* is a collection of investigations into and fascinations with the scale of objects. It questions how the shape and size of a book governs the way its contents are presented. The book takes as inspiration home-improvement and homecraft manuals. Cutting and folding techniques are employed throughout in the highly creative presentation of a host of disparate objects—buttons, a die-cut mug, a set of perforated pull-out postcards—all presented at their actual size.

The book's dimensions dictate how objects are displayed, whether on one page or across a series of pages. By showing these objects at life size within the format of the book, the reader is encouraged to engage with them in a different way. Readers also encounter a number of objects that can be used within real-life situations, such as a place setting at a dining table. By incorporating such objects, the designers question the function of the book and push the boundaries of what a book can be.

Henry Hobson

PROJECT ABOLISH THE FOREST BOOK
DESIGNER HENRY HOBSON
CLIENT SELF-INITIATED

PAPER FACTS:
STOCK GF SMITH COLORPLAN FOREST GREEN 135gsm
SIZE 148.5 × 210mm (5⅞ × 8¼in)
PRINT TECHNIQUE COVER: SILKSCREEN WITH CEMENT—INK REPLACED WITH CONCRETE
PRINTER SELF-PRINTED
BINDING FRENCH FOLD, PERFECT BOUND

SPECIAL CONSIDERATIONS:
"The fine Portland cement was mixed with a textile base and printed with standard mesh screens. The textile base gave it the flexibility that paper demands yet cement does not traditionally allow."

Henry Hobson, UK

To accompany Abolish the Forest, a movie he produced in conjunction with illustrator Adam Hayes, Henry Hobson reflected the provocative title with an equally radical solution. Screenprinting with cement on virgin paper stock was the perfect metaphor for concreting over virgin forests.

The promotional material comprises a book and poster. The book catalogs the travel journal, research material, and background to the movie and the poem it animates.

The innovative technique was key to the project. By printing with such a destructive medium, Hobson felt he was able to convey perfectly the inherent tension in the title. In this way, medium and message are cleverly combined.

Printing the piece himself, Hobson's diligent research into the optimum silkscreen method to achieve flexibility, superfine image reproduction, and color matching paid off with an Innovations in Concrete award, sponsored by the British Cement Association.

GUM

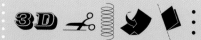

PROJECT GUM 2
DESIGNERS KEVIN GRADY, COLIN METCALF
CLIENT SELF-INITIATED

PAPER FACTS:
STOCK COVER: SMART PAPERS, CARNIVAL HOPSACK STELLAR WHITE 90lb; TEXT: PORCELAIN GLOSS TEXT 100lb AND COUGAR OPAQUE SMOOTH TEXT 100lb
SIZE 5 × 7in (127 × 178mm)

PRINT TECHNIQUES COVER: FOUR-COLOR PRINT WITH OVERALL SATIN AQUEOUS; PAGES 1–132: FOUR-COLOR PRINT + PMS 504 WITH OVERALL GLOSS AQUEOUS; PAGES 133–184: FOUR-COLOR PRINT + PMS 504 WITH OVERALL SATIN AQUEOUS
ADDITIONAL TECHNIQUES CARDBOARD DIE-CUT, PERFORATED, AND FOLDED TO MAKE AN OUTER BOX WITH A GUMBALL DISPENSER AT THE BOTTOM
PRINTER THE POND-EKBERG COMPANY
BINDING PERFECT BOUND

GUM is an award-winning art and design collectible, published occasionally by design duo Kevin Grady and Colin Metcalf. Intended to appeal to the creative inner child in its readers, it is described by its creators as "a piñata filled with Pop-Art goodies." The materials used and the print and finishing techniques employed all work together to achieve the playful effect. The outer box holds a gumball dispenser at the bottom. Open up the box and a wealth of goodies is revealed—including the *GUM* book, an activity book, a View-Master reel, ten trading cards, Puma candy gummies, and three gumballs.

After printing, the paper was too thick for the size of the signatures that were to be used in the book, making the folding and binding very difficult. The team overcame this production issue with advice from an experienced binder.

On their release, *GUM* and its follow-up *GUM2* were both met with fanatical praise, being described by *Anthem Magazine* as "perhaps the most innovative product to hit the street market in years."

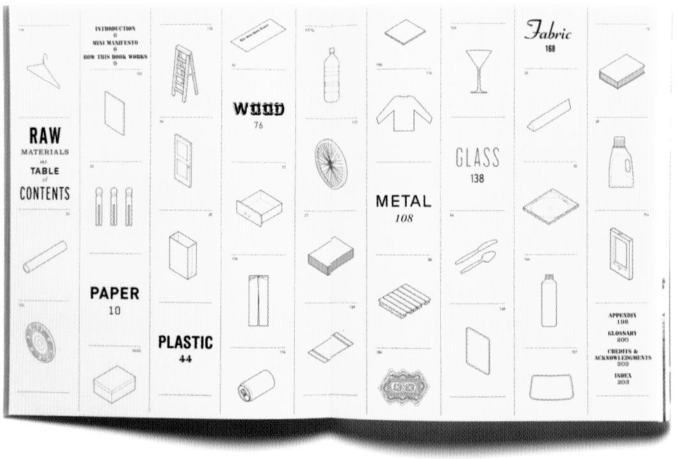

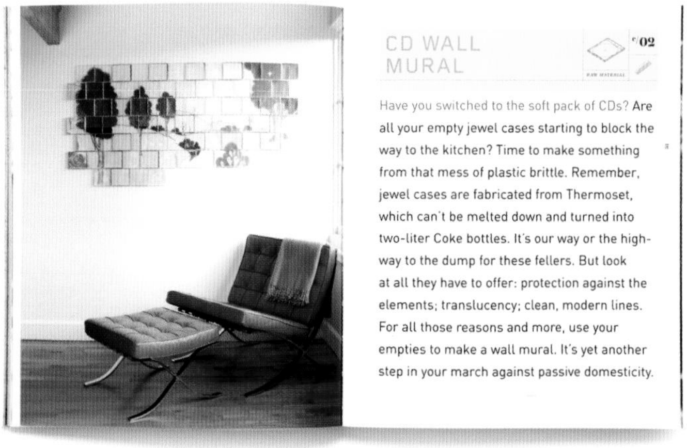

CD WALL MURAL
02
Have you switched to the soft pack of CDs? Are all your empty jewel cases starting to block the way to the kitchen? Time to make something from that mess of plastic brittle. Remember, jewel cases are fabricated from Thermoset, which can't be melted down and turned into two-liter Coke bottles. It's our way or the high-way to the dump for these fellers. But look at all they have to offer: protection against the elements; translucency; clean, modern lines. For all those reasons and more, use your empties to make a wall mural. It's yet another step in your march against passive domesticity.

Volume Inc.

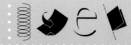

PROJECT READYMADE: HOW TO MAKE (ALMOST) EVERYTHING
DESIGNER VOLUME INC.
CREATIVE DIRECTORS ADAM BRODSLEY, ERIC HEIMAN, ELIZABETH FITZGIBBONS, AKIKO ITO
ILLUSTRATOR KATE FRANCIS
PHOTOGRAPHER JEFFERY CROSS
CLIENTS READYMADE/SHOSHANA BERGER, GRACE HAWTHORNE

PAPER FACTS:
STOCK COVER: EXPOSED CHIPBOARD; INSIDE: JAPANESE WHITE A PAPER MATTE 140gsm
SIZE 7½ × 9in (191 × 229mm)
PRINT TECHNIQUE FOUR-COLOR OFFSET LITHO
ADDITIONAL TECHNIQUES COVER: FOIL STAMPING, BLIND DEBOSSING, ADHESIVE STICKERS (PRINTED OFFSET), SILKSCREENED TAPE BINDING
PUBLISHER CLARKSON POTTER
PRINTER ASIA PACIFIC OFFSET
BINDING SECTION-SEWN, THREE-PIECE CASE WITH EXPOSED FRONT AND BACK BOARD; SPINE IS IMITATION CLOTH

SPECIAL CONSIDERATIONS:
"Since the book's content was structured much more like a magazine, we had to free ourselves from the trappings of traditional book design, including how we considered the packaging. We put a lot of our money into the cover packaging, which uses foil stamping, blind debossing, adhesive stickers, silkscreened tape binding, and exposed chipboard, so we had to settle for simple white matte paper and four-color offset printing on the inside."

Eric Heiman, Volume Inc., US

Written by the cofounders of US magazine *ReadyMade*, this book bears a family resemblance to the magazine, but with a distinct visual identity. Based on the reuse of six key building materials, the design nonetheless stays away from the usual brown recycled-paper look of environmentalism. The book itself is reusable: the spine doubles as a ruler and a perforated back panel becomes a picture frame. Readers are invited to interact by signing the *ReadyMade* manifesto, proposing their own projects, and suggesting alternative uses for the book.

Yang Rutherford

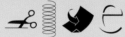

PROJECT CECIL GEE LOOKBOOK SPRING/SUMMER 2007
DESIGNERS JIMMY YANG, TOM RAPACIOLI at YANG RUTHERFORD
CLIENT MOSS BROS GROUP

PAPER FACTS:
STOCK BOOK: INCADA SILK 350gsm
BAND: CHALLENGER OFFSET 190gsm
SIZE 190 × 130mm (7½ × 5⅛in)
PRINT TECHNIQUES BOOK: FOUR-COLOR OFFSET LITHO ONE SIDE WITH SPECIAL GRAY ON THE REVERSE
BAND: SPECIAL GRAY ONE SIDE ONLY

ADDITIONAL TECHNIQUES ALL BOOK PAGES MATTE-LAMINATED ONE SIDE AND DIE-CUT TO GIVE ROUND CORNERS; FRONT PAGE SILVER-FOIL BLOCKED
PRINTER PEARL PRINT
BINDING COLLATED INTO ORDER, DRILLED WITH ONE HOLE IN THE TOP LEFT-HAND CORNER, BOUND TOGETHER WITH NICKEL BINDING SCREWS. CREASED IN FOUR POSITIONS, TRIMMED, WRAPPED AROUND THE BOOK, AND TAPED IN ONE POSITION TO HOLD CLOSED

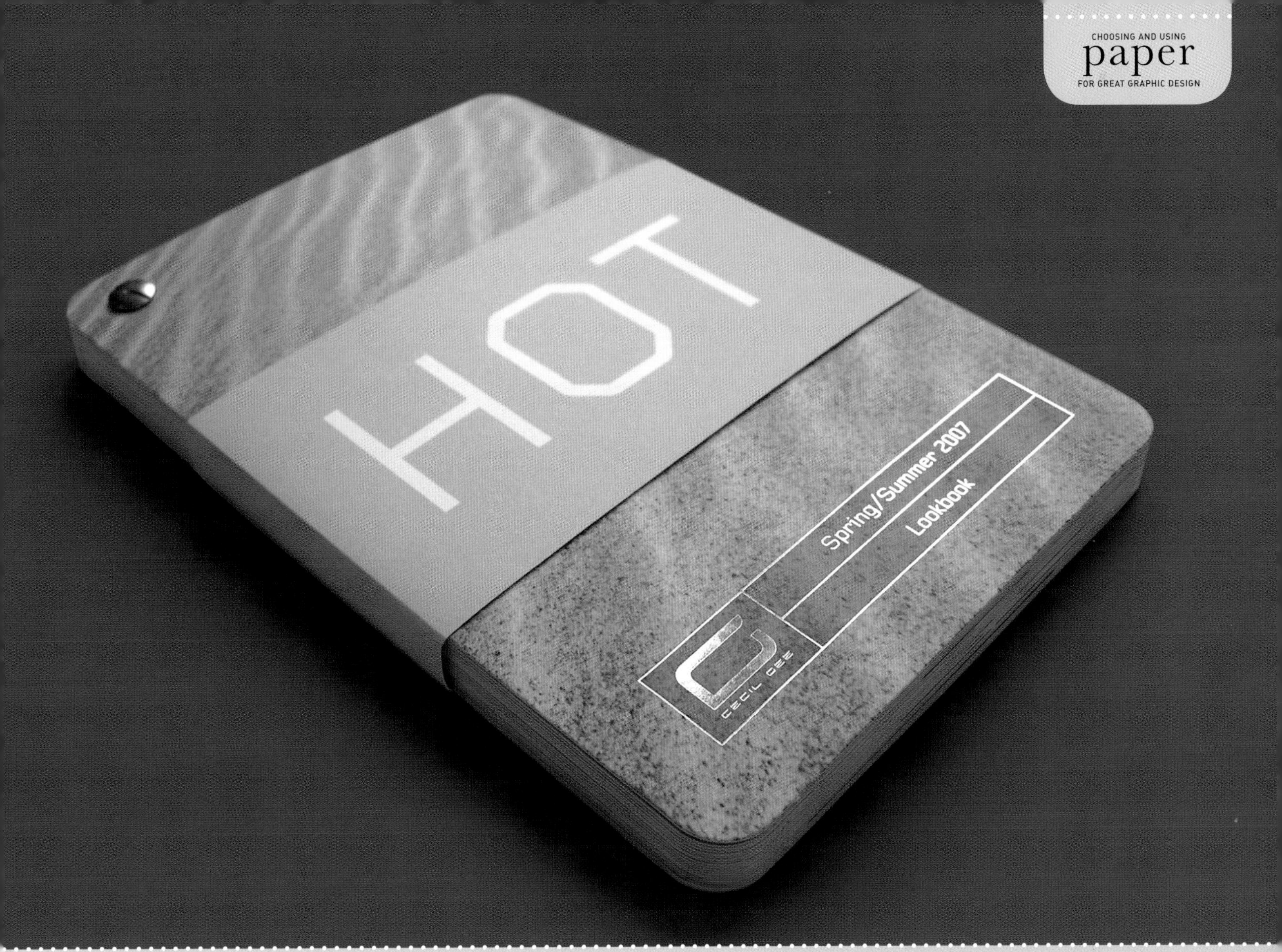

Achieving standout requires out-of-the-box thinking if you don't want your mailer filed in the circular filing-cabinet—in this case, "out-of-the-book" thinking. International creative consultants Yang Rutherford eschewed the usual brochure solution when conceiving the design for Cecil Gee's Spring/Summer 2007 Lookbook in favor of a striking swatch book that is as hot as its printed bellyband claims.

The unconventional approach started with the choice of paper. The book uses 350gsm Incada Silk, a boxboard usually used for packaging. Coated one side with a matte reverse, the stock offers the book a substantial and tactile quality, with a different effect created on each side. A host of finishes offer depth and appeal, from the die-cut rounded corners to nickel binding screws that allow a swivel action. Eye-catching silver-foil blocking adorns the cover.

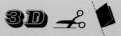

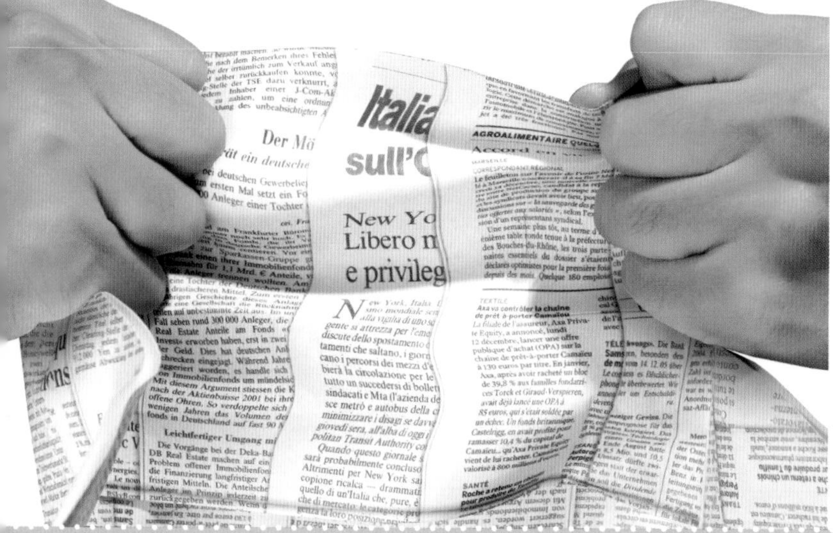

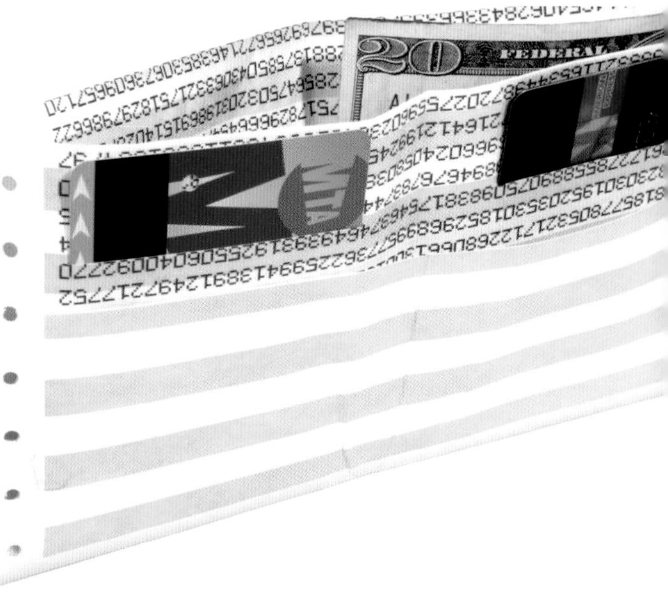

PUSHING THE BOUNDARIES

Terrence Kelleman

3D

PROJECT PAR AVION WALLETS
DESIGNER TERRENCE KELLEMAN
CLIENT DYNOMIGHTY

PAPER FACTS:
STOCK TYVEK®
SIZE 3¼ × 8in (83 × 203mm) OPEN

SPECIAL CONSIDERATIONS:
"Stitching is always the first thing that rips in a wallet, so I designed this wallet without any parts or stitches. It is simply one single sheet of hi-tech Tyvek®, folded to create this seamless design."

Terrence Kelleman, Dynomighty, US

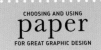

The Par Avion wallet is intended to evoke that youthful excitement you felt when you first received an international mail envelope. The wallet is made from Tyvek®, a material that feels like paper, but is actually made of thousands of long plastic fibers, creating a surface that is lightweight yet durable, superthin while also tear-resistant. As it contains 25% postconsumer recycled content, products made from Tyvek® are also environmentally friendly and can be recycled.

The clever construction of the wallet from a single folded sheet offers a number of features. The tucked-in flaps allow the wallet to expand gradually with use, providing extra room as needed—capacity can expand from 5 to 25 credit cards. The flaps also offer a secret storage area. The Tyvek® will wear and become supple, but will not break. And because Tyvek® is water-resistant, it will protect against the humidity inside the pocket that destroys the leather of a traditional wallet.

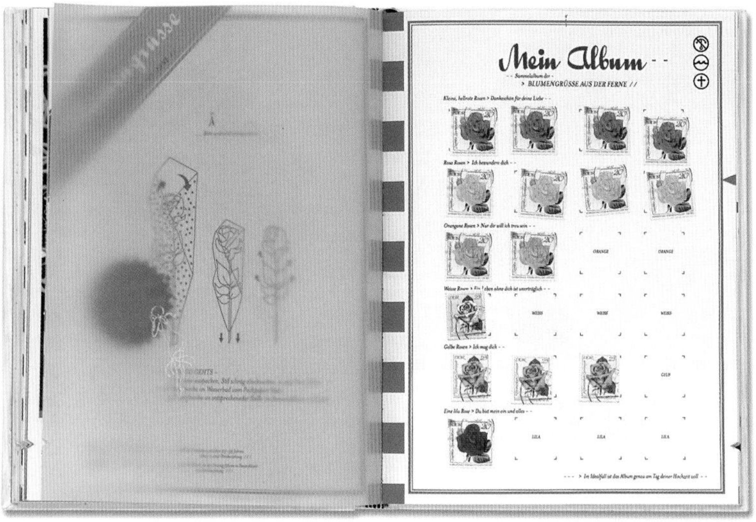

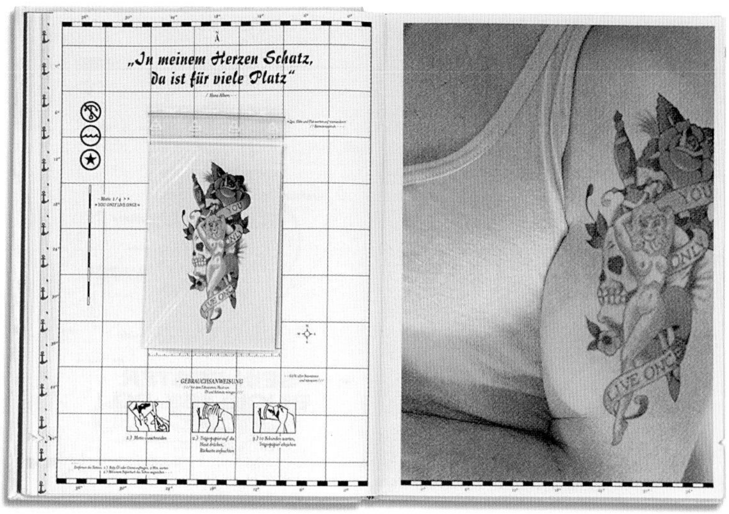

Jenny Orel

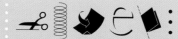

PROJECT LOGBOOK OF LOVE
DESIGNER JENNY OREL
CLIENT STATE ACADEMY OF ART AND DESIGN, STUTTGART

PAPER FACTS:
STOCK SCHNEIDERSÖHNE LUXOSATIN 135gsm, GMUND ALEZAN CULT GAZELLE 200gsm, ZANDERS EFALIN FEINLEINEN 120gsm, ZANDERS SPECTRAL 100gsm, GMUND TRANSPARENCE FLEUR 80gsm, DECORATIVE CAKE PAPERS
SIZE 180 × 240mm (7$\frac{1}{16}$ × 9$\frac{1}{2}$in)

PRINT TECHNIQUE SCREENPRINT
ADDITIONAL TECHNIQUES PERFORATION, EMBOSSING, DIE-CUTTING, MIXED PAPERS, HOT-FOIL STAMPING, PACKAGED IN WATERPROOF BAG
PRINTER DRUCKEREI AICKELIN
BINDING CASEBOUND

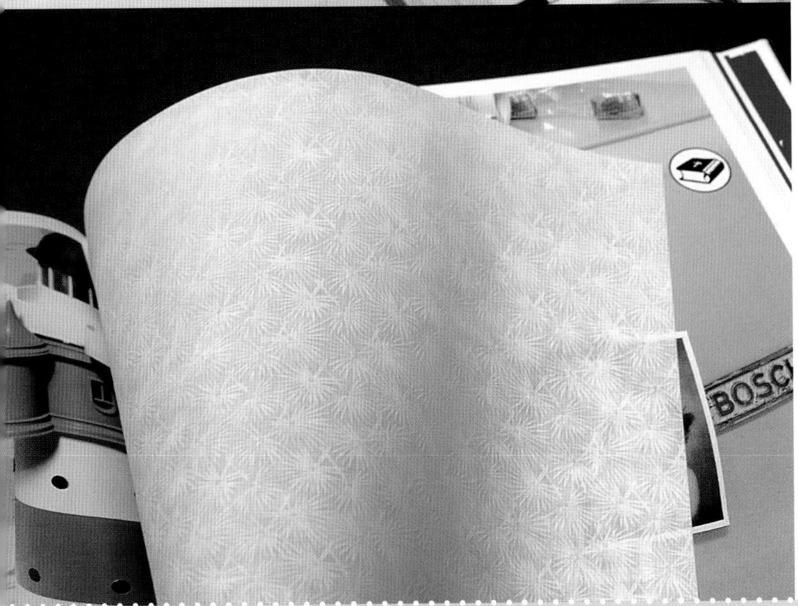

"My bounty is as boundless as the sea, my love as deep," wrote William Shakespeare in *Romeo and Juliet*. Fascinated with the many expressions in art and literature connecting love with the sea, Jenny Orel created a book entitled Verliebt, Verlobt, Verheiratet—Logbuch der Liebe (In Love, Engaged, Married—Logbook of Love) for her diploma thesis in Communication Design at the State Academy of Art and Design, Stuttgart, Germany. The book's layout and graphic style was developed based on the different symbols and graphic elements associated with love and the sea.

Using a whole range of print and finishing techniques, including perforation, embossing, die-cutting in various shapes, stickers, and hot-foil stamping, Jenny chose different paper types to communicate a number of themes. Zanders Efalin Feinleinen gives the impression of a painting on canvas; Gmund Transparence Fleur simulates the parchment interleaves of an old family album. Even decorative cake paper is used to give a sense of celebration. And to complete the sea theme and emphasize the preciousness of its paper construction, the book is packaged in a waterproof bag.

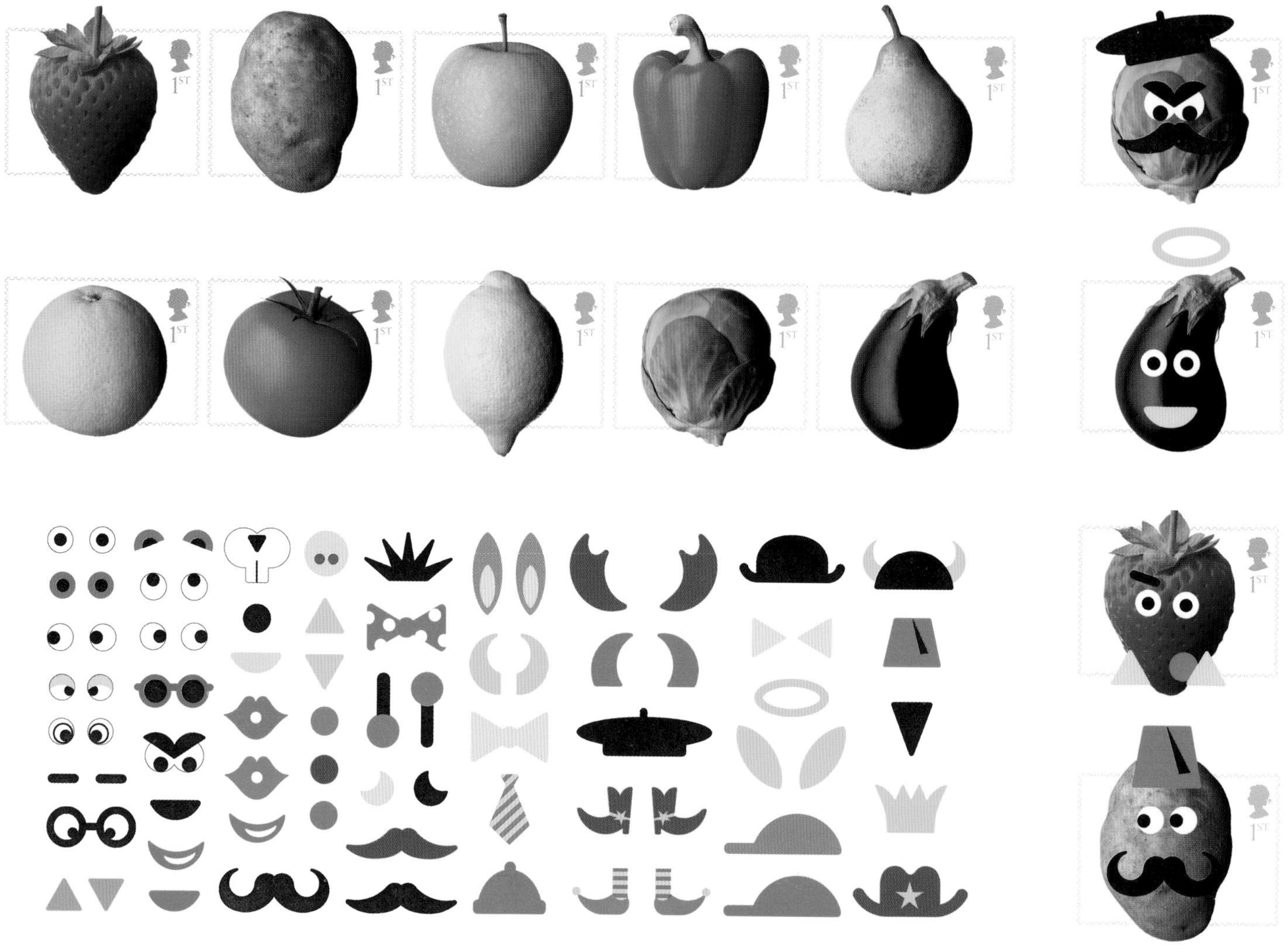

PUSHING THE
BOUNDARIES

johnson banks

PROJECTS FRUIT AND VEG SMILERS® STAMPS, BEATLES STAMPS
DESIGNER JOHNSON BANKS
CLIENT ROYAL MAIL

PAPER FACTS:
STOCK AVERY SASS LAMINATE GLAD FILTER FACE PAPER
PRINT TECHNIQUE GRAVURE

ADDITIONAL TECHNIQUES FRUIT AND VEG SMILERS® STAMPS: PERFORATION, STICKERS; BEATLES STAMPS: DIE-CUTTING, SELF-ADHESIVE
PRINTER WALLSALL SECURITY PRINTERS

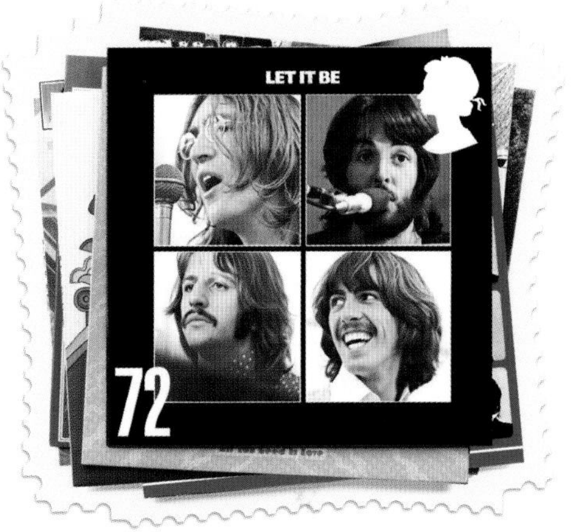

Good design is often about adding value to the everyday items we take for granted. With their children's stamps for Royal Mail, UK consultancy johnson banks made poetry from the prosaic. Driven by childhood memories of Fuzzy-Felt faces, Mr Potato Head, and Giuseppe Arcimboldo's vegetable paintings, they came up with a range of customizable stamps. Ten sticky-back fruit and vegetable stamps and 76 die-cut stickers make up a philatelic kit of parts that offers endless combinations and limitless fun.

Royal Mail sold half a million sets, and the stamps became one of johnson banks's best-known projects. So when it sought the consultancy's services to design stamps to celebrate the Beatles' cultural contribution to Britain, Royal Mail was right not to expect a square solution. Six iconic albums spanning the band's career were chosen to feature on the stamps. Using the same paper as standard stamps, the magic lies in the irregular shapes that evoke a jumbled pile of vinyl albums, with the edges die-cut to simulate the perforations on traditional stamps.

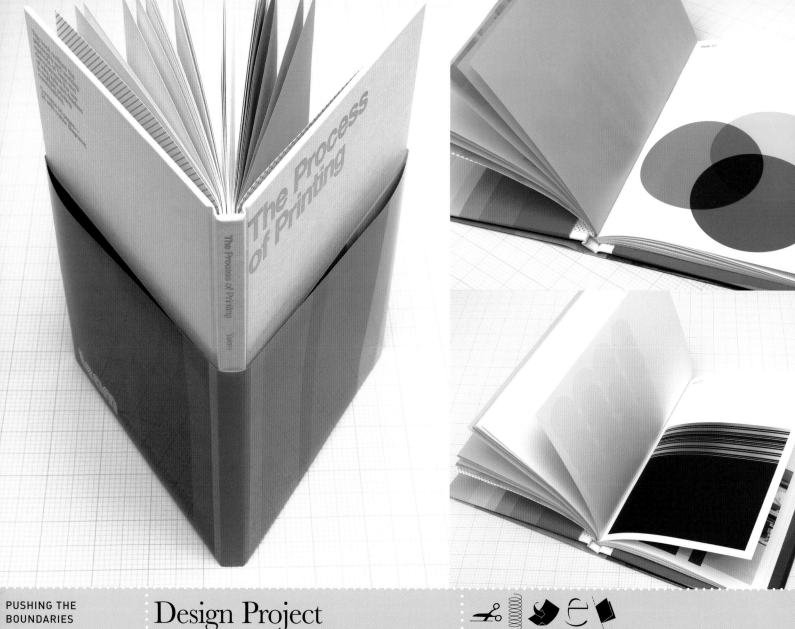

PUSHING THE BOUNDARIES

Design Project

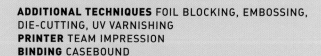

PROJECT THE PROCESS OF PRINTING
DESIGNERS JAMES LITTLEWOOD, ANDY ROBERT at DESIGN PROJECT
CLIENT TEAM IMPRESSION

PAPER FACTS:
STOCK JACKET: HELLO SILK 90gsm
PAGES: KASKAD LEAFBIRD GREEN 80gsm, PARILUX MATT 150gsm
PRINT TECHNIQUES OFFSET LITHO IN A MIXTURE OF 15 PROCESS AND SPECIAL COLORS; FRONT 16 PAGES: SINGLE-COLOR FLUORESCENT GREEN ONTO A LIGHT-GREEN PAPER STOCK

ADDITIONAL TECHNIQUES FOIL BLOCKING, EMBOSSING, DIE-CUTTING, UV VARNISHING
PRINTER TEAM IMPRESSION
BINDING CASEBOUND

SPECIAL CONSIDERATIONS:
"Most of the sections were put through the press two or three times to get all the colors and techniques down. This is not common practice and can cause major problems, but as the job was a small run we managed to navigate the problem with preplanning, foresight, and organization at artwork stage."

James Littlewood, Design Project, UK

Dissatisfied with the quality of design and information being sent out by companies in the printing industry, Design Project set about developing a piece to showcase how they thought print should be demonstrated. Their relationship with Team Impression (a Leeds-based printer) offered the opportunity to design, develop, and produce The Process of Printing. The piece outlines the philosophy and working methods of Team Impression, and demonstrates the use of inks, foils, and finishes in multiple-printing combinations to demonstrate the use of print technique coupled with choice of substrate.

The design was kept deliberately simple, with written information in the front 16 pages, printed in one color to contrast with the materials, colors, and processes used in the 24 plates at the back of the book. The jacket, printed in full color with a gloss-laminate finish, wraps around the base of the book to accentuate the materials used in the book. An uncoated, unprinted white binding paper was used to cover the boards. The book has won many awards and resulted in significant company growth for Team Impression.

CHAPTER 2

corporate literature

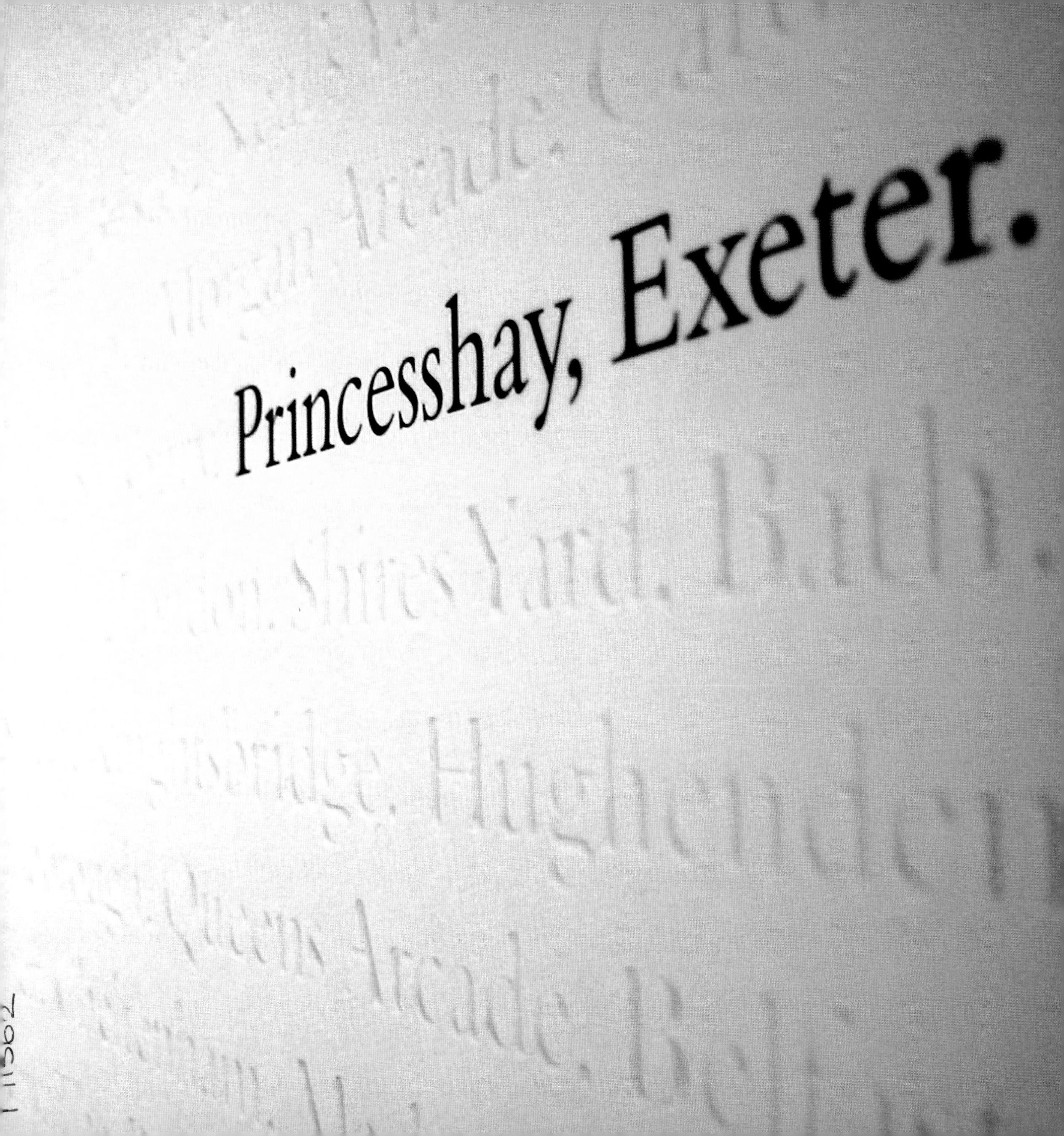
Princesshay, Exeter.

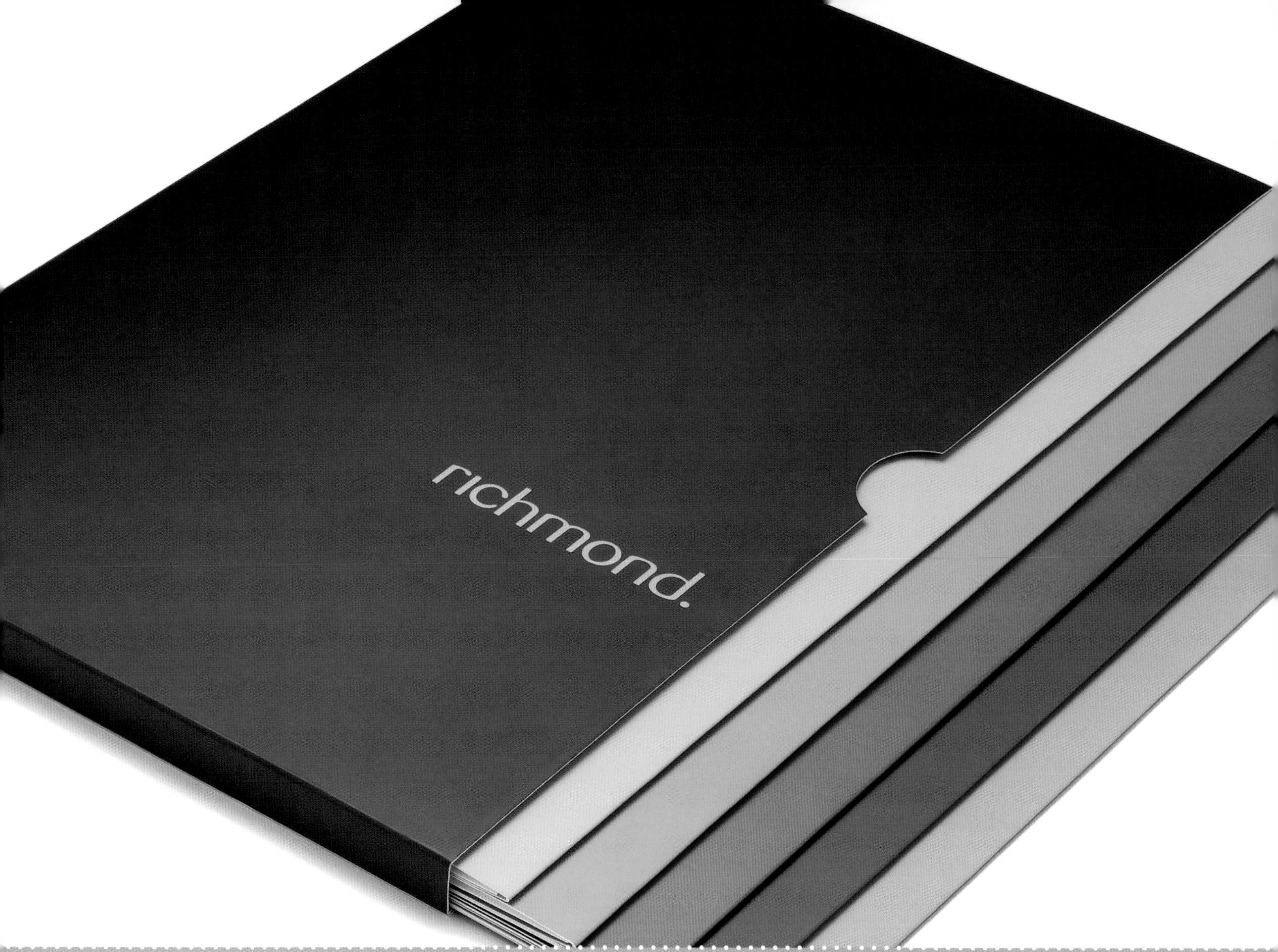

Curious

PROJECT RICHMOND BROCHURE
DESIGNER LOUISE DESBOROUGH at CURIOUS
ART DIRECTOR PETER RAE
CLIENT RICHMOND INTERNATIONAL

PAPER FACTS:
STOCK SLIPCASE: CHROMOMAT 300gsm
COVERS: CHROMOMAT 300gsm
INSIDE: CHROMOMAT 170gsm

SIZE 180 × 298mm (7 × 11¾in)
PRINT TECHNIQUE BROCHURES: FOUR-COLOR DUOTONE
ADDITIONAL TECHNIQUES BROCHURES: SILK LAMINATION ON BOTH SIDES; SLIPCASE: CLEAR-FOIL BLOCKED LOGO
PRINTER SOLWAYS
BINDING SIX-PAGE ROLLFOLD

Having designed the branding and identity for Richmond International, a hotel and leisure design consultancy, London agency Curious were tasked with creating a brochure that would showcase different examples of the company's work throughout the world. Its solution was to create a series of mini-brochures presented in a slipcase with the flexibility to hold five or six brochures.

High-end luxury characterizes Richmond International's work, so attention to detail was key to the success of the suite of literature. This is reflected in the choice of a quality coated stock and the range of finishes used. The logo is foil blocked on the cover, while the inside of the slipcase was color printed for an unexpected touch of opulence. The brochure covers, bearing duotone photographs printed in four colorways, have silk lamination on both sides.

Bruketa&Žinić

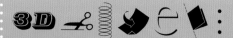

PROJECT ANNUAL REPORT: FEED ME
DESIGNER BRUKETA&ŽINIĆ
CLIENT PODRAVKA

PAPER FACTS:
STOCK AGRIPINA 140gsm
SIZE 220 × 250mm (8¾ × 9¾in)
PRINT TECHNIQUE FOUR-COLOR OFFSET LITHO
ADDITIONAL TECHNIQUES DIE-CUTTING, PERFORATION, FOIL STAMPING
PRINTER PRINTING OFFICE IBL
BINDING FRENCH FOLD

SPECIAL CONSIDERATIONS:
"As well as the classic punch press, French binding, and expanded plastic, with this annual report we found out how sexy white folio print can look on white paper."

Ana Muhar, PR Coordinator,
Bruketa&Žinić

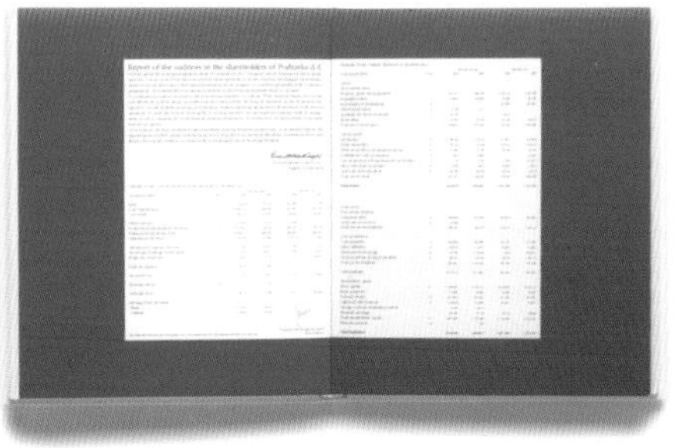

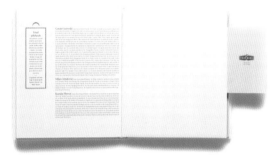

Podravka is the largest food company in eastern Europe and the Balkans, and the Croatian company has a reputation for quality food and creative advertising. Design agency Bruketa&Žinić was briefed for the fifth time to design Podravka's annual report. The result is Feed Me, a hardback volume that comes in cardboard packaging. Designed predominantly in Podravka's brand colors of black, white, and red, the report uses paper techniques to create an impression of quality and innovation while remaining rooted in traditional values.

Podravka's brand communication is one of food prepared with heart. Knowing that the annual report sits in the libraries of bankers, stockbrokers, and shareholders, the agency brought the proposition to life with die-cut heart shapes and perforated cut-out-and-keep recipe cards, peppered throughout the corporate information. Another innovation was to highlight the central Auditors' Report section; printed in red and French-folded, its pages are cut 55mm (2⁵⁄₃₂in) shorter than the rest of the book.

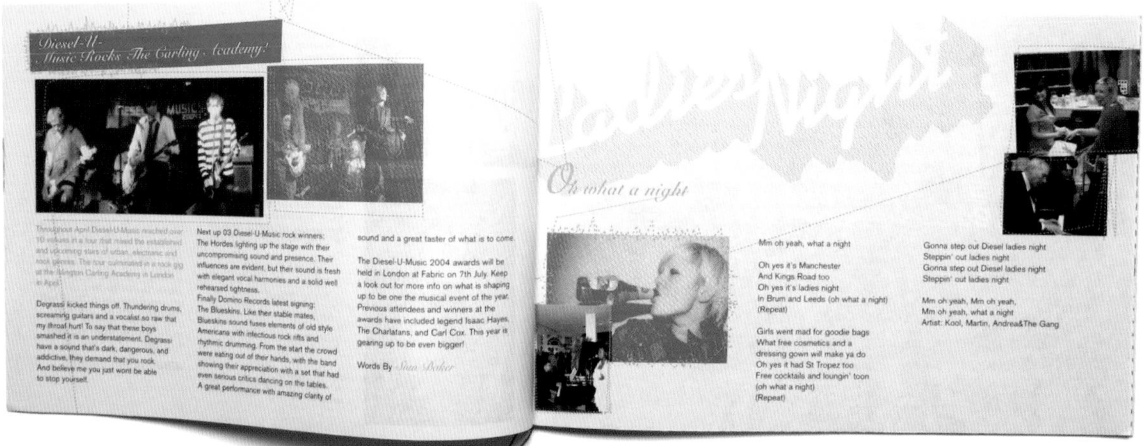

theFarm

PROJECT SON OF DIESEL PLANET MAGAZINE
DESIGNER theFarm
CLIENT DIESEL

PAPER FACTS:
STOCK NEWSPRINT 50gsm
SIZE 210 × 135mm (8¼ × 5¼in)
PRINT TECHNIQUE FOUR-COLOR OFFSET LITHO
ADDITIONAL TECHNIQUES HAND-SEWN IMAGE ON COVER, EMBROIDERED LABEL
PRINTER CALVERTS
BINDING SINGER-SEWN

ABOVE: SON OF DIESEL PLANET MAGAZINE
Photography: Victoria Woolhead © theFarm

Diesel produces an internal magazine to accompany the launch of each collection. It asked theFarm to produce a magazine that related to a clothing collection that made use of hand-sewing and embroidery. Every element of the production and design of the piece supports these themes. Icons and headlines were designed as sewn graphics. The format allows imagery and content from several sources to work harmoniously and creates a desirable, informative, and compelling piece of communication.

Litho-printed onto newsprint, the stock was chosen to replicate sewing-pattern paper. The lightweight paper also facilitated the decision to have the piece Singer-sewn-bound by a local hosiery company. A stitched label mimics school name tags and loose threads give a crafted appeal so that each issue feels unique. The image on the cover was hand-sewn specially for this project. Graphic detailing of stitches throughout complete the theme.

Carter Wong Tomlin

PROJECT BROCHURE
DESIGNER CARTER WONG TOMLIN
CLIENT CAPITAL CITY ACADEMY

PAPER FACTS:
STOCK TEXT: MODO GRAPHIC SILK 300gsm, 150gsm
TIP IN: CLASSIC TRANSLUCENT 90gsm
SIZE 170 × 230mm (6¾ × 9in) + POCKET
PRINT TECHNIQUE FOUR-COLOR OFFSET LITHO

ADDITIONAL TECHNIQUE UNCOATED STOCK USED THROUGHOUT WITH TRACE OVERLAYS
PRINTER FERNEDGE PRINTERS
BINDING SADDLESTITCH

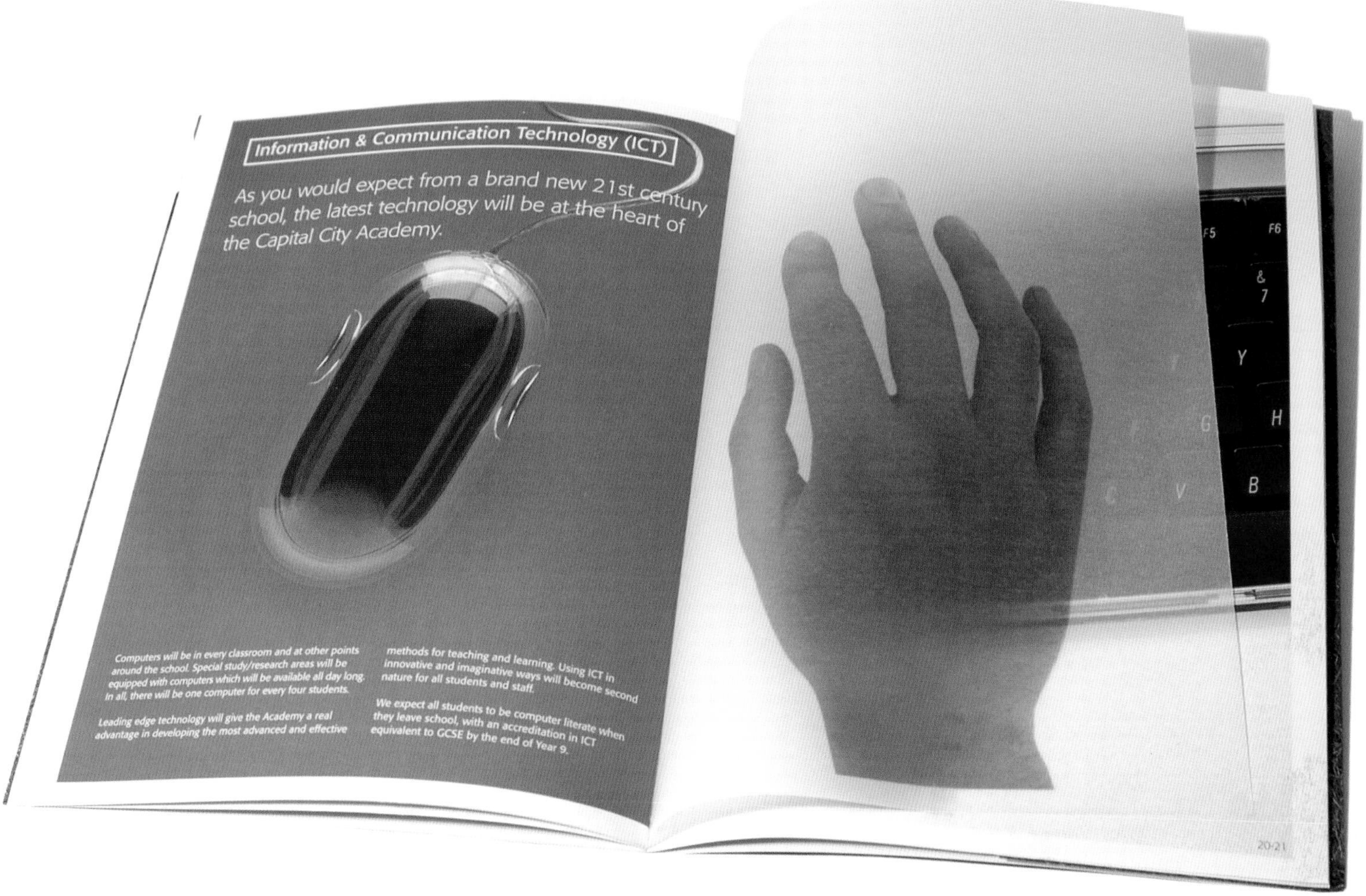

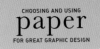

How do you produce a prospectus for a school that doesn't exist yet? Approached by London's Capital City Academy to do just this, UK design agency Carter Wong Tomlin turned to the school curriculum for inspiration.

The new school was to be housed in a landmark building designed by Foster and Partners, but that was some way off completion. With no visual material to back up the prospectus content, it was decided to communicate the school's subjects and skills through the language of education. Thus, mathematics communicated funding; geography indicated the school's location.

The concept was brought to life by the use of uncoated paper stock throughout, contrasted with trace overlays, which add an extra dimension of meaning and visual interest. This creative approach helped set the new school apart and raised its profile among members of the local community.

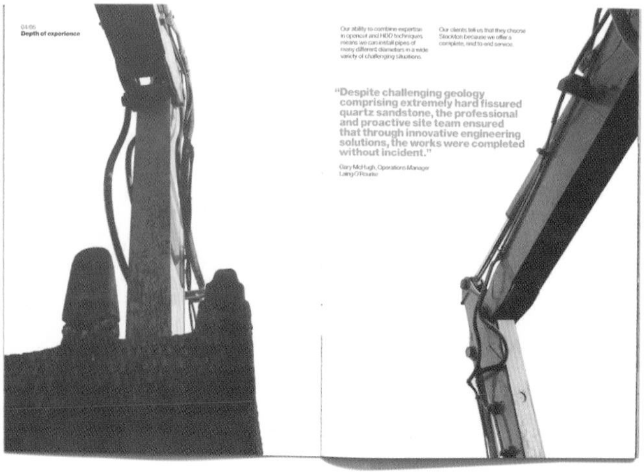

B&W Studio

PROJECT STOCKTON DRILLING BROCHURE
DESIGNER STEVE WILLS at B&W STUDIO
PHOTOGRAPHER MARCUS GINNS
CLIENT STOCKTON DRILLING

PAPER FACTS:
STOCK PAPERBACK: FLUTE BOARD 220gsm, CYCLUS OFFSET 140gsm
SIZE 200 × 148mm (7⅞ × 5¾in)
PRINT TECHNIQUE FOUR-COLOR OFFSET LITHO
ADDITIONAL TECHNIQUE DEBOSSED COVER
PRINTER PROCO
BINDING SADDLESTITCH

B&W Studio designed a corporate brochure for specialist UK pipeline contractor Stockton Drilling as part of an overall identity program. Two concepts guided the design: the new logo that emphasizes the "O" in the name was to evoke the idea of drilling a hole; and the brochure was to have an earthy feel in line with the company's business. The debossed circle on the flute-board cover brings to mind pipes and gives a stonelike effect, while Cyclus Offset paper offered the recycled earthiness the brand demanded.

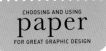

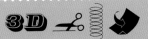

Carter Wong Tomlin

PROJECT BROCHURE
DESIGNER CARTER WONG TOMLIN
CLIENT OCTAGON SPORTS MARKETING

PAPER FACTS:
STOCK MONADNOCK ASTROLITE SMOOTH 216gsm, 118gsm, HOLLANDER 100gsm
SIZE MAIN SECTION: 280 × 240mm (11 × 9³⁄₈in); INSERT SECTION: 120 × 120mm (4³⁄₄ × 4³⁄₄in)
PRINT TECHNIQUE FOUR-COLOR OFFSET LITHO
PRINTER WESTERHAM PRESS
BINDING SMALL COATED PAGES BOUND INTO EACH UNCOATED SPREAD THROUGHOUT

Octagon is a worldwide sports and entertainment marketing company that describes its philosophy as "Passion, Engagement, Results." To reflect this singular vision, Carter Wong Tomlin felt the design of the brochure should focus on arresting sports imagery, and the informative text should be kept separate. The solution was to produce a book within a book. Large-format uncoated pages carry full-bleed color images of sports. Each spread has a smaller insert on coated paper that contains the text. A gatefold at the back was cut to insert the business card of the relevant marketing representative.

CORPORATE LITERATURE

Wink

PROJECT JEWELRY KIT
DESIGNER WINK
ART DIRECTORS SCOTT THARES, RICHARD BOYNTON at WINK; GREG CLARK at MARSHALL FIELD'S
DESIGNER/ILLUSTRATOR: SCOTT THARES at WINK
PHOTOGRAPHY MARSHALL FIELD'S HISTORICAL ARCHIVES, GETTY IMAGES
CLIENT MARSHALL FIELD'S

PAPER FACTS:
STOCK OUTER HOLDER: BROWN BOOKBOARD INTERIOR PAGES: MOHAWK ARCHIVAL PAPER 80lb AND STRATHMORE ENVELOPES
SIZE INTERIOR PAGES: 8¾ × 10¾in (222 × 273mm)
PRINT TECHNIQUES OUTER HOLDER: THREE-COLOR SCREENPRINT; INTERIOR PAGES, COVER: TWO-COLOR LETTERPRESS; STICKERS: LETTERPRESS, DIGITAL
ADDITIONAL TECHNIQUES OUTER HOLDER: DIE-CUT PAGES: HAND-TIED AND DRILLED BY KENT ALDRICH
PRINTER NOMADIC PRESS
BINDING FRENCH FOLD, JAPANESE STAB SEWN

Department store Marshall Field's wanted to inform its jewelry vendors about 150 years of the brand's retail heritage and update partners on some recent dramatic changes. With just 100 copies being produced, the retailer wanted the piece to have a handmade feel. Creative agency Wink's solution was a pack in the form of a lady's purse, utilizing traditional design techniques such as letterpress, die-cutting, silkscreened illustration, and hand-tied tags.

The jewelry-kit holder was made from die-cut and two-color silkscreened brown bookboard. Within this, a 16-page book has interior pages run off on a large-scale digital-format press using archival paper, bound in a Japanese stab-sewn style using blue linen wax-coated binding thread. The books were hand-tied and drilled by the proprietor. The front and back covers of the book are made up of large envelopes, which contain photos and an introductory letter, all sealed by stickers that were letterpressed using a 106-year-old Chandler and Price clamshell-platen letterpress machine.

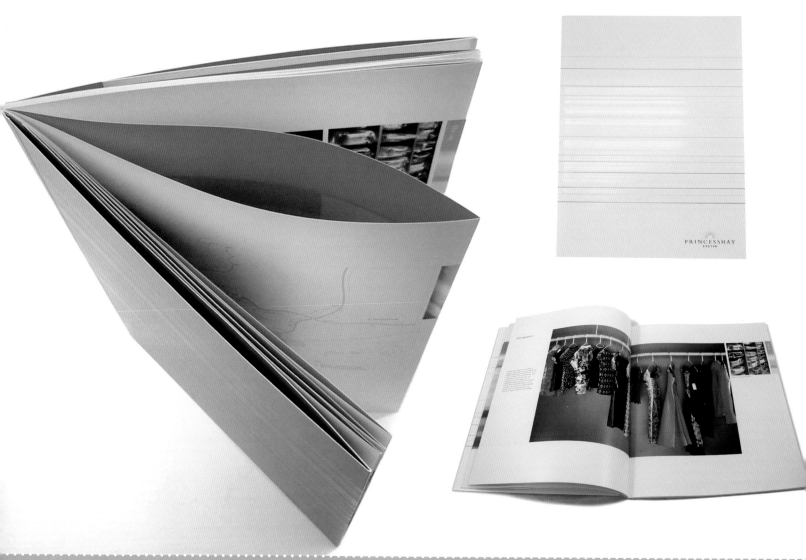

nextbigthing

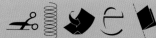

PROJECTS PRINCESSHAY, EXETER BROCHURES
DESIGNER NEXTBIGTHING
CLIENT LAND SECURITIES

PAPER FACTS: RETAIL BROCHURE
STOCK COVER: ROBERT HORNE HELLO SILK 270gsm; TEXT: ROBERT HORNE HELLO SILK 105gsm
SIZE 245 × 315mm (9⅝ × 12½in)
PRINT TECHNIQUE LITHO
ADDITIONAL TECHNIQUES UV VARNISH COVER, FRENCH FOLD, DIE-CUTTING
PRINTER PEGASUS
BINDING PERFECT BOUND, GATEFOLD COVER

PAPER FACTS: NICHE RETAIL BROCHURE
STOCK MUNKEN LYNX 270gsm
SIZE 245 × 315mm (9⅝ × 12½in)
PRINT TECHNIQUES FOUR-COLOR OFFSET LITHO, TRITONES, THREE SPECIAL COLORS
ADDITIONAL TECHNIQUES BLIND EMBOSSING AND FRENCH-FOLDED COVERS
PRINTER ST. IVES WESTERHAM PRESS
BINDING SINGER-SEWN

One development, two brochures. nextbigthing used different papers for two design briefs to promote the Princesshay scheme in Exeter, UK, by property developer Land Securities. The first brief was to target big retailers with a distinctive and premium brochure. With color banding printed on the inside of French-folded spreads, the choice of Robert Horne Hello Silk was crucial to achieving the right balance of showthrough without interfering with the design. Also key to the end result was ensuring the die-cut holes registered with the folds.

Next, Land Securities wanted to highlight the potential for niche retailers in the development. A smaller-format brochure was designed with more artisan cues, including black-and-white photography, embossed typography, a tactile stock and Singer-sewn binding. Munken Lynx was chosen for its ability to carry black-and-white images well. The weight of the covers was kept light in order to achieve a definite impression when blind-embossing, then French-folded to give them sufficient weight and synergy with the first brochure.

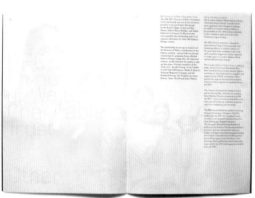

CORPORATE
LITERATURE

Egelnick and Webb

PROJECTS REPORTS OF ACTIVITIES 2002 AND 2003
DESIGN EGELNICK AND WEBB
CLIENT BRITISH FASHION COUNCIL

PAPER FACTS: 2002 REPORT
STOCK COVER: ARJOWIGGINS IMPRESSIONS TEXTURES RIVES DESIGN, MISTY GREY 250gsm; INNER STOCK: NATURAL WHITE 120gsm (KINDLY DONATED BY ARJOWIGGINS)
SIZE 188 × 298mm (7⅜ × 11¾in)
PRINT TECHNIQUE TWO-COLOR OFFSET LITHO
PRINTER SANDYPRESS
BINDING OVERLOCKED

PAPER FACTS: 2003 REPORT
STOCK PRINT SPEED 300gsm, 70gsm (KINDLY DONATED BY ANTALIS)
SIZE 188 × 298mm (7⅜ × 11¾in)
PRINT TECHNIQUE TWO-COLOR OFFSET LITHO
ADDITIONAL TECHNIQUE EMBOSSED TITLE TO FRONT AND REVERSE OF COVER
PRINTER SANDYPRESS
BINDING SADDLESTITCH

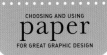

Design studio Egelnick and Webb took up the challenge of designing an annual report for the British Fashion Council. Their brief was to reflect the vitality of the British fashion industry, but within a limited budget. They sourced a special textured paper to imitate fabric, and juxtaposed elegant typography with the picture layout to give a workbook feel. Playing with channels and multi-ink colors ensured a wide range of hues within the limits of two inks, lending richness to the finished print. With no budget for binding, their fashion-designer neighbor's work-experience person overlocked all 1,500 books.

The following year brought another challenge: how to unify diverse imagery from a variety of sources. Using a bitmap dither screen, images were blown up to create a supersized feel from fairly low-resolution catwalk shots. Using a very thin stock they managed to achieve a showthrough effect, so that the large images "glowed" from behind the text. To keep print costs down to just two sets of plates, the inside consists of two A2 sheets, folded down and left untrimmed at the top.

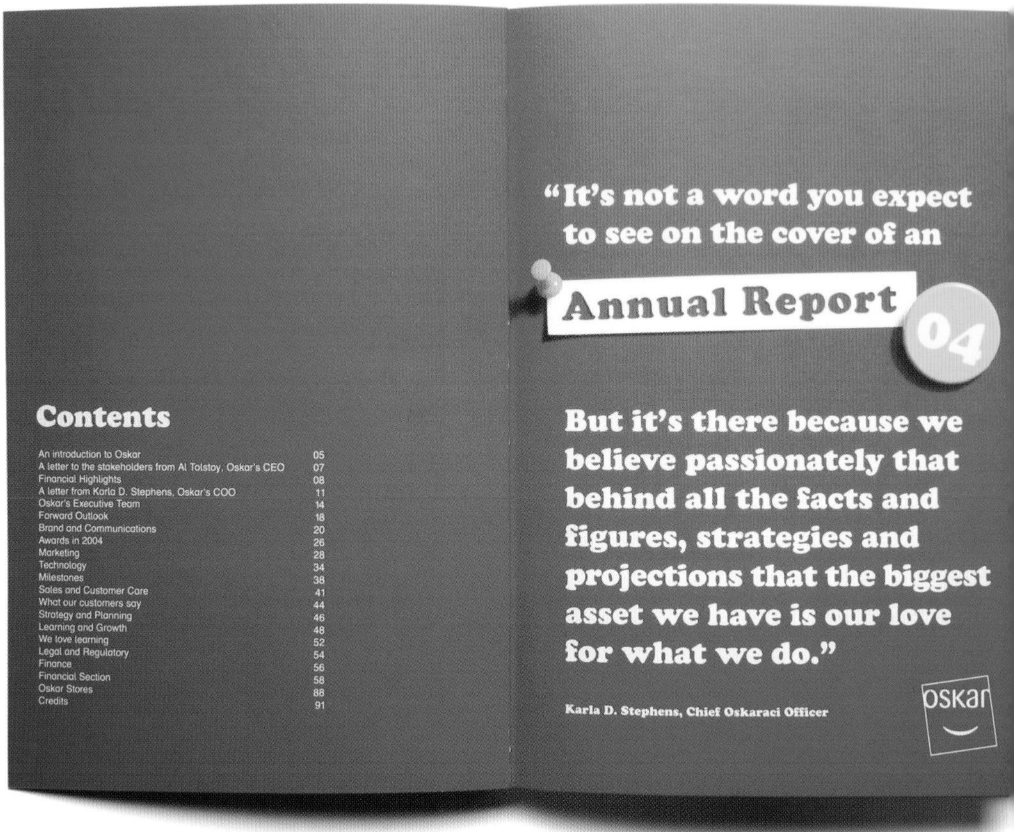

CORPORATE LITERATURE

theFarm

PROJECT OSKAR ANNUAL REPORT
DESIGNER theFarm
CLIENT OSKAR

PAPER FACTS:
STOCK COVER: OFFSET 350gsm
PAGES: OFFSET 170gsm
SIZE 170 × 240mm (6¾ × 9⅜in)
PRINT TECHNIQUE FOUR-COLOR OFFSET LITHO

ADDITIONAL TECHNIQUES EACH SPREAD LAID OUT IN 3D USING LASER-CUT HEADLINES AND IMAGERY, THEN SHOT USING ROSTRUM PHOTOGRAPHY
PRINTER BOOMERANG
BINDING SECTION-SEWN THEN PERFECT BOUND

PASSION
the thread that runs through Oskar...
Passion: Our greatest strength
It's the southern Europeans who have a reputation for passion. The Italians, the Spanish, the French. Maybe it's something in the olive oil that makes them so hot-blooded, fiery and impulsive. But we'd like to redress the balance. Here in the Czech Republic, we believe we're a match for anyone. And at Oskar in particular, passion is right at the heart of what we do.
Love story No.47
100 km to work
Oskar ECO
Lonely Hearts
Karla D. Stephens
Vivacious super-venus with bags of style in search of stratospheric success...
Muriel Anton
Focused and determined professional with head for figures and a thirst for adventure

ABOVE: OSKAR ANNUAL REPORT
Photography: Victoria Woolhead
© theFarm

Oskar was a mobile phone network in the Czech Republic. theFarm designed an award-winning annual report for the company, their final one, prior to being rebranded as Vodafone CZ. Unlike most annual reports, this also had to serve as a staff memento, charting a five-year success story. The theme of "love" runs through the book, focusing on Oskar's human values, making a normally dry, corporate publication into an engaging book and reflecting the unique culture of the organization.

A scrapbook concept was created, which helped to overcome a number of issues. First, it made a virtue of limited availability of stock and print techniques within the Czech Republic—the limitations actually enhanced the concept. Second, it helped unite a diverse pool of supplied imagery under one coherent theme. Each spread was laid out in 3D using laser-cut headlines and imagery. The spreads were then shot using rostrum photography. Since the annual report was produced in Czech and English, each spread needed to be shot twice.

Squires & Company

PROJECTS FELCOR ANNUAL REPORTS
DESIGNER SQUIRES & COMPANY
CLIENT FELCOR LODGING TRUST

PAPER FACTS: 2003 ANNUAL REPORT
STOCK WEYERHAEUSER COUGAR OPAQUE 65lb COVER
SIZE BOOK: 6 × 9in (152 × 229mm); SUPPLEMENT: 8½ × 11in (216 × 279mm)
PRINT TECHNIQUE FOUR-COLOR OFFSET LITHO
ADDITIONAL TECHNIQUE THE 6 × 9in BOOK WAS BOOGER GLUED TO THE 8½ × 11in SUPPLEMENT
PRINTER BEST PRESS
BINDING SADDLESTITCH

PAPER FACTS: 2005 ANNUAL REPORT
STOCK UTOPIA ONE × 80lb COVER
SIZE 8¼ × 11¾in (210 × 298mm)
PRINT TECHNIQUES FOUR COLOR + ONE SPOT COLOR
ADDITIONAL TECHNIQUE SPOT VARNISH
PRINTER THE GRAPHICS GROUP
BINDING SADDLESTITCH

In 2003, US real-estate investment trust FelCor wanted to communicate to their shareholders and the investment community that they were working through difficult times post-9/11, so Squires & Company developed the metaphor of a journey through the wilderness for FelCor's annual report. With budget a primary factor, they proposed printing a smaller book to carry the story, booger glued to the larger financial supplement for a portion of the quantity. Custom black-and-white illustration and maps were scanned and spot color added. An uncoated stock felt down-to-earth and suited the adventure-book feel.

The investment community commended FelCor for their frugality and creativity. Fast-forward to 2005 and the company wanted the annual report to communicate the "new" FelCor, highlighting some major management and portfolio changes. Squires & Company came up with the idea of a highly stylized product parody to connote the "new-and-improved" company. Bright, four-color photography printed on a coated gloss stock with a gloss varnish ensured an over-the-top book that was so shiny it was almost garish.

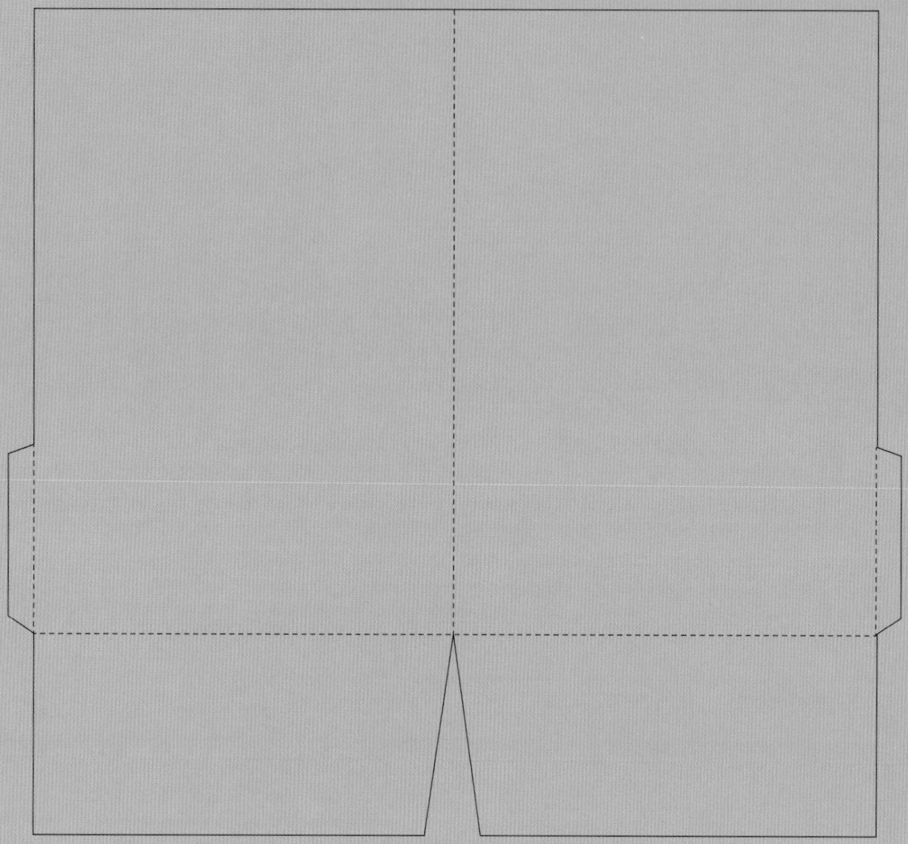

pocket folder styles

STANDARD TWO-POCKET
FOLDER

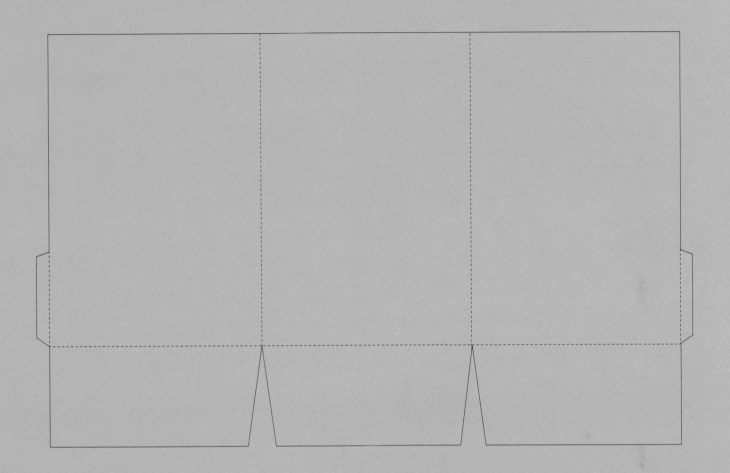

STANDARD THREE-POCKET FOLDER

Pocket folders are an easy way to bring together different pieces of documentation, and are an effective method of branding paper presentations and corporate literature. Always use a cover stock between 270gsm and 325gsm, and have a dummy made in your chosen weight to determine if your folder is suitable to hold the documents for which it is intended. Most printers will have ready-made dies for folders, which will save time and expense, so it is worth checking with your chosen printer what they have available before getting to the design stage.

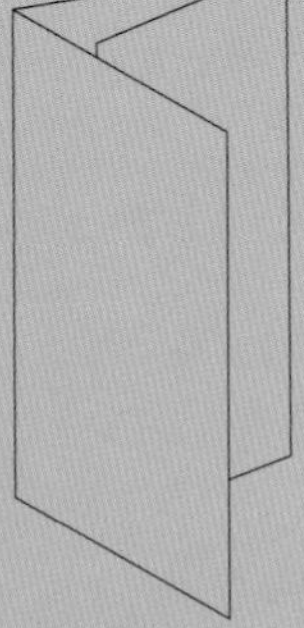

TWO-POCKET FOLDER WITH BOX SIDE FLAPS

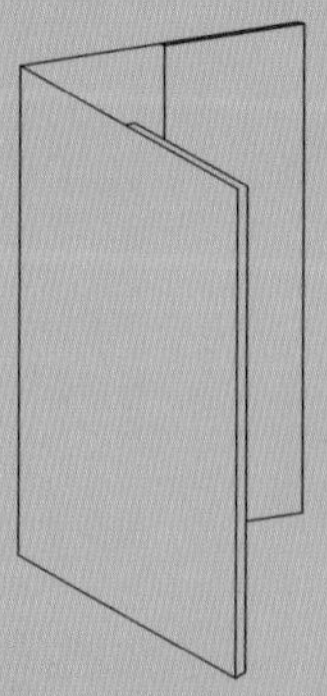

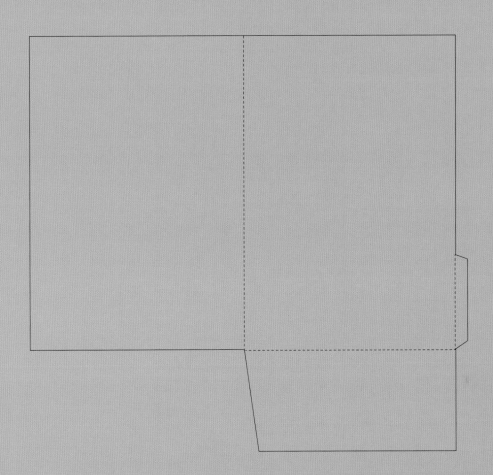

SINGLE-POCKET
FOLDER

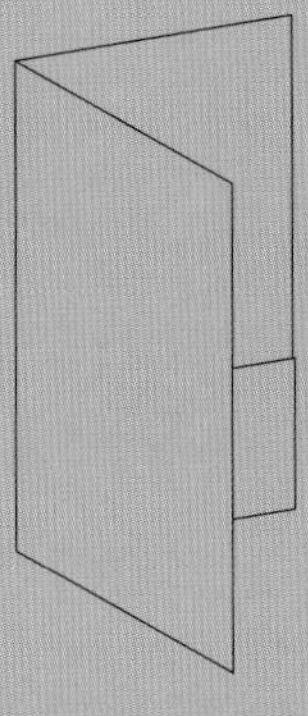

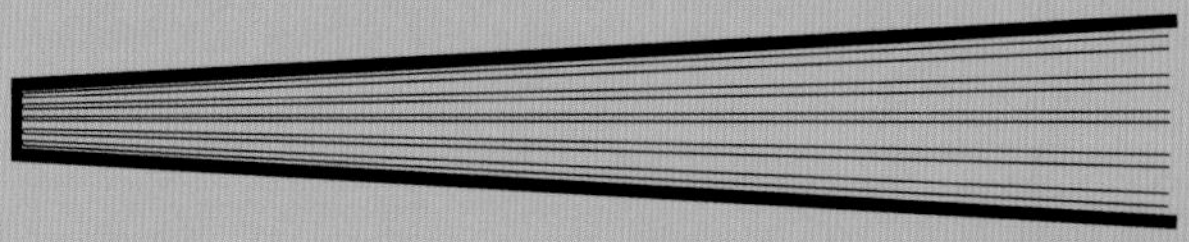

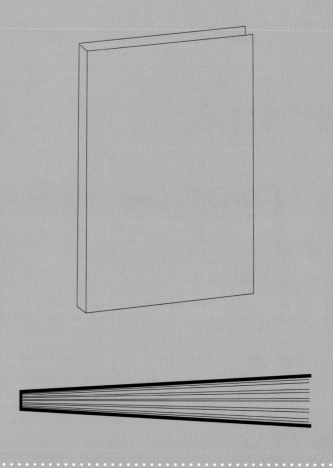

binding styles

PERFECT BINDING

A style of binding in which all pages are trimmed at the binding edge and held together by glue or thermoplastics. An alternative to stitched bindings, most paperback books are produced by this method.

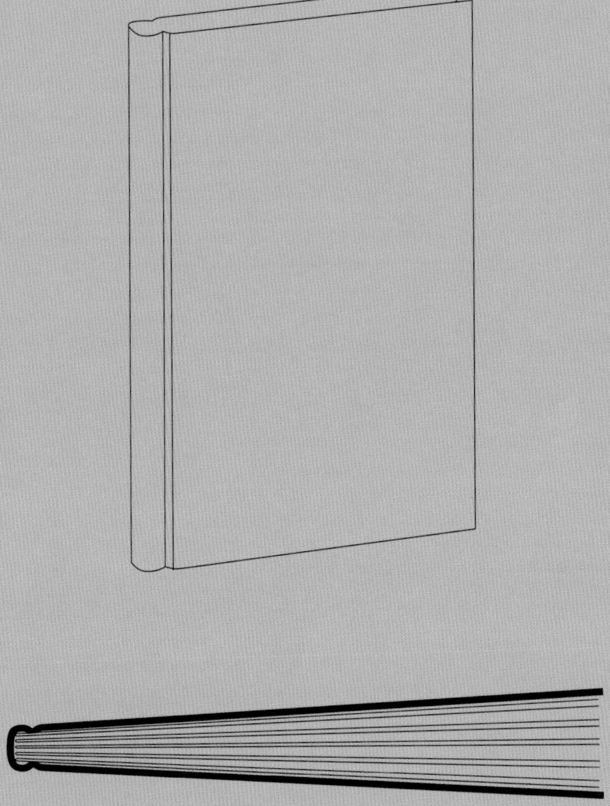

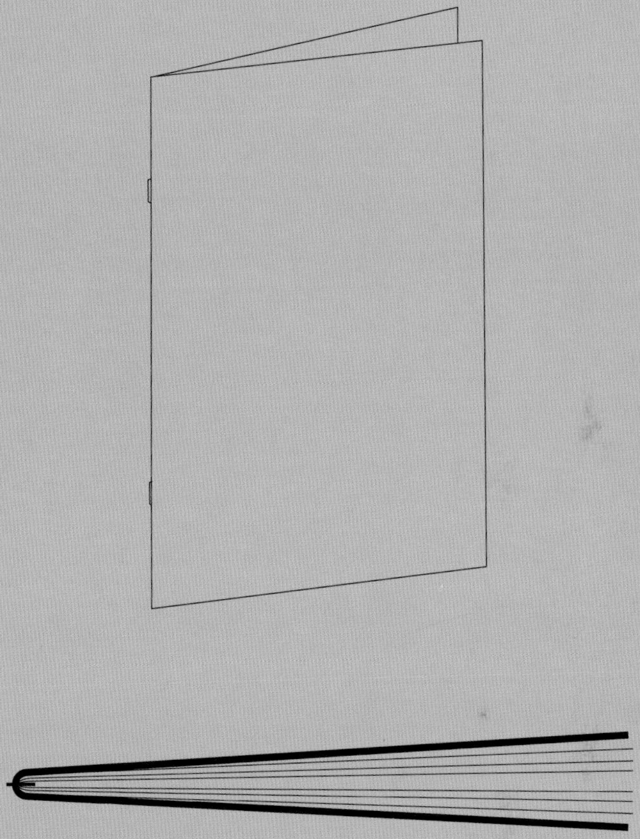

CASE BINDING

The pages of each section—or signature—are sewn together along the spine. The sewn book is then glued to the endpapers and binder's boards at the spine.

SADDLESTITCH BINDING

The covers and sections are placed over a "saddle" or chain and then stapled along the spine.

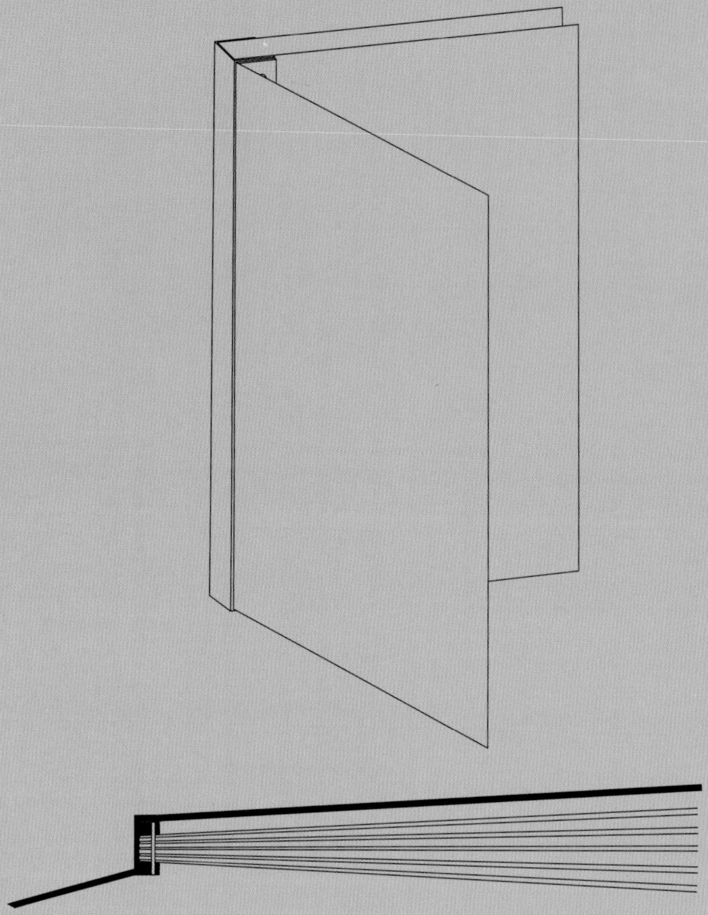

SCREW-AND-POST BINDING

Pages are stacked, drilled, and fastened with a post with adjustable screw heads, which can be unscrewed if new pages are to be added later.

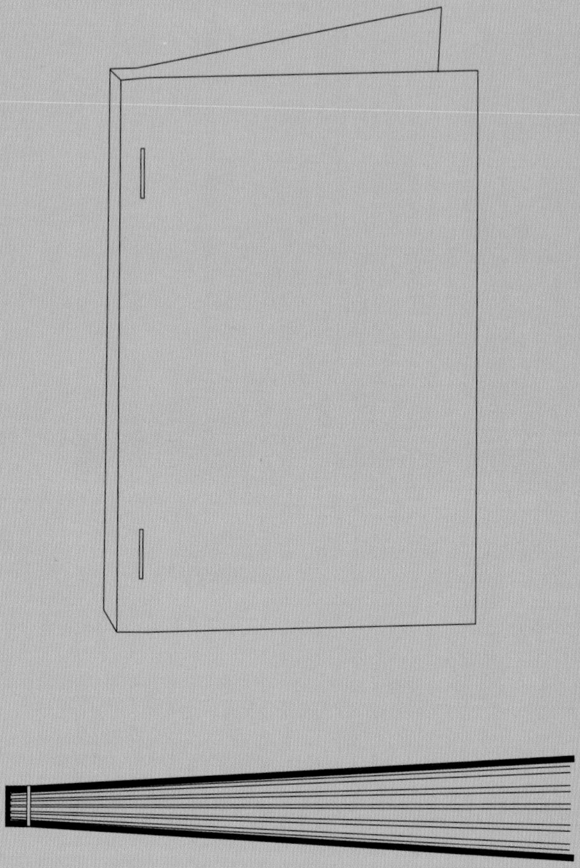

SIDE-STITCH BINDING

The cover and signatures are stacked and wire-stitched at the bound edge.

TAPE BINDING

Covers and signatures are stacked and then a glued flexible cloth tape is applied to one edge, overlapping the front and back covers. Heat is applied to melt the glue, which spreads so binding the covers and signatures together.

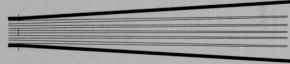

FRENCH FOLD, SINGER-SEWN BINDING

Each sheet of paper is folded in half and bound together at the open edge by mechanically sewing the collated sheets.

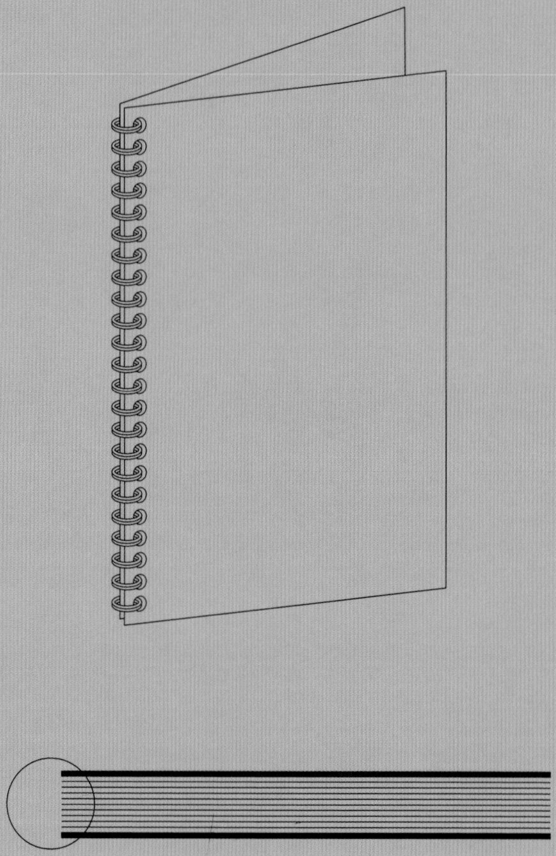

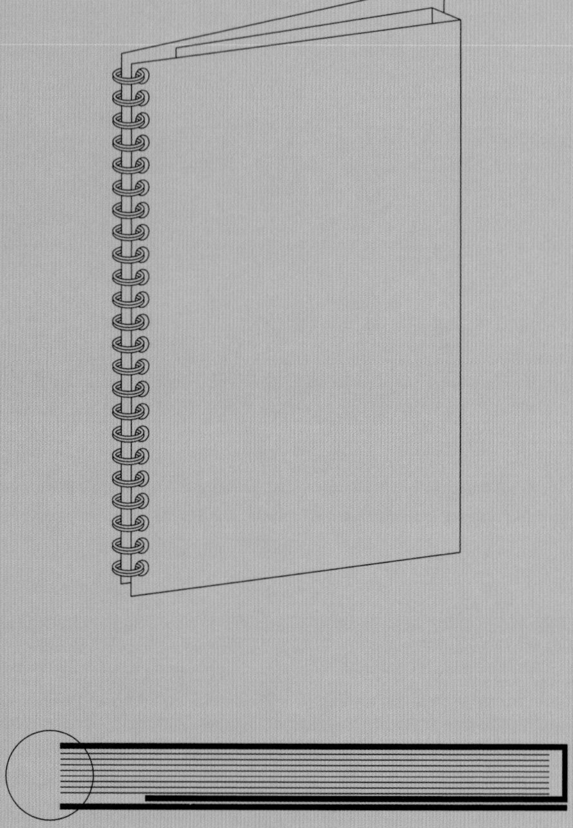

STANDARD WIRE-O BINDING

The wire loops penetrate the front and back covers and individual pages, leaving the wire exposed on the spine.

STANDARD WIRE-O BINDING WITH SPINE FLAP

The wire loops penetrate the front and back covers and individual pages, leaving the wire exposed on the spine—but the cover has an extended flap that folds around the text forming a spine at the foredge of the book or document.

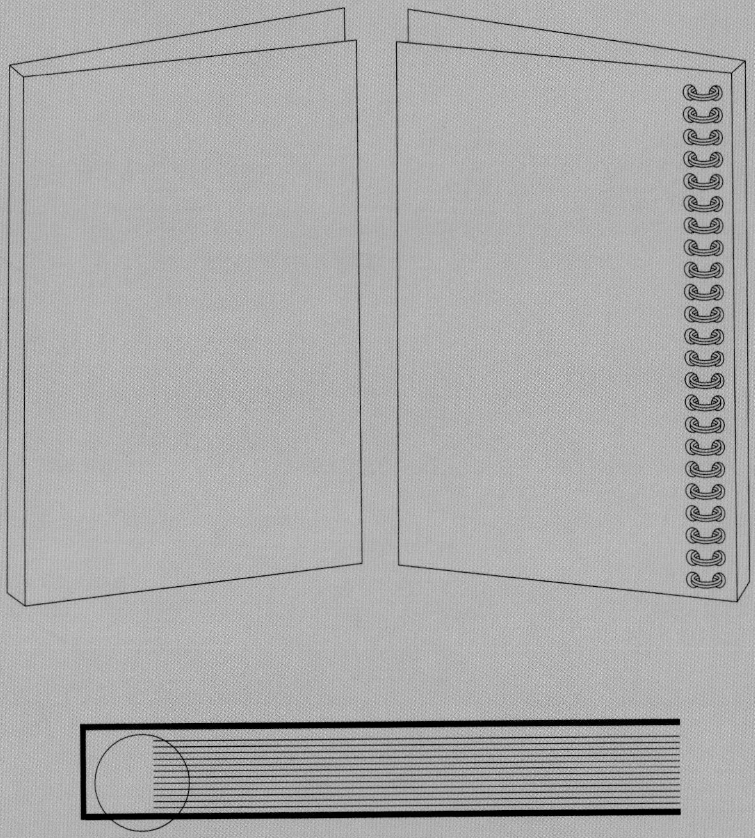

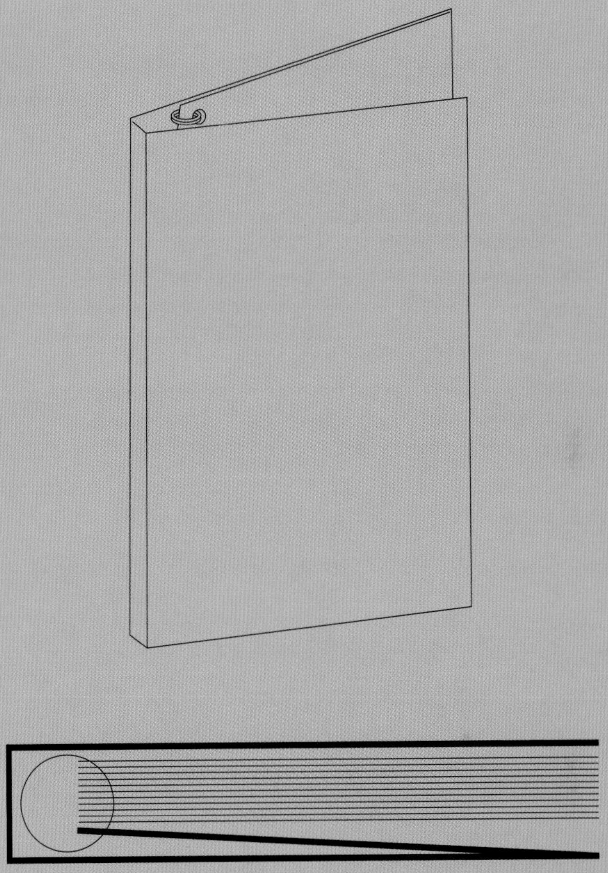

**HALF-CANADIAN
WIRE-O BINDING**

The wire loops go through either the back or the front cover allowing for a visible, printed spine.

**REVERSE-FOLD STANDARD
WIRE-O BINDING**

The wire loops penetrate the text and one end of the cover. The back cover folds back on itself to form a double thickness and visible spine.

CHAPTER 3

mailers + pr

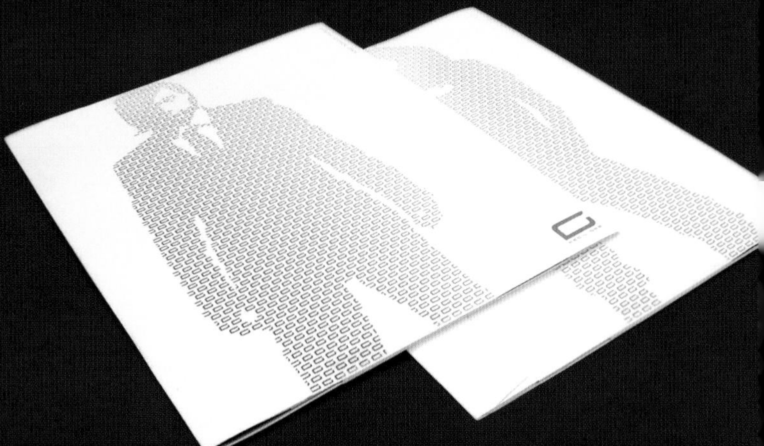

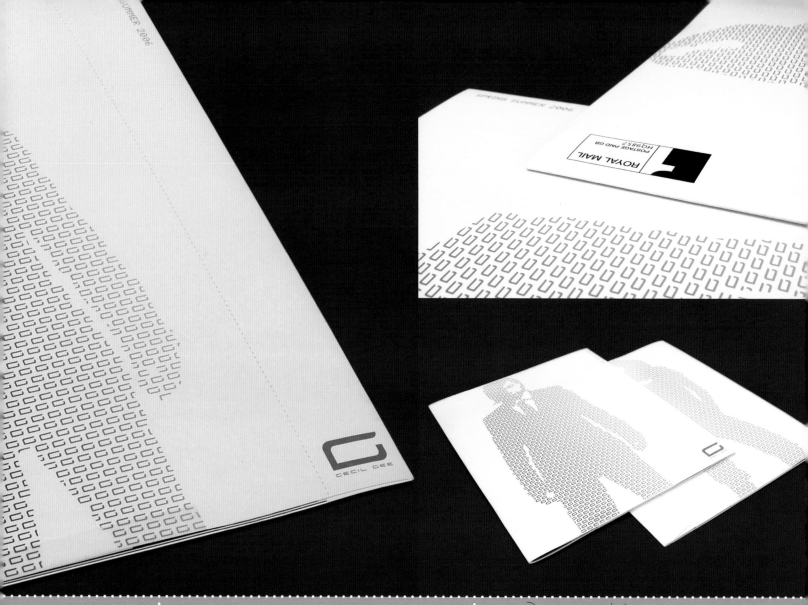

MAILERS + PR

Yang Rutherford

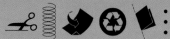

PROJECT CECIL GEE LOOKBOOK SPRING/ SUMMER 2006
DESIGNER JIMMY YANG at YANG RUTHERFORD
CLIENT MOSS BROS GROUP

PAPER FACTS:
STOCK REVIVE UNCOATED 325gsm, 150gsm
SIZE COVER: 370 × 290mm (14½ × 11½in); TEXT: 370 × 250mm (14½ × 9¾in)
PRINT TECHNIQUE UNCOATED DIGITAL PROOFS PRINTED ON 200-LINE SCREEN WITH SPECIALLY FORMULATED INKS TO ALLOW DOTS TO BE SHARPER ON CHOSEN SUBSTRATE

ADDITIONAL TECHNIQUES DIE-CUT, CREASED, AND PERFORATED COVER, TRIMMED AND FOLDED TEXT, GATHERED, TRIMMED FOREDGE OF TEXT TO 40mm (1⅝in) SHORTER THAN THE COVER, FLAP AFFIXED WITH DOUBLE-SIDED TAPE TO BE OPENED AT A LATER DATE WITH USE OF PERFORATED TEAR STRIP
PRINTER GRANITE COLOUR
BINDING SADDLESTITCH TWO WIRES

Each year, fashion retailer Cecil Gee requires a spring/summer fashion lookbook to showcase its latest own-label collection. Sent in the post to fashion journalists, the lookbook has to be immediately appealing to attract busy fashion editors when it arrives on their desks. When briefing creative consultants Yang Rutherford, the company made a further request: avoid using expensive envelopes, keeping waste and budget to a minimum.

The consultancy took the unusual step of making an envelope from the front and back covers. Sealed with a perforated strip on the side, the brochure could be mailed as one piece. The recipient tears the strip away, and it opens as a conventional brochure. A recycled substrate—Revive Uncoated—provided green credentials, but necessitated printing on a 200-line screen with specially formulated inks to achieve a sharper result for the images.

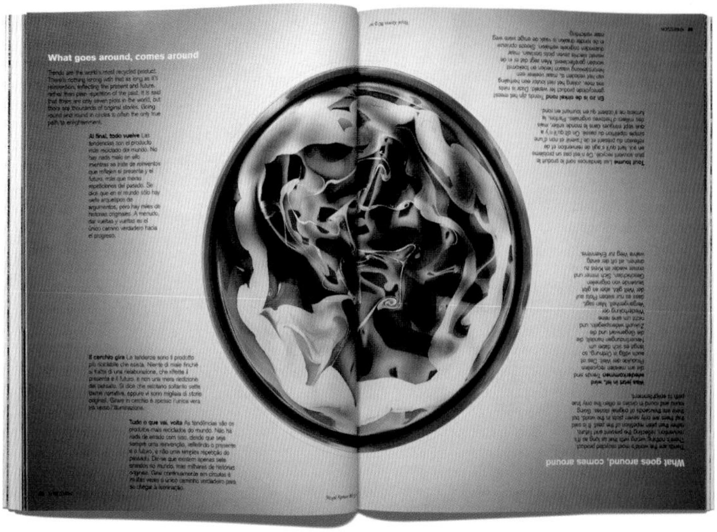

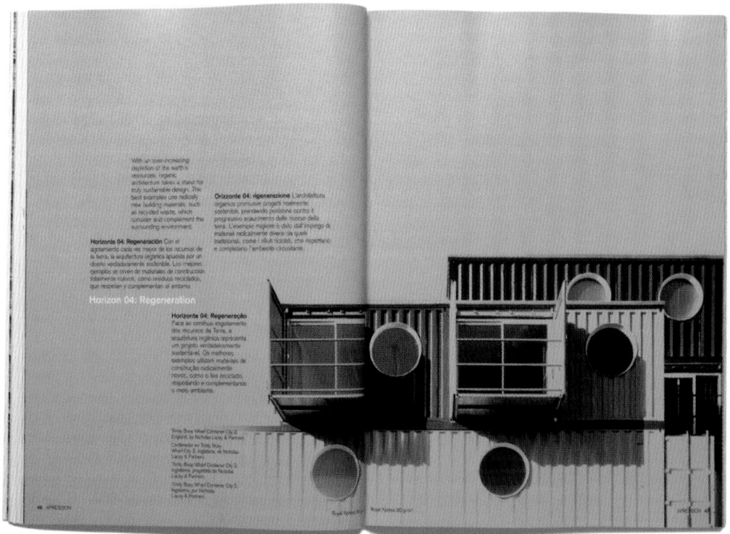

Curious

PROJECT SAPPI ROYAL XPRESSION MAGAZINE
DESIGNERS GARY SMITH, DAVID BAIRD at CURIOUS
PHOTOGRAPHER ANDY CAMERON
CLIENT SAPPI FINE PAPER EUROPE

PAPER FACTS:
STOCK COVER: SAPPI MAGNO SATIN 350gsm
PAGES: SAPPI ROYAL XPRESS 80gsm

SIZE 220 × 165mm (8⅝ × 6½in)
PRINT TECHNIQUE OFFSET PRINTING
ADDITIONAL TECHNIQUE COVER: SILK LAMINATION
PRINTER ELLER REPRO+DRUCK GMBH
BINDING PERFECT BOUND

Sappi Royal Xpress paper is primarily used for printing quality magazines and product catalogs. Asked to design and produce a promotional mailer for the paper, Curious of London felt the most important issue was to find an appropriate format to demonstrate the paper's print performance. Hence, a 160-page magazine was conceived, designed to showcase as many of the paper's qualities as possible, including its opacity and how well different print jobs and styles—full color, text only, bleeds, for instance—work on it.

Taking the name *Xpression*, the magazine is an honest expression of ink on paper—the print is everything. Produced by offset printing, the only extra finish used is a silk lamination on the cover. Designed to be sent out throughout Europe, it has a "top-to-tail" configuration.With the book turned one way up, pages 1 to 80 are printed in English, Italian, Spanish, and French; turn it over, and the first 80 pages are in English, Portuguese, German, and Dutch.

Yang Rutherford

PROJECT OZWALD BOATENG LOOKBOOK
DESIGNER JIMMY YANG at YANG RUTHERFORD
CLIENT OZWALD BOATENG

PAPER FACTS:
STOCK COVER: MAINE CLUB GLOSS 400gsm; TEXT: 200gsm
SIZE 75 × 155mm (2 15/16 × 6 1/8in)
PRINT TECHNIQUE FOUR-COLOR OFFSET LITHO

ADDITIONAL TECHNIQUES MATTE LAMINATION, SILVER-FOIL BLOCKING, CONCERTINA FOLDED
PRINTER FRANKLY DEVILISH
BINDING DOUBLE-SIDED TAPE TO STICK TEXT INTO COVER

Ozwald Boateng has championed the cause of British menswear and tailoring for two decades. His ability to unify classic bespoke tailoring with a unique sense of color, cut, and detail has allowed him to create a distinctive, recognizable, and widely acclaimed style. Every year he stages two fashion shows, one in Milan and the other in Paris. By utilizing photographs taken from the shows, creative consultancy Yang Rutherford produces a lookbook to showcase his collection.

With consistent format and branding, the design of each lookbook is influenced by the theme and color scheme prevalent in any particular season. Two weights of Maine Club Gloss offer a unified feel to the cover and concertina-folded insert. The glossy stock is the ideal substrate to show off both vibrant color and sleek black, the two signature elements of Ozwald Boateng's branding.

Aloof Design

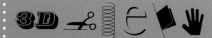

PROJECT PRESS NOTEBOOK
DESIGNER LEIGH SIMPSON at ALOOF DESIGN
CLIENT MULBERRY

PAPER FACTS:
STOCK COVER: COLORPLAN/ACCENT SMOOTH 350gsm; TEXT: COLORPLAN/ACCENT SMOOTH 160gsm
SIZE 105 × 148mm (5¾ × 4⅛in)
PRINT TECHNIQUE OFFSET LITHO
ADDITIONAL TECHNIQUES CREATION OF SPECIAL DEBOSSING TOOL WITH MOCK-CROC TEXTURE, DEBOSSING, DIE-CUTTING, HOT-FOIL BLOCKING, HAND-FINISHING

BINDING FULL-CANADIAN BINDING WITH COVER WRAPPING AROUND SPINE TO CONCEAL WIRE-O
PRINTER BENWELL SEBARD

Aloof Design created an alternative press giveaway to coincide with Mulberry's menswear fashion show in Florence. The all-paper notebook was inspired by Mulberry's iconic leather agenda. The eight-page cover was made from a single sheet of card, folded back on itself, glued, die-cut, and debossed with a specially created tool giving a mock-croc texture. The full-Canadian binding means the cover wraps around the spine to conceal the Wire-O.

Squires & Company

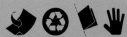

PROJECT TWO PEAS IN ONE POD
DESIGNER SQUIRES & COMPANY
CLIENTS NOEL ELLISON, MEREDITH MARTINDALE

PAPER FACTS:
STOCK COVER: SEED PACKS 60lb; CARDS: MOHAWK TEXTURES, FLAX, BROWN KRAFT ENVELOPES
SIZE CARDS: 4 × 6in (102 × 152mm)
PRINT TECHNIQUE DIGITAL
PRINTER PADGETT PRINTING COMPANY

US design consultancy Squires & Company was approached by two friends needing an announcement for the birth of their two boys. The humorous concept uses readily available brown kraft envelopes and packets of real pea seeds to create an engaging mailer with a vintage feel. The budget dictated digital printing. A number of stocks and weights of paper were tested on the digital press. The final choice was a stock with recycled content that soaked in more of the digital-press ink, giving the appearance of a more traditional printing or silkscreened method.

JHI

PROJECT DIFFERENTIA
DESIGNER JHI
CLIENT SELF-INITIATED

PAPER FACTS:
STOCK WAUSAU PAPERS, EXACT OPAQUE, NATURAL TEXT, 50lb
SIZE 34½ × 23in (876 × 584mm) FLAT
PRINT TECHNIQUES FOUR-COLOR OFFSET LITHO, TWO PMS, AND INLINE SPOT-GLOSS VARNISH; ALL FOUR-COLOR IMAGES MANIPULATED TO ALLOW MINIMAL DOT GAIN ON THE UNCOATED SHEET; LINE SCREEN 200dpi

ADDITIONAL TECHNIQUES VARYING FOLDS: SOME COPIES FOLDED JUST ONCE ON THE LONGEST AXIS, THEN COLLATED THREE SHEETS TOGETHER; OTHERS, ONCE COLLATED, WERE REFOLDED VIA A SECOND PASS ON THE FOLDER TO 11 × 17in (279 × 432mm); SOME WERE THEN FOLDED TO 8½ × 11in (273 × 216mm) FOR MAILING
PRINTER CENVEO

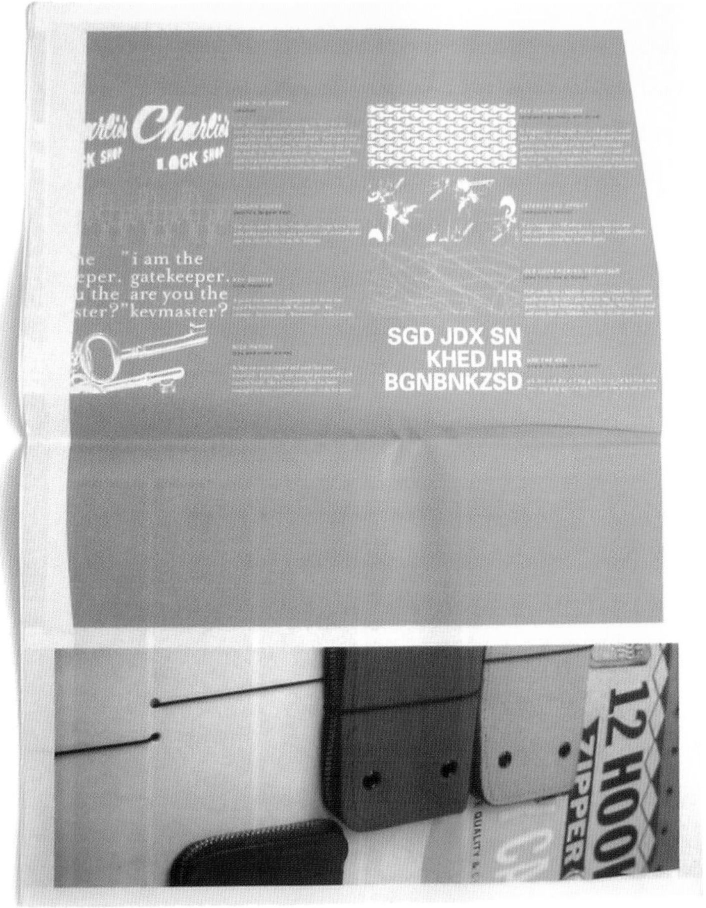

JHI is a strategic creative-services company based in Richmond, Virginia, and *Differentia* was created as a new business tool, targeting like-minded clients who would connect with it on an emotional level. The piece celebrates uniqueness by focusing on how someone's key ring holds information about his or her day-to-day life. Its oversized design is enhanced by the stock chosen, which offers just enough intended showthrough to add a subtle extra layer of design value.

The paper's weight and dimensions also offer the piece greater flexibility. Folded as a newspaper, it becomes a guerrilla-marketing tool, dropped in building lobbies, waiting rooms, bookstores, and restaurants. Folded to envelope size, the recipient can open it as a conventional piece of direct mail.

Differentia was a huge success for JHI, winning numerous design awards, and it was included in a traveling show sponsored by the New York Art Director's Club.

Squires & Company

PROJECT NASCAR INVITATION
DESIGNER SQUIRES & COMPANY
CLIENT HILLWOOD

PAPER FACTS:
STOCK FRENCH PAPER
CONSTRUCTION WHITEWASH 100lb
SIZE VARIOUS, TO FIT A STANDARD A7 ENVELOPE
(74 × 105mm; 2 15/16 × 5 3/4in)
PRINT TECHNIQUES ENVELOPE: TWO COLOR
INSERTS: FOUR-COLOR DIGITAL
ADDITIONAL TECHNIQUE HAND-ASSEMBLY
PRINTER PADGETT PRINTING COMPANY

Hillwood wanted fun invitations to draw clients and employees to a private party at the Texas Motor Speedway during the NASCAR races, and to educate participants about the colorful history of the races. Squires & Company created a set of trading cards featuring NASCAR's Most Popular Drivers from the preceding five decades. Photos, vintage logos, and memorabilia were hand-distressed and arranged to appear authentic. The glossy nature of digital printing mixed with the uncoated paper stock gave the design an appropriately lo-fi look. A printed bellyband was wrapped around the cards to keep them together.

B&W Studio

PROJECT 75TH ANNIVERSARY ANNUAL APPEAL
DESIGNERS LEE BRADLEY, STEVE WILLS at B&W STUDIO
PHOTOGRAPER JOHN ANGERSON
CLIENT ST. GEORGE'S CRYPT

PAPER FACTS:
STOCK GF SMITH COLORPLAN 270gsm
SIZE 300 × 222mm ($11\frac{13}{16} \times 8\frac{3}{4}$in)
PRINT TECHNIQUE ONE-COLOR OFFSET LITHO
ADDITIONAL TECHNIQUE SILVER-FOIL BLOCKING
PRINTER HARROGATE PRINT LTD.

St George's Crypt is a Leeds-based charity that provides shelter and advice to homeless, rootless, and disadvantaged people. For their 75th-anniversary appeal, they asked B&W Studio to create a mailer that would help raise £750,000 (US $1.5 million). Using simple typography and layout on eight different colors of GF Smith Colorplan paper, the solution centers on the house-shaped outline formed by an open envelope that was to be used to send in a donation. The strapline "Help put a roof over somebody's head" ties the whole concept together. The piece won gold in the Direct Mail section of the Roses Design Awards 2005.

B&W Studio

PROJECT ANNUAL APPEAL 2007
DESIGNERS LEE BRADLEY, STEVE WILLS, ANDREW DROOG at B&W STUDIO
PHOTOGRAPHER JOHN ANGERSON
CLIENT ST. GEORGE'S CRYPT

PAPER FACTS:
STOCK MCNAUGHTON CYCLUS PRINT 115gsm
SIZE 210 × 148.5mm (8¼ × 5 13/16in)
PRINT TECHNIQUE TWO-COLOR OFFSET LITHO
ADDITIONAL TECHNIQUE BADGE WITH LOGO APPLIED
PRINTER HARROGATE PRINT LTD.

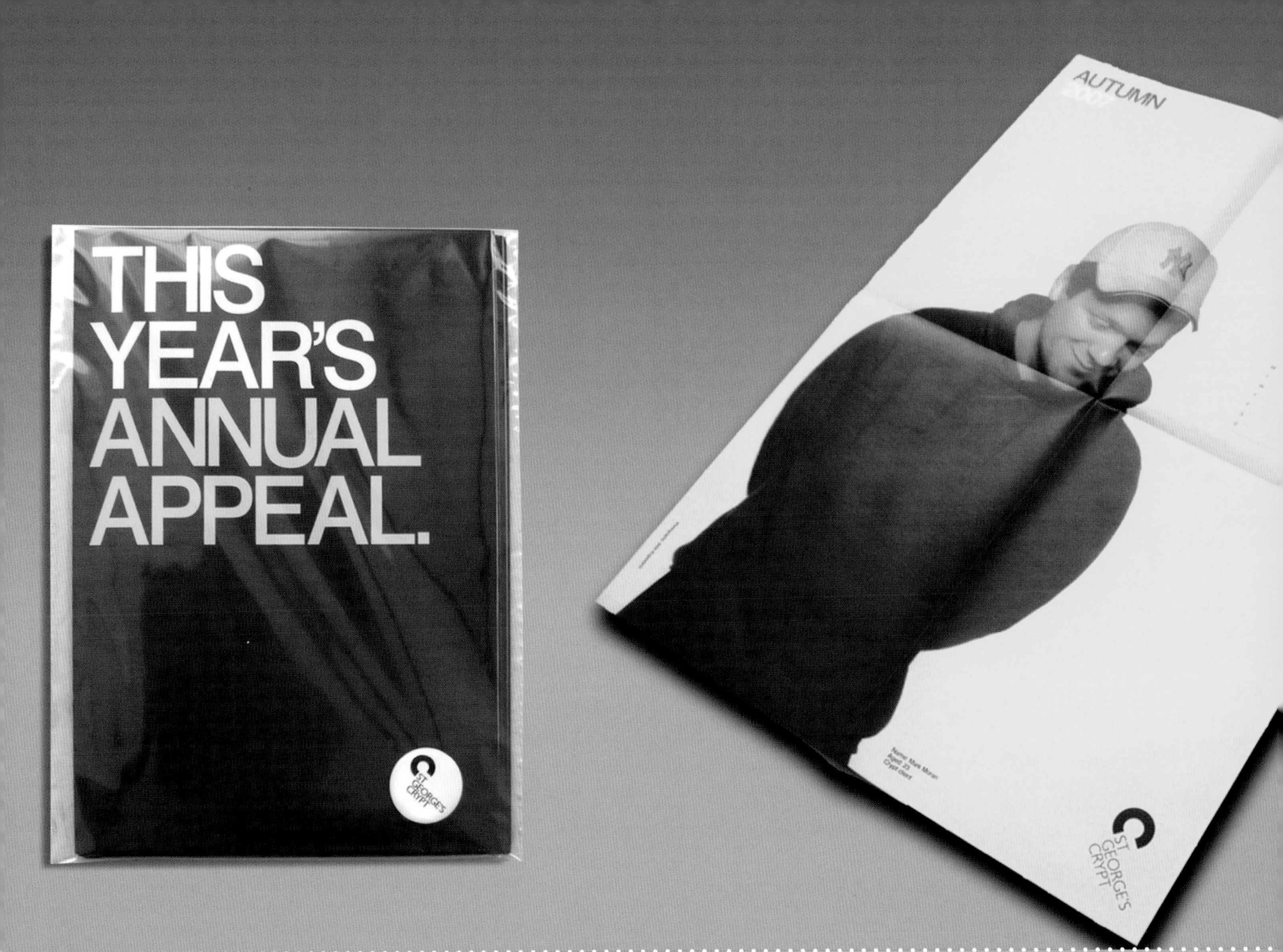

Charity St. George's Crypt's annual appeal is designed to raise money for the homeless. The 2007 brief to B&W Studio was to communicate how the money is spent and how the charity's clients benefit from the donations as well as updating donors on the previous year's activities. Direct messaging and the bold use of high-contrast yellow and black were chosen to ensure the piece would really stand out.

A recycled paper stock was chosen for its lightweight quality—a practical choice to help keep postage costs down. The plastic mailing-bag houses four A3 (297 × 420mm; 11¾ × 16½in) calendar posters, one for each season, folded to make a 16-page loose-leaf brochure. The final touch—a free badge bearing the charity's logo—gives the overall feel of a mailer with added extras.

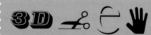

johnson banks

PROJECT SEND A LETTER
DESIGNER JOHNSON BANKS
CLIENT SELF-INITIATED

PAPER FACTS:
STOCK TWO LAMINATED SHEETS OF 270gsm COLORPLAN
ADDITIONAL TECHNIQUES SILVER-FOILED ON THE REVERSE, HAND-COLLATED
PRINTER BENWALL SEBARD

SPECIAL CONSIDERATIONS:
"If you can name all the fonts, you qualify for a free alphabet. Best attempt we've had so far is 21."

Michael Johnson, johnson banks, UK

Invited to take a stall at the Victoria and Albert Museum's annual summer fete in London, UK, design consultancy johnson banks decided to run its own post office. They needed some product to sell, and the idea of "sending a letter" evolved into the creation of 26 actual die-cut letters, making up a playful postcard alphabet.

Each card consists of two laminated sheets of Colorplan, with a selection of bright colors used face up and lighter colors on the backs. Twenty-six different "fat" fonts were chosen so that the letters would be robust enough to be die-cut to shape. Suitable postcard prompts—such as a stamp-positional rectangle—were silver-foiled on the reverse. A mammoth hand-collating session resulted in either multicolored single-letter bundles or a full alphabet of 26 different letters, all tied up with string.

Aloof Design

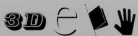

PROJECT SEASONAL SELLING CAMPAIGN SS05
DESIGNER LEIGH SIMPSON at ALOOF DESIGN
CLIENT GEORGINA GOODMAN

PAPER FACTS:
STOCK ZEN 300gsm
SIZE 3.8m (12½ft) UNFOLDED
PRINT TECHNIQUE FOUR-COLOR OFFSET LITHO
ADDITIONAL TECHNIQUE DEBOSSED COVER
PRINTER GENERATION

SPECIAL CONSIDERATIONS:
"There are always difficulties with this kind of production. The skill is to keep communicating with your printer, problem-solve, and focus on getting the right result. At Aloof, we pride ourselves on our ability to push our manufacturers into new territories."

Michelle Kostyrka, Aloof Design, UK

Aloof Design created a brand identity and range of packaging for couture shoe designer Georgina Goodman to coincide with the opening of her flagship store in London's Mayfair. Each season, Aloof creates a lookbook and product guide for the designer that is sent to journalists and fashion buyers worldwide as the basis of a promotional campaign. Their enthusiasm in pushing the limits of print and production techniques has ensured Georgina Goodman's marketing campaigns have become synonymous with innovation.

The formats of the books have varied, to some extent dictated by the maximum printable area of the paper stock. Depending on the origin of the stock, the sheet sizes vary from SRA2 (450 × 640mm; 17¾ × 25¼in) to B1 (1,000 × 1,414mm; 39¼ × 55¾in). In one case, with the Autumn/Winter 04 lookbook, Aloof enlisted the help of a European paper mill that agreed to produce an oversized sheet specially for the job. For the Spring/Summer 05 concertina lookbook, the pages for one book fitted onto a sheet of B1 paper. They were cut out and joined together by hand to create a foldout book nearly 4m (13ft) in length.

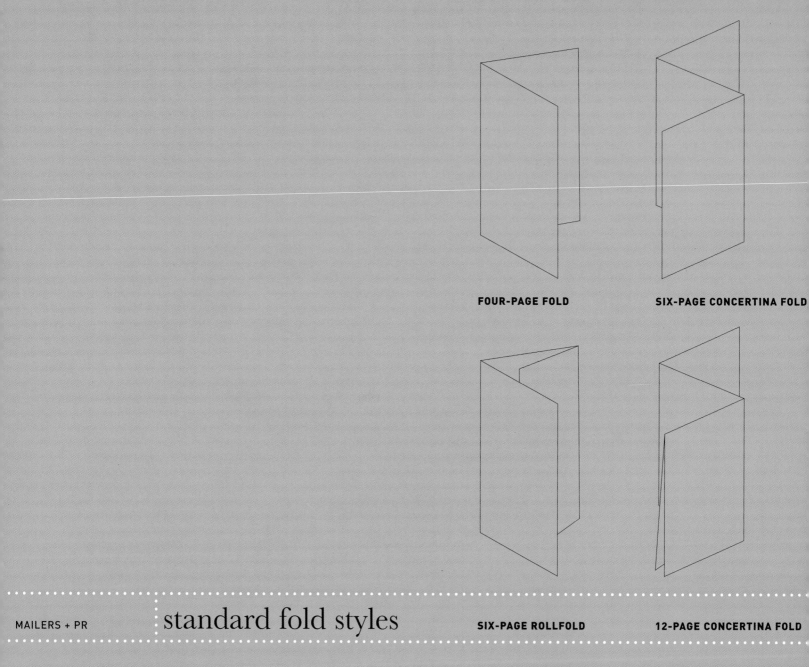

standard fold styles

FOUR-PAGE FOLD

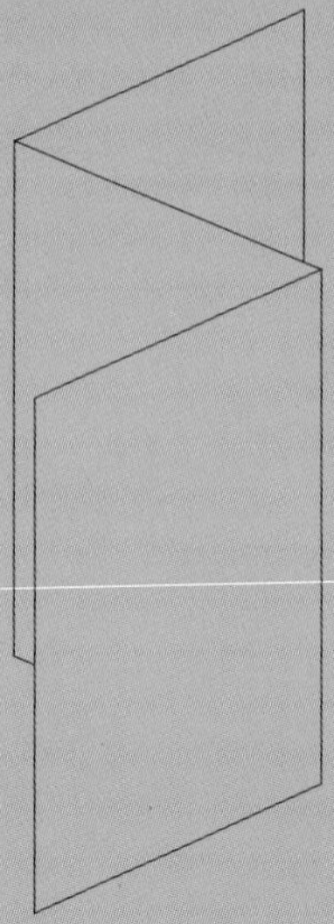

SIX-PAGE CONCERTINA FOLD

SIX-PAGE ROLLFOLD

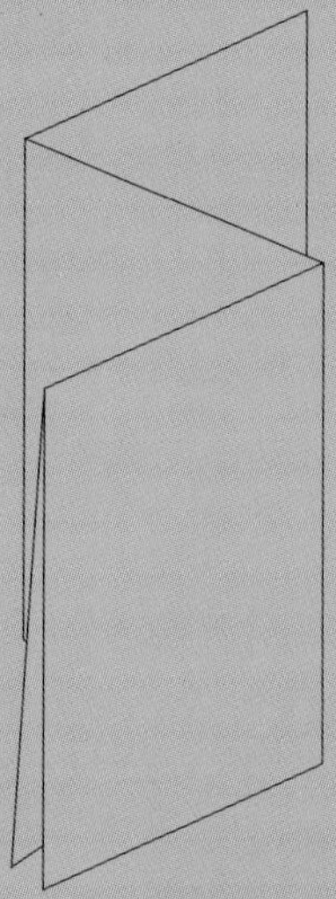

12-PAGE CONCERTINA FOLD

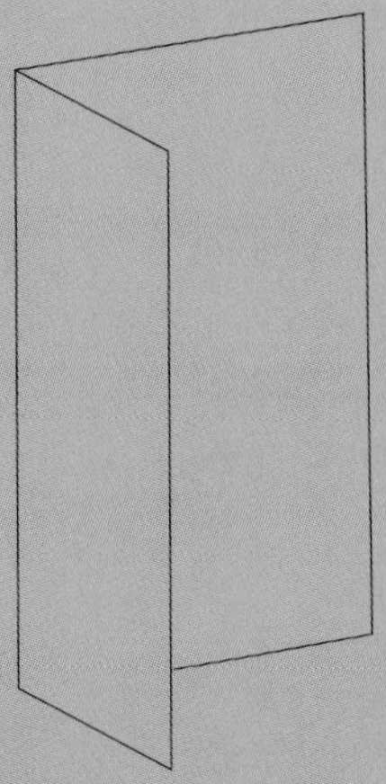

FOUR-PAGE SHORT FOLD

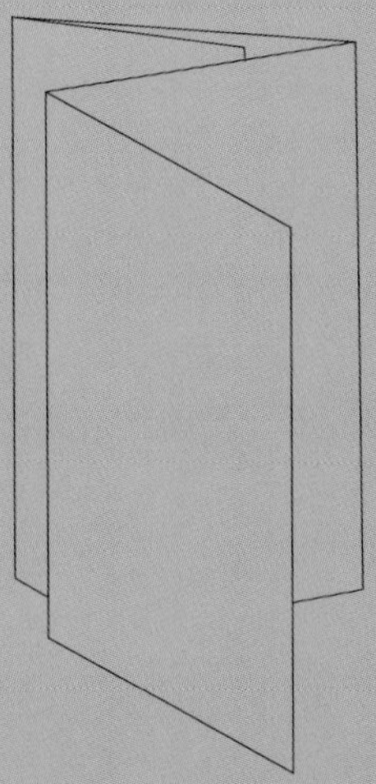

PARALLEL MAP FOLD

EIGHT-PAGE GATEFOLD

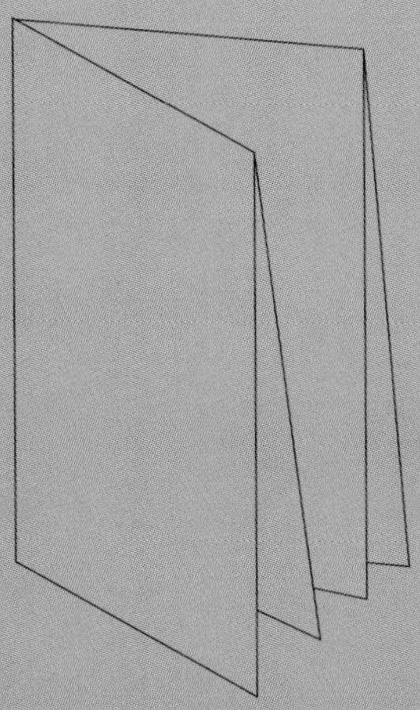

EIGHT-PAGE FRENCH FOLD

EIGHT-PAGE PARALLEL FOLD

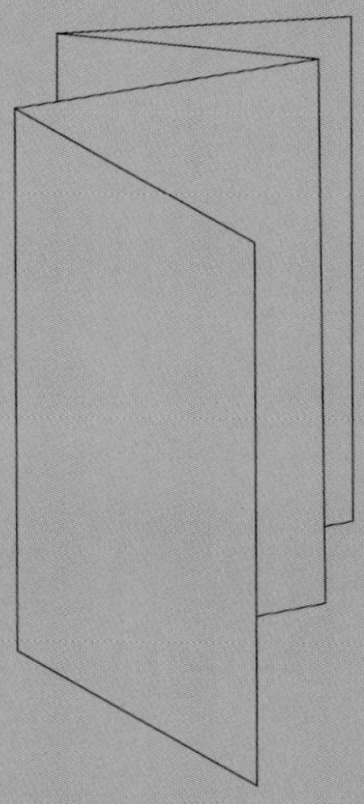

EIGHT-PAGE CONCERTINA FOLD

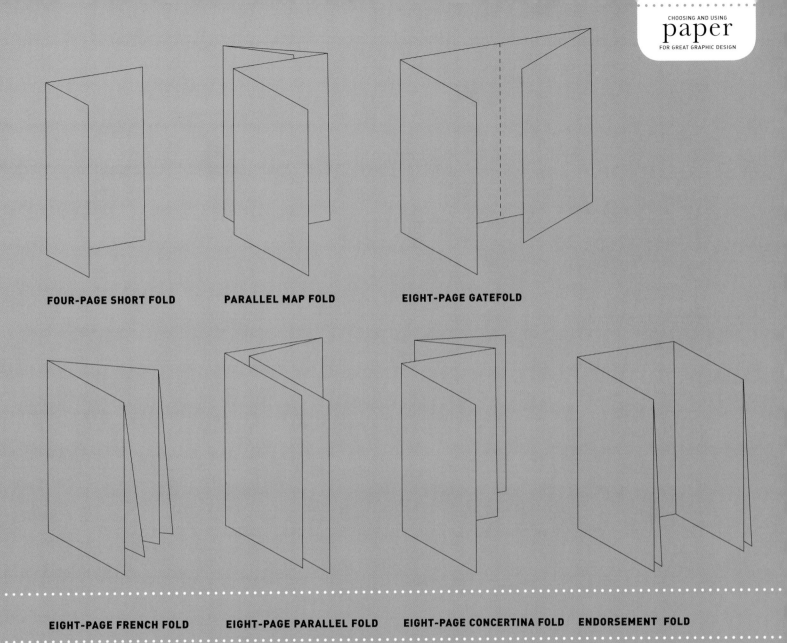

ENDORSEMENT FOLD

CHAPTER 4

paper manufacturers' promotions

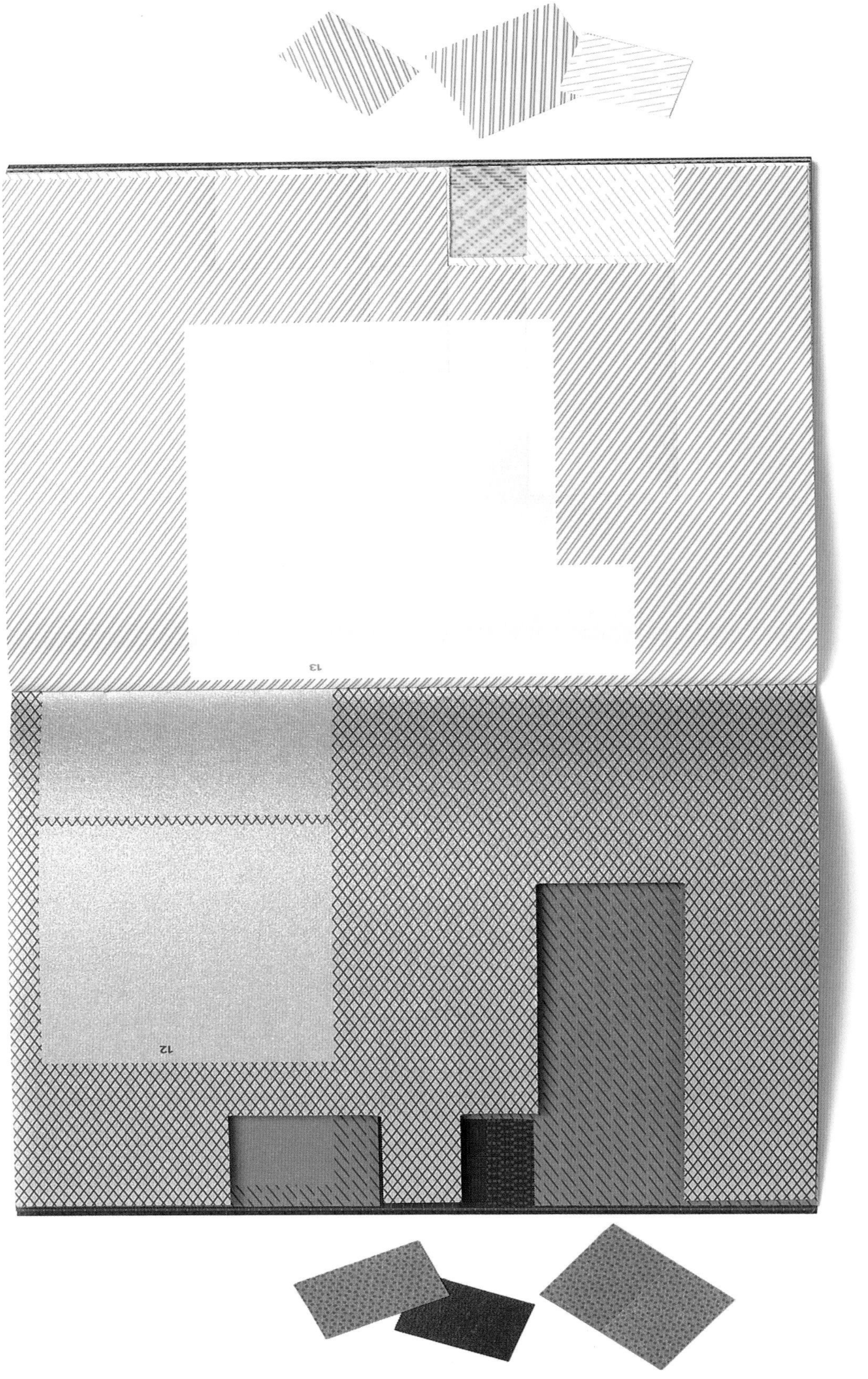
13
12

PAPER MANUFACTURERS' PROMOTIONS

JHI

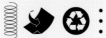

PROJECT WAUSAU ASTROBRIGHTS MORE PROMOTION
DESIGNER JHI
CLIENT WAUSAU PAPER

PAPER FACTS:
STOCK WAUSAU PAPER ASTROBRIGHTS, ALL COLORS, VARIOUS WEIGHTS
SIZE 7½ × 5in (191 × 127mm)
PRINT TECHNIQUE METALLIC INKS USED THROUGHOUT
PRINTER PROGRESS PRINTING COMPANY
BINDING WIRE-O

SPECIAL CONSIDERATIONS:
"The client deeply appreciated JHI's multilevel strategic thinking, which has proved much more effective than a straightforward design solution."

John Homs, JHI, US

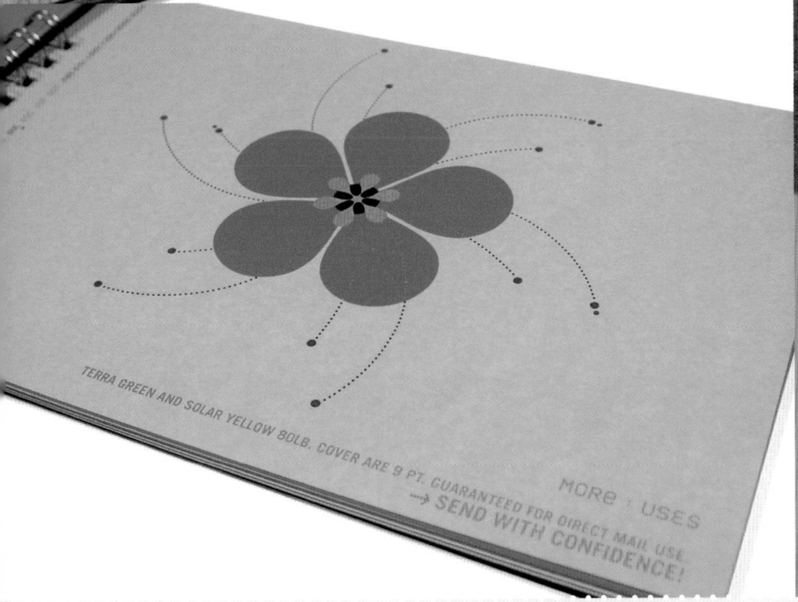

The challenge for Wausau Papers was to differentiate their line of bright papers in what is considered a commoditized category. US creative-services company JHI initiated a strategic-positioning process to define clearly the aspects of the product that set it apart. The result was the concept of More: Wausau offers more colors, more weights, more cut sizes, better service. The book was designed to be small enough to sit on the counters of small printshops where most of these papers are purchased and used.

Metallic inks were used throughout to offer maximum appeal and inspiration to designers, showing how they reacted on such intensely colored surfaces. The book was bound with Wire-O for easy handling. And since Wausau Papers also offers the most black in their black-paper stock, JHI chose to include black-paper samples from other manufacturers so that customers could make a side-by-side comparison for themselves.

PAPER MANUFACTURERS' PROMOTIONS

Curious

PROJECT SAPPI MAGNO CORNER POSTER
DESIGNER CURIOUS
ART DIRECTOR GARY SMITH
DESIGNER AND ILLUSTRATOR JOE HARRIES
PHOTOGRAPHER HELEN MCARDLE
CLIENT SAPPI FINE PAPER EUROPE

PAPER FACTS:
STOCK SAPPI MAGNO SATIN 170gsm
SIZE 800 × 600mm (31½ × 23⅝in)

PRINT TECHNIQUE FOUR-COLOR OFFSET LITHO
ADDITIONAL TECHNIQUE SPOT VARNISH ON ILLUSTRATIONS
PRINTER BLONDE

Achieving intensity of color is something that paper manufacturers constantly strive to demonstrate. Sappi Fine Paper Europe came up with an ingenious competition to promote their Magno range. The public were invited to send in photographs on the theme "intensity in nature." Curious, London, created color-coded 3D collages from over 600 submitted images, which were then photographed to create a promotional poster.

The symmetrical nature of the images prompted the decision to create a corner poster, one folded down the vertical axis to be used on either the concave or convex corner of a room. This creates the illusion of movement and offers the flat poster format the chance to occupy a 3D space. The use of a spot varnish on the illustrations, printed on high-white Sappi Magno Satin, enhances the photographic quality of the images. The poster was offered via a teaser-mailer campaign, and high response rates validated the effectiveness of the concept.

This 64 page specimen booklet utilises 16 unusual printing surfaces taken from the Curious Collection.
Unusual printing surfaces
Experimenting with paper, board and plastic substrates
The Curious Collection is a unique laboratory developed range of papers, boards and plastics—all with enhanced aesthetic and surface properties. The collection is made up of five ranges: Translucents, Particles, Metallics, Touch and Plastics.
The objective of this booklet for the designer is to provide an access point to the ranges and encourage further investigation of the collection.
Particles are recycled sheets with variations of pronounced fibres, all with differing characteristics. Some grades have thermochromic qualities (altering in colour after a temperature change) while others shimmer in the light or have colour coordinated flecks that add a unique dimension to the surface.
Range includes 12 colours, 3 weights (100–250g), 2 envelopes (C5 and DL)
Page 19.20 45.46 Hot Ice 100g
Translucents
Particles
Metallics
Touch
Plastics

Design Project

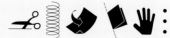

PROJECT UNUSUAL PRINTING SURFACES
DESIGNER DESIGN PROJECT
CLIENT ARJOWIGGINS

PAPER FACTS:
STOCK SLIPCASE: CURIOUS COLLECTION, TOUCH-ARCHES CRIMSON 250gsm; 64-PAGE SPECIMEN BOOKLET: CURIOUS COLLECTION, TRANSLUCENT PLUM IRIDESCENT 100gsm, METALLIC METAL INFERNO 120gsm, TRANSLUCENT RED 100gsm, METALLIC METAL BRONZE ORE 120gsm, METALLIC METAL GOLD LEAF 120gsm, METALLIC METAL LUSTRE 120gsm, STOCK PLASTICS MELLOW HINT OF SILVER 120gsm, TOUCH-ARCHES VELOUR BRIGHT WHITE 120gsm, TRANSLUCENT SPACE DUST 112gsm, PARTICLES HOT ICE 100gsm, METALLIC IRIDESCENT AQUA FIZZ 120gsm, TRANSLUCENT JADE 100gsm, TRANSLUCENT KIWI IRIDESCENT 100gsm, METALLIC IRIDESCENT CITRIC BUZZ 120gsm, TRANSLUCENT GOLD 100gsm, TOUCH WET ALASKA 120gsm
SIZE SLIPCASE: 145 × 198mm (5¾ × 7 13/16in); BOOKLET: 165 × 195mm (6½ × 7 11/16in)
PRINT TECHNIQUES SLIPCASE: HOLOFOIL-BLOCKED BOTH SIDES; BOOKLET: PRINTED THROUGHOUT IN 21 SPECIAL COLORS, INCLUDING FLUORESCENTS, METALLICS, UV VARNISHES, AND CLEAR-FOIL BLOCKING

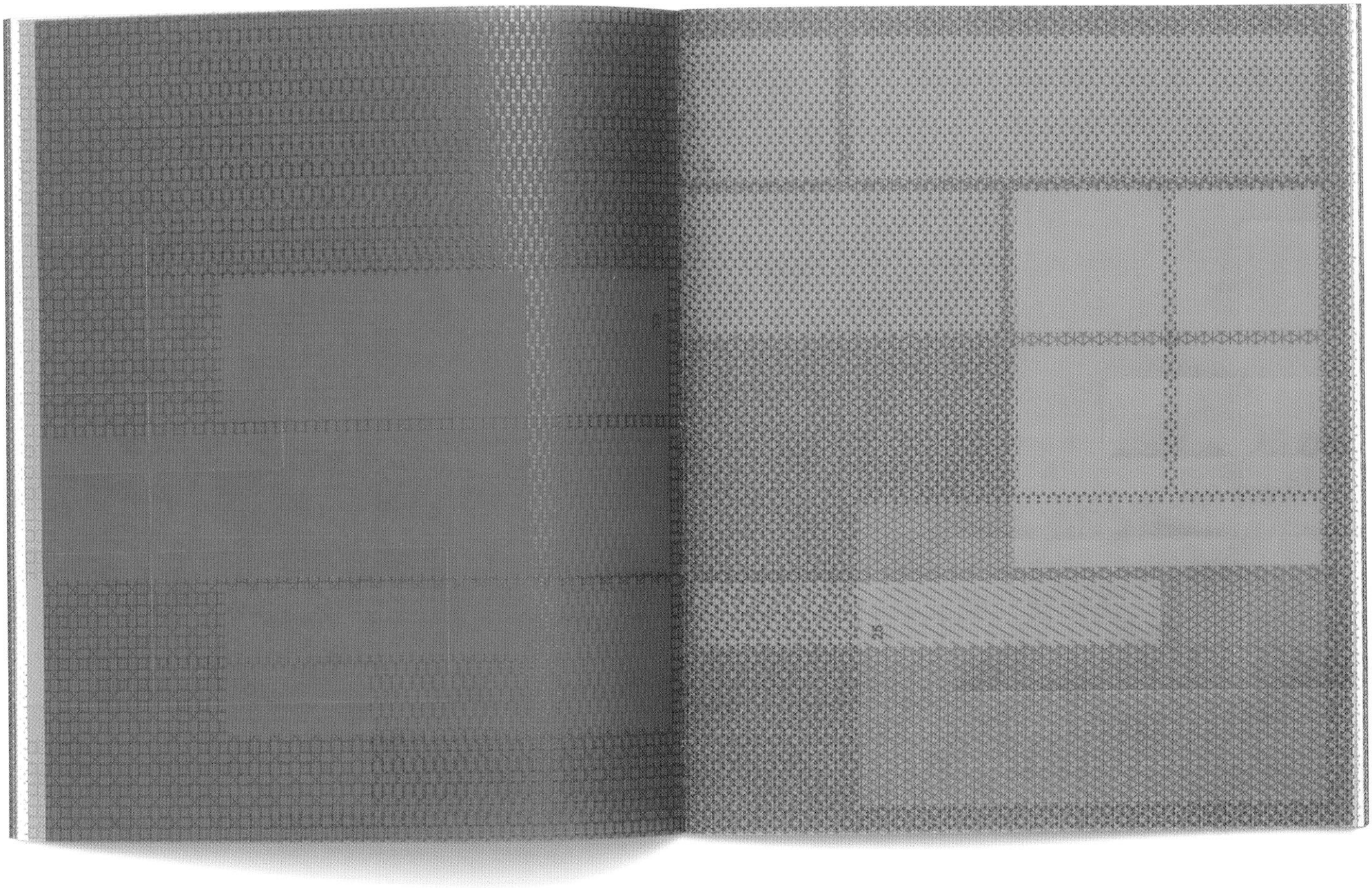

ADDITIONAL TECHNIQUES SLIPCASE: DIE-CUT, CREASED, HAND-FOLDED, AND GLUED; BOOKLET: MICROPERFORATED THROUGHOUT IN MULTIPLE POSITIONS TO ENABLE DESIGNERS TO DECONSTRUCT THE PAGES FOR SAMPLES AND REFERENCE
PRINTER TEAM IMPRESSION
BINDING HANDBOUND

Unusual Printing Surfaces was created to promote the Arjowiggins Curious Collection, a range of papers, boards, and plastics developed in the laboratory. A series of graphic patterns mask out and highlight the unprinted areas of the pages, allowing the designer to become immersed in the colors and surface properties of the papers. The copy on the shortfall slipcase acts as vital reference information. Getting production right was a hands-on process. Over 30 press passes were needed, adjusting pressures on press to ensure the right effect of translucent inks and opaque metallics on the 17 diverse substrates used.

PAPER MANUFACTURERS' PROMOTIONS

Various

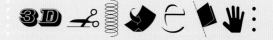

PROJECT VARIOUS PAPER PROMOTIONS
DESIGNER ODEN MARKETING AND DESIGN
CLIENT INTERNATIONAL PAPERS

PAPER FACTS: FORGET APPLES TO APPLES
STOCK ACCENT® OPAQUE COVER 100 WHITE SMOOTH
PRINT TECHNIQUES FOUR-COLOR OFFSET LITHO + MATCH GREEN TOUCH PLATE, DENSE BLACK
ADDITIONAL TECHNIQUES EMBOSSING, CLEAR FOIL

PAPER FACTS: IS WHITE THE ABSENCE OF COLOR?
STOCK ACCENT® OPAQUE WHITE SMOOTH
PRINT TECHNIQUES FOUR-COLOR OFFSET LITHO WITH FLUORESCENT INK ADDED TO M/Y, MATCH OPAQUE GRAY, DENSE BLACK
ADDITIONAL TECHNIQUE DOT-TO-DOT VARNISH

PAPER FACTS: POP
STOCK ACCENT® OPAQUE COVER WHITE SMOOTH 100lb
PRINT TECHNIQUES FOUR-COLOR OFFSET LITHO WITH FLUORESCENT INK ADDED TO M/C, MATCH GRAY, MATCH RED
ADDITIONAL TECHNIQUES SPOT DULL VARNISH, SCULPTURED EMBOSSING WITH CLEAR-FOIL STAMP

PAPER FACTS: THE THRILL OF SPRINGHILL®
STOCK POCKET FOLDER: SPRINGHILL VELLUM BRISTOL

COVER WHITE 80lb; PROPELLER: SPRINGHILL TAG MANILA 200lb; POSTER: SPRINGHILL OPAQUE OFFSET SMOOTH CREAM 70lb; TICKET: SPRINGHILL INDEX BLUE 140lb; GOGGLES: SPRINGHILL OPAQUE OFFSET COVER IVORY 65lb **PRINT TECHNIQUES** POCKET FOLDER: FOUR-COLOR OFFSET LITHO WITH FLUORESCENT INK ADDED TO M/Y, MATCH OPAQUE GRAY, DENSE BLACK; PROPELLER: FOUR-COLOR OFFSET LITHO WITH FLUORESCENT INK ADDED TO M/Y; POSTER: FOUR-COLOR OFFSET LITHO WITH FLUORESCENT INK ADDED TO M/Y; TICKET: MATCH OPAQUE BROWN; GOGGLES: FOUR-COLOR OFFSET LITHO **ADDITIONAL TECHNIQUES** POCKET FOLDER: DOT-TO-DOT SPOT DULL VARNISH BOTH SIDES, DIE-CUTTING, SCORING; PROPELLER: DOT-TO-DOT SPOT DULL VARNISH, DIE-CUTTING, EYELET TO POCKET FOLDER; POSTER: DOT-TO-DOT SPOT DULL VARNISH, SCORING, PERFORATION, FOLDING; TICKET: DOT-TO-DOT SPOT DULL VARNISH; GOGGLES: DOT-TO-DOT SPOT DULL VARNISH, TWO-LEVEL REGISTERED EMBOSSING, DIE-CUTTING, SCORING, FOLDING

These promotions highlight different properties of Accent® Opaque. It is an economical opaque that performs well; it has a uniform luminosity; and with embossing, the image pops off the page. The Thrill of Springhill promotion reminds customers about the wide selection of weights, sizes, and distinctive colors that the Springhill range offers.

PAPER MANUFACTURERS' PROMOTIONS

Charles S. Anderson

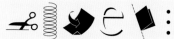

PROJECTS SWATCH BOOKS AND PROMOTIONS
DESIGNER CHARLES S. ANDERSON DESIGN
IMAGES CSA IMAGES
CLIENT FRENCH PAPER

PAPER FACTS:
STOCK SWATCH BOOKS: SPECKLETONE, DUR-O-TONE, PARCHTONE, MOD-TONE IN VARIOUS WEIGHTS; PERFECT MATCH/GO FRENCH PROMOTION: FRENCH SMART WHITE 140lb
SIZE 8½ × 11in (216 × 279mm)

PRINT TECHNIQUE FOUR-COLOR OFFSET LITHO
ADDITIONAL TECHNIQUES LIQUID EMBOSSING, DIE-CUTTING, PERFORATIONS
PRINTER WILLIAMSON PRINTING CORP.
BINDING SWATCH BOOKS: SPIRAL AND DOUBLE-LOOP WIRE BINDING

Based in Michigan, family-owned French Paper is a real gem of a company. In their own words: "We treat our customers as if they live next door. And while we could probably get some computerized robotic arm to do it cheaper, French paper is still hand-checked for quality, which might lead you to believe that we haven't quite caught on to this 21st-century thing. Not true! We're more than a little ahead of our time. Sure, some of our equipment has been around a while, but most of it is brand spanking new. No stranger to high-techno, we even designed some of the machines ourselves."

For many years they have enjoyed a relationship with neighboring Michigan company Charles S. Anderson Design, who are responsible for all of French Paper's brand communications. French Paper is Charles S. Anderson's paper of choice, and their passion for the quality, look, and feel of the various paper types comes across in these promotions. Combining witty range names with vintage-styled typography and pop-culture-inspired imagery, they convey the meticulous standards and warmth of service on which the company prides itself.

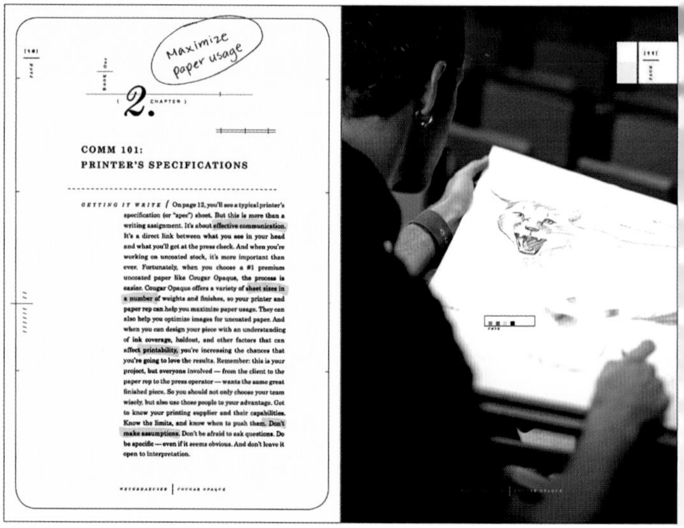

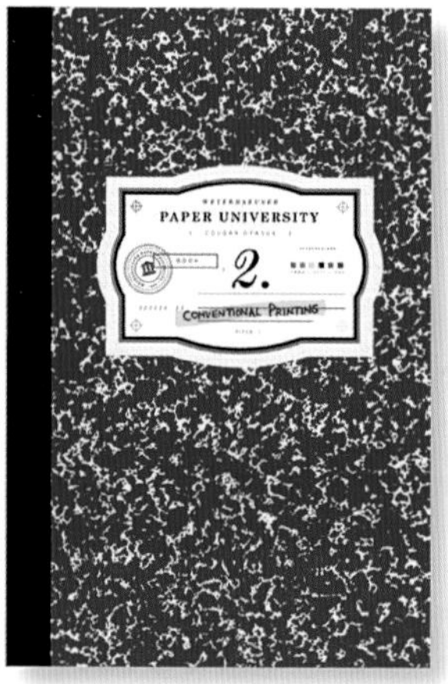

PAPER MANUFACTURERS' PROMOTIONS

Squires & Company

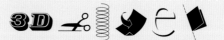

PROJECT PAPER UNIVERSITY
DESIGNER SQUIRES & COMPANY
CLIENT WEYERHAEUSER PAPER COMPANY

PAPER FACTS:
STOCK COVER: 170gsm; TEXT: WEYERHAEUSER COUGAR OPAQUE 60lb, 70lb, 100lb, 120lb
SIZE 6 × 9in (152 × 229mm)

PRINT TECHNIQUE FOUR-COLOR OFFSET LITHO
ADDITIONAL TECHNIQUES UV PROCESS, STOCHASTIC PRINTING, SOY INKS, METALLIC INKS, NUMEROUS SPOTS, DIE-CUTTING, EMBOSSING, FOIL STAMPING
PRINTER WILLIAMSON PRINTING CORP.
BINDING PERFECT BOUND WITH FOLDOUTS

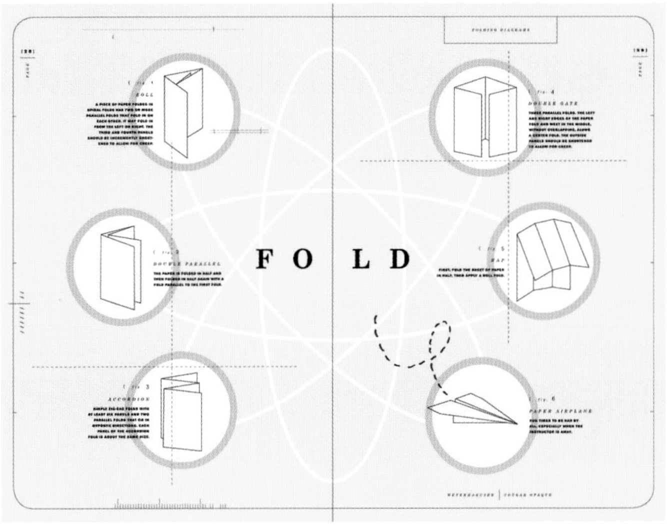

Weyerhaeuser wanted to create a piece to educate the market about how to print on uncoated paper, addressing the common misconception by printers and designers that you can't print deep, rich color on an uncoated surface. One of the primary lessons was to show how to manipulate curves in prepress so as to avoid dot gain on press. The creative concept of the Weyerhaeuser Paper University provided a humorous and engaging vehicle for such an instructive piece.

Because of the amount of information, it was deemed necessary to create three separate books: Prepress, Conventional Printing, and Specialty Printing and Techniques. To demonstrate the paper's versatility, Squires & Company utilized conventional four-color process, UV process, stochastic printing, soy inks, metallic inks, numerous spots, die-cutting, embossing, and foil stamping. Containing photography, color illustration, and spot black-and-white illustrations and icons, the books were very popular and even used as teaching aids on design courses.

PAPER MANUFACTURERS' PROMOTIONS

Cocken, Bolitho

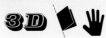

PROJECT OKI CITY AND URBAN ENVIRONMENT
DESIGNERS PAUL COCKEN, MARK BOLITHO
PHOTOGRAPHER PAUL COCKEN
CLIENT OKI

PAPER FACTS:
STOCK CITY, SKYSCRAPERS, OFFICE BLOCKS: OKI A3 BANNER PAPER 160gsm, A4 BANNER PAPER 100gsm, A4 BRIGHT WHITE PRESENTATION PAPER 100gsm
SIZE CITY: 297 × 900mm ($11\frac{3}{4} \times 35\frac{1}{2}$in); SKYSCRAPERS: 215 × 900mm ($8\frac{1}{2} \times 35\frac{1}{2}$in); OFFICE BLOCKS: 215 × 300mm ($8\frac{1}{2} \times 11\frac{3}{4}$in)

TECHNIQUE ORIGAMI CITY AND OFFICE MADE USING ORIGAMI TECHNIQUES BY MARK BOLITHO
www.creaselightning.co.uk

SPECIAL CONSIDERATIONS:
"During the delivery of the origami to Paul's studio I made a paper airplane for him which subsequently made a surprise appearance in the sky over the city."

Mark Bolitho, Creaselightning, UK

ABOVE: OKI CITYSCAPE
Photography: Paul Cocken
Paul Cocken Photography & Digital Imaging

OKI commissioned Paul Cocken to produce a photographic project that would showcase their papers in an interesting way. Paul contacted origami expert Mark Bolitho to design an origami city and office environment using products from the OKI paper range. With the choice of paper a prerequisite of the creative concept, Mark designed all the models using only folded OKI paper.

The office was created using classic origami techniques. The tables and desks were composed of several sheets, generally A4 (210 × 297mm; 8¼ × 11¾in). The six boardroom chairs were each made from a single A4 sheet; the rotating office chairs used two. Model buildings constructed from larger A3 (297 × 420mm; 11¾× 16½in) and A4 banner sheets make up a dramatic city skyline. As the entire installation is made from plain, unprinted paper, Mark's paper-creasing techniques and Paul's clever lighting offer the suggestion of windows and cladding.

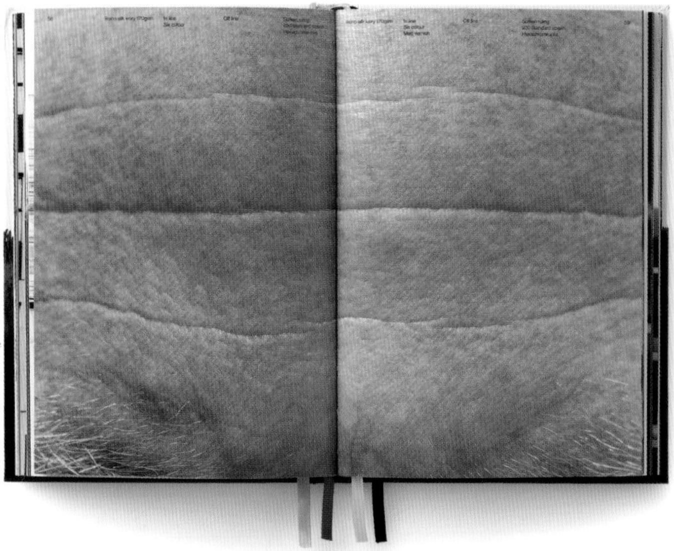

Roundel

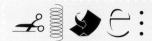

PROJECT IKONO IN LINE OFF LINE
DESIGNER ROUNDEL
CLIENT ZANDERS/M-REAL

PAPER FACTS:
STOCK IKONO SILK, IKONO SILK IVORY, IKONO GLOSS, IKONO MATT 170gsm, 250gsm
SIZE A5 (148 × 210mm; 5 13/16 × 8 1/4in)

PRINT TECHNIQUES 350dpi SCREEN RULING, 200dpi STANDARD SCREEN RULING, 350dpi SCREEN RULING FOUR-COLOR CMYK, 200dpi STANDARD SCREEN RULING FOUR-COLOR CMYK, OVERPRINTING, BLACK AND SILVER DUOTONES, GLOSS VARNISH, SEAL/SPOT SEAL, HEXACHROME INKS, FLUORESCENT INKS, STOCHASTIC SCREEN RULING, STOCHASTIC FOUR-COLOR CMYK, METALLIC INKS, TRITONES, DUOTINTS
ADDITIONAL TECHNIQUES 3D EMBOSSING, GLOSS VARNISH, UV GLOSS VARNISH, MATTE VARNISH, GOLD HOLOFOIL BLOCKING, PERFORATIONS, DIE-CUTTING
PRINTER VENTURA LITHO
BINDING CASEBOUND

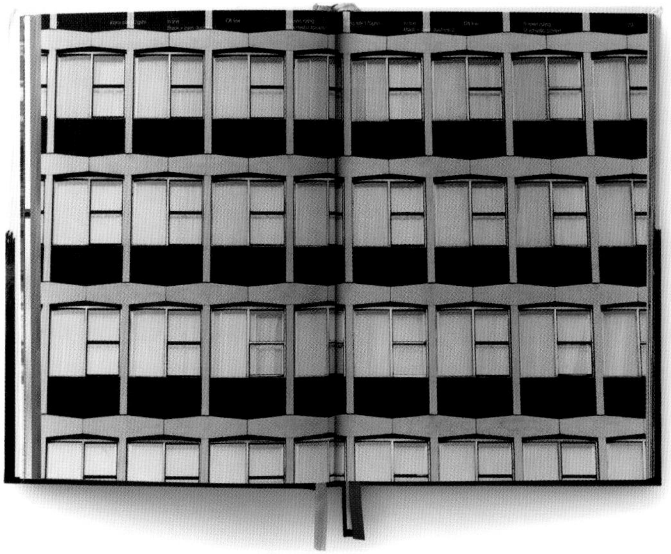

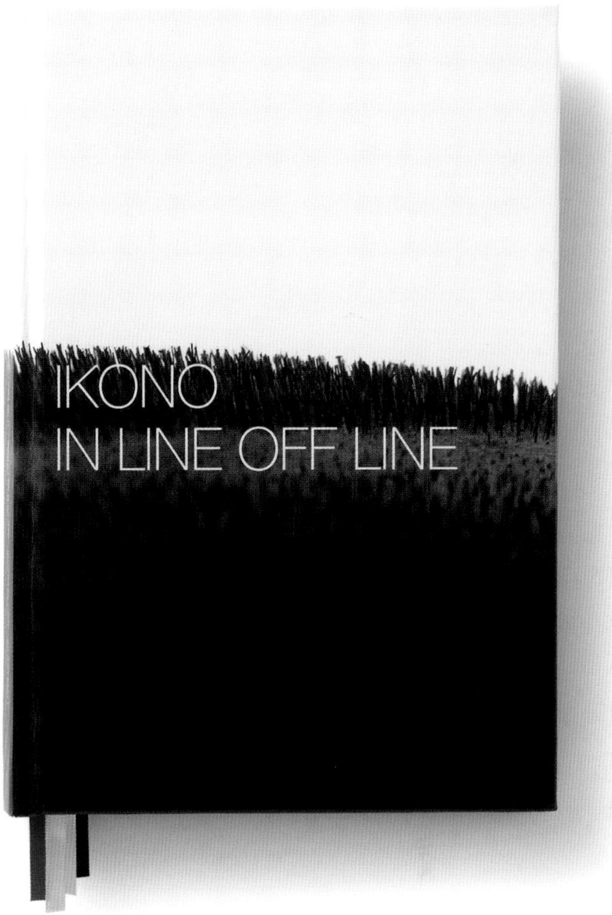

Zanders wanted to demonstrate the benefits of their Ikono range and showcase its ability to take both in-line and off-line print techniques and finishes. Inspired by the terminology of printing, London design consultants Roundel chose a graphic concept that uses diverse photographic imagery united by a linear theme, emphasized by the title of the book, *In Line Off Line*.

The casebound book is split into four sections, each showcasing a surface from the range, and each filled with a wealth of figurative and graphic imagery that employs a multitude of print techniques and finishes to demonstrate the benefits of the Ikono range. The result is a beautiful, comprehensive source of visual and technical material that demonstrates Ikono's consistently reliable product performance.

Roundel

PROJECT IKONO HANDBOOK
DESIGNER ROUNDEL
CLIENT ZANDERS/M-REAL

PAPER FACTS:
STOCK IKONO SILK, IKONO SILK IVORY, IKONO GLOSS, IKONO MATT 170gsm
SIZE A5 LANDSCAPE (210 × 148mm; 8¼ × 5 13/16in)

PRINT TECHNIQUES FOUR-COLOR OFFSET LITHO, FOUR-COLOR BLACK AND WHITE, BLACK HALFTONE, DUOTONE
ADDITIONAL TECHNIQUES BLIND DEBOSSING, SILK LAMINATION, TINTED MATTE VARNISH, TINTED MATTE HALFTONE, MACHINE-SEALED VARNISH (OIL- AND SPIRIT-BASED)
PRINTER VENTURA LITHO
BINDING CASEBOUND

Following the In Line Off Line project, Roundel was once again asked by Zanders to promote the Ikono range by creating a piece aimed at the designer-specific market. The design concept uses excerpts from conversations with specifiers, and these quotes are combined with photography and strong graphic layouts for maximum visual impact and variety.

Four separate landscape casebound books were collated within one large slipcase. Each book showcases one of Ikono's surfaces: Ikono Silk, Ikono Silk Ivory, Ikono Gloss, and Ikono Matt, demonstrating how the paper performs using various printing and finishing techniques, including debossing, silk lamination, and a number of varnishes.

All day confidence
The new Zeta bespoke watermark system,
added company prestige, enhanced corporate image

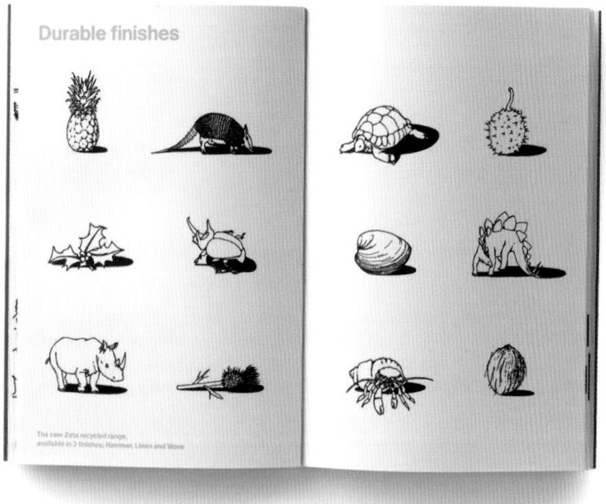

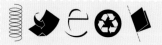

Roundel

PROJECT NUT FREE
DESIGNER ROUNDEL
CLIENT ZANDERS/M-REAL

PAPER FACTS:
STOCK COVER: ZANDERS ZETA RECYCLED 250gsm;
TEXT: ZANDERS ZETA RECYCLED 90gsm
SIZE A5 (148 × 210mm [5 13/16 × 8 1/4in])

PRINT TECHNIQUE OFFSET LITHO
ADDITIONAL TECHNIQUES BESPOKE WATERMARK, WHITE-FOIL BLOCKING, DOUBLE HITS
PRINTER FULMAR
BINDING FRENCH FOLDING, SINGER-SEWN

Low maintenance
The new Zeta bespoke watermark system,
simple and quick to order and available in small quantities

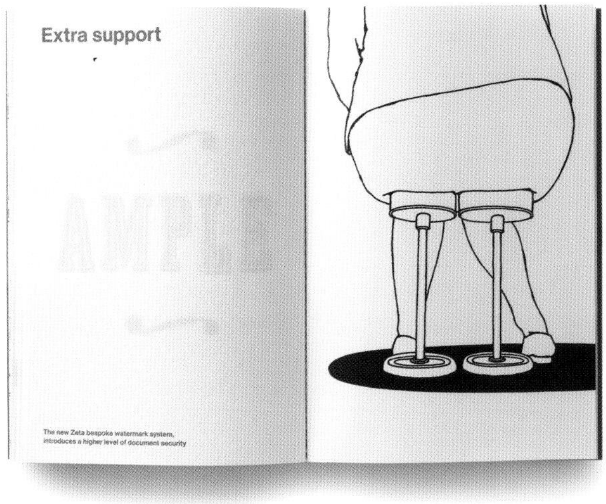

Extra support
AMPLE
The new Zeta bespoke watermark system,
introduces a higher level of document security

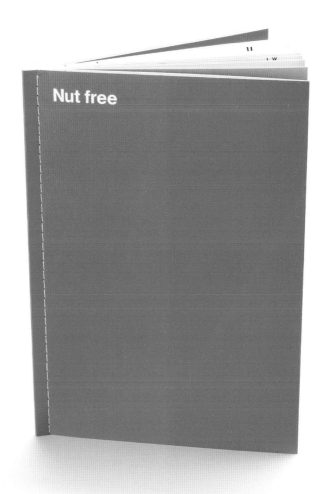

When asked by Zanders to design a piece promoting their new Zeta range of recycled paper and its bespoke watermarking service, Roundel created a series of tongue-in-cheek benefits promoting the environmental and design advantages of the new product and service in a spirit that would appeal to the target audience of designers. Working closely with an illustrator, they refined ideas and developed a series of images to be used throughout the campaign.

The piece needed to showcase the full range of Zeta surfaces and a number of specific print techniques used on them. Key to this was the bespoke watermark facility, but also white-foil blocking and double hits. French-folded sheets and a Singer-sewn binding give the piece a tactile quality that also feels honest and simple, in line with the recycled credentials of the paper.

CHAPTER 5

identity + self-promotion

IDENTITY + SELF-PROMOTION

konnectDesign

PROJECT AUSTIN WALSH IDENTITY
DESIGNERS KAREN KNECHT, DAVID WHITCRAFT at konnectDESIGN
CREATIVE DIRECTOR KAREN KNECHT
CLIENT AUSTIN WALSH PHOTOGRAPHY

PAPER FACTS:
STOCK BUSINESS CARDS: MOHAWK BRILLIANT WHITE 120lb DOUBLE-THICK COVER; MINI PICS: MOHAWK BRILLIANT WHITE 120lb DOUBLE-THICK COVER; STICKERS: FASSON CRACK'N'PEEL PREMIUM
SIZE BUSINESS CARDS: $3\frac{1}{2} \times 2$in (89 × 51mm); MINI PICS: $2\frac{1}{4} \times 2$in (57 × 51mm); STICKERS: $2\frac{1}{2} \times 1\frac{5}{8}$in (89 × 41mm)
PRINT TECHNIQUE FOUR-COLOR, SHEETFED
ADDITIONAL TECHNIQUES THE IMAGE ON EACH CARD WAS DEBOSSED, AND THE TYPE WAS ENGRAVED, FOLLOWED BY ADDITIONAL PRINTING AND VARNISHING AT A LETTERPRESS HOUSE
PRINTER COLORNET PRESS BURDGE, INC. (LITHOGRAPHY, DEBOSSING, ENGRAVING)

ABOVE: AUSTIN WALSH IDENTITY
Photography: JoDean Bifoss for konnectDesign

Photographer Austin Walsh approached konnectDesign to create an identity system that would position him as an emerging photographer who shoots lifestyle and stills. Based on the premise that an image initiates dialogue, the identity features a speech bubble containing various images by Walsh—a design that will allow the identity to evolve and change as his body of work grows. The suite includes a series of business cards with debossed areas to highlight an image, square-format mini pictures, stickers used for impromptu correspondence, and bold, oversized postcards.

The tactile presentation of the images conveys Walsh's work in a professional yet playful manner. Debossing and engraving were key processes to the project, as they establish a sense of the handmade and encourage the individual holding the card to really connect with the image. Austin Walsh says that the cards inspire play. "The photos give people something to talk about. They flip the cards back and forth and rub their thumbs across them. It appeals to their sense of touch—the card feels good."

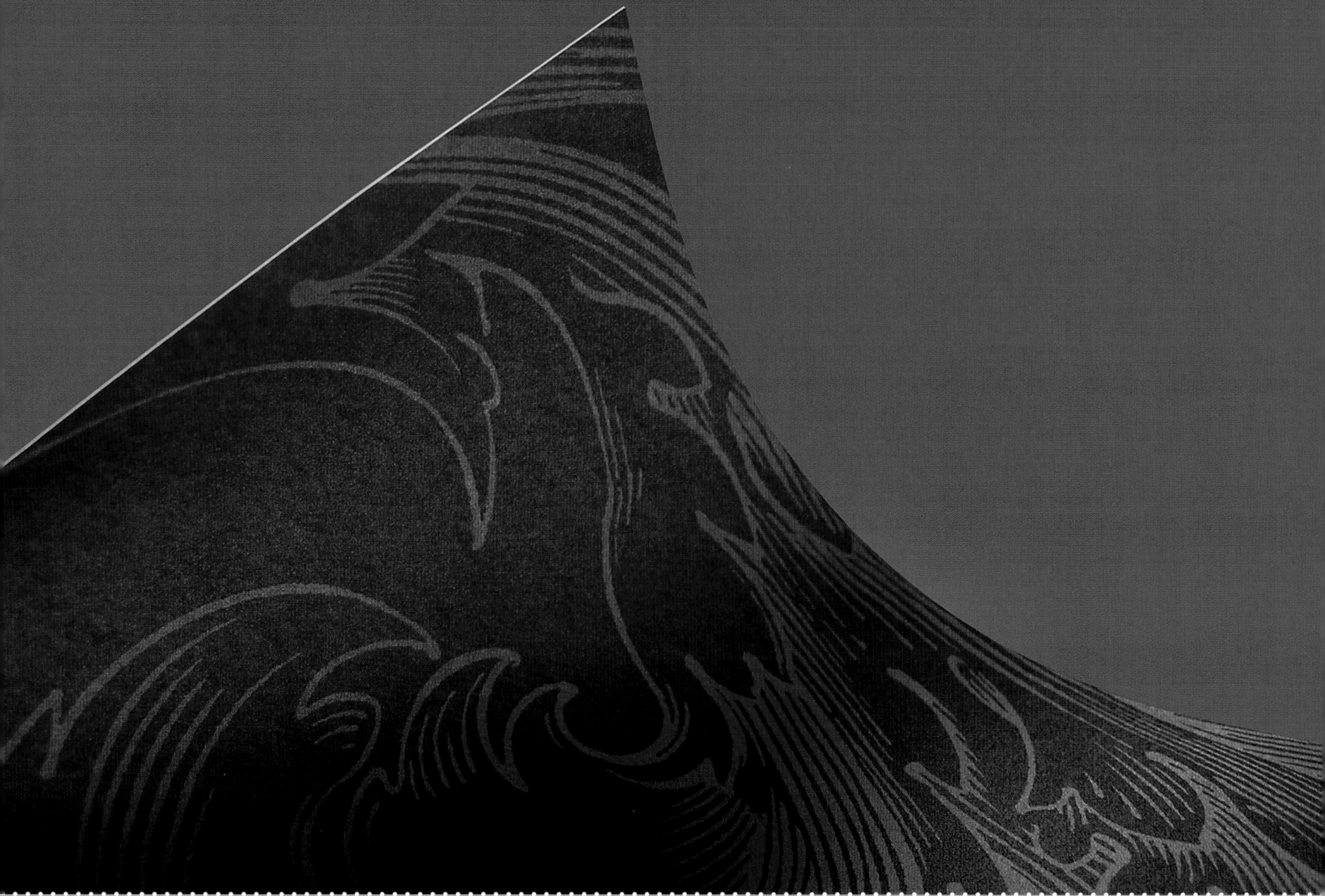

IDENTITY +
SELF-PROMOTION

Yang Rutherford

PROJECT L'HOTEL REBRANDING
DESIGNER JIMMY YANG at YANG RUTHERFORD
CLIENT A CURIOUS GROUP OF HOTELS

PAPER FACTS:
STOCK FENNER MATRISSE COTTON 110gsm
SIZE A4 (210 × 297mm; 8¼ × 11¾in)
PRINT TECHNIQUES OFFSET LITHO, TWO SPECIAL COLORS ON THE FRONT AND TWO SPECIAL COLORS ON THE REVERSE
PRINTER ATELIERS MODERNES D'IMPRESSIONS

L'Hotel is an iconic hotel on Paris' Left Bank, within walking distance of the Boulevard Saint-Germain, the Louvre, and Notre-Dame. Oscar Wilde's last home, and the heart of Parisian society in the Swinging Sixties, the hotel has been remodeled by the acclaimed designer Jacques Garcia. International creative consultants Yang Rutherford were commissioned to create an identity that would reflect the ornate nature of the hotel's interior.

Communicating a sense of luxury depends as much on touch as it does on visual communication. Taking inspiration from the interior decor, the choice of Fenner Matrisse Cotton paper for the letterhead and stationery allowed the designers to simulate the texture of a wallpaper finish. The sophisticated restraint of the typography complements a variety of patterned backgrounds on the reverse that reflect the opulent wallpapers used throughout the hotel.

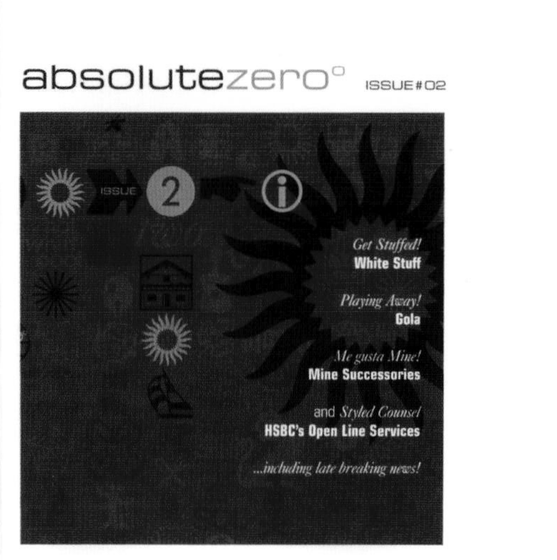

absolutezero°
ISSUE#03
3
NEW WORK
featuring
Art of the matter Spectrum Fine Art See here Southwark Council
Dream Building Dwell Developments Exposure! DMP Media
...including late breaking news and
Dossier a-z° archive

absolutezero°
ISSUE#04
FOUR
NEW WORK including...
Cuddle up with the results
of the absolute zero degrees
field trip to Portmeirion STEEL TOWN Illustrative work for a revamped
housing development HUE & SATURATION Colormatch by Ali Hanan
ROAD TRIP new identity work with an illustrative bent
THE BUG! The new DAB radio from hemingwaydesign and Pure
Digital...and so much more!

absolutezero°
ISSUE#05
5
24 HOUR PARTY PEOPLE° Illustrative work for Glastonbury
KISS AND TELL° Pout packaging and promotional stuff
MORE SURF - LESS BORED° Bulldog broadband event graphics
THE BIG FREEZE Southwark Council's Frost fair
AND much more...

IDENTITY +
SELF-PROMOTION

Absolute Zero°

PROJECT PROMOTIONAL MAGAZINES
DESIGNER ABSOLUTE ZERO°
CLIENT SELF-INITIATED

PAPER FACTS:
STOCK ERA SILK 130gsm
SIZE 230 × 195mm (9 × 7$^{11}/_{16}$in)
PRINT TECHNIQUE DIGITAL
PRINTER INKOLOR
BINDING SADDLESTITCH

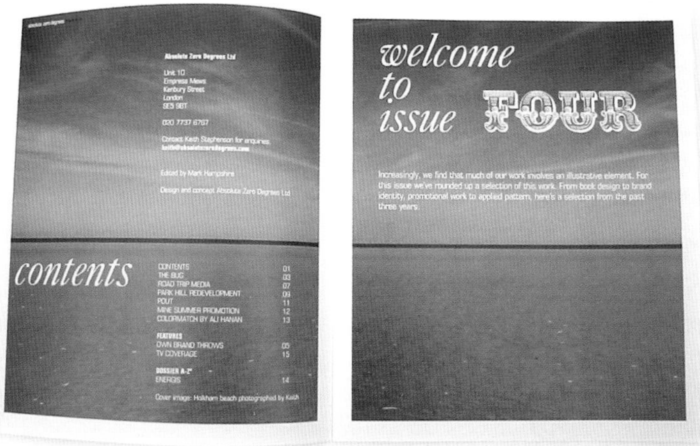

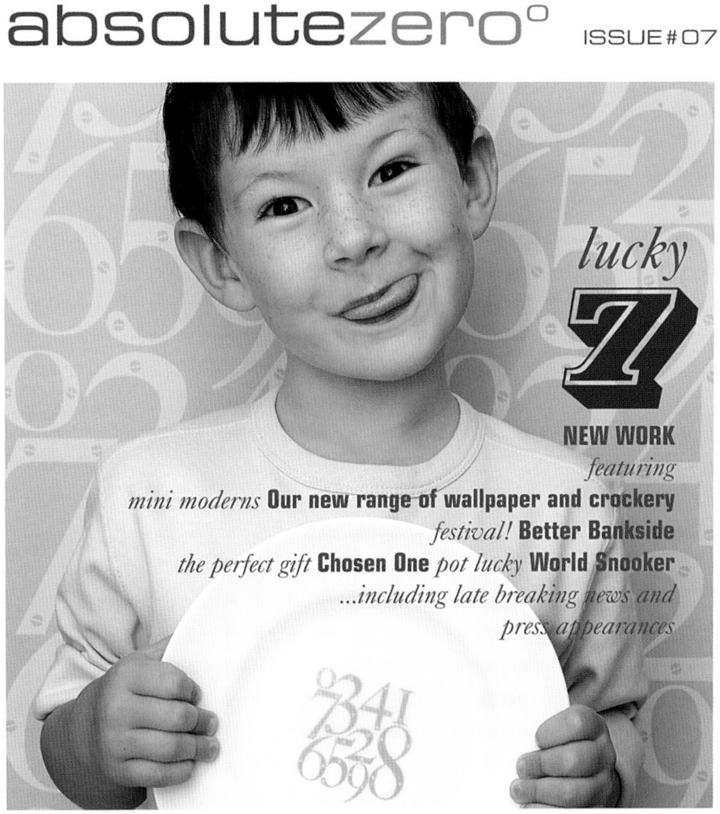

Absolute Zero° is a branding and design agency working in a broad range of disciplines across a number of sectors. To produce a corporate brochure showcasing their work was deemed too inflexible. Instead, it was decided to take an editorial approach that would communicate topicality and diversity, taking inspiration from fanzines. The result is a series of magazines, each edition produced whenever there is enough new work to show. Short runs, as few as 50 at a time, can be produced by digitally printing with a trusted printer.

The recycled stock was chosen for its ability to stand high momentary temperature during printing and finishing. Each new edition offers a reason to make contact, giving the agency's current and prospective clients a broader taste of their work. Sometimes, happy coincidence allows projects to be grouped thematically—for example, Issue 3 features brand identity and Issue 4 focuses on illustration. Case-study "supplements" are produced in-house, using Epson paper and an Epson printer, to expand on the projects' coverage in the main issues.

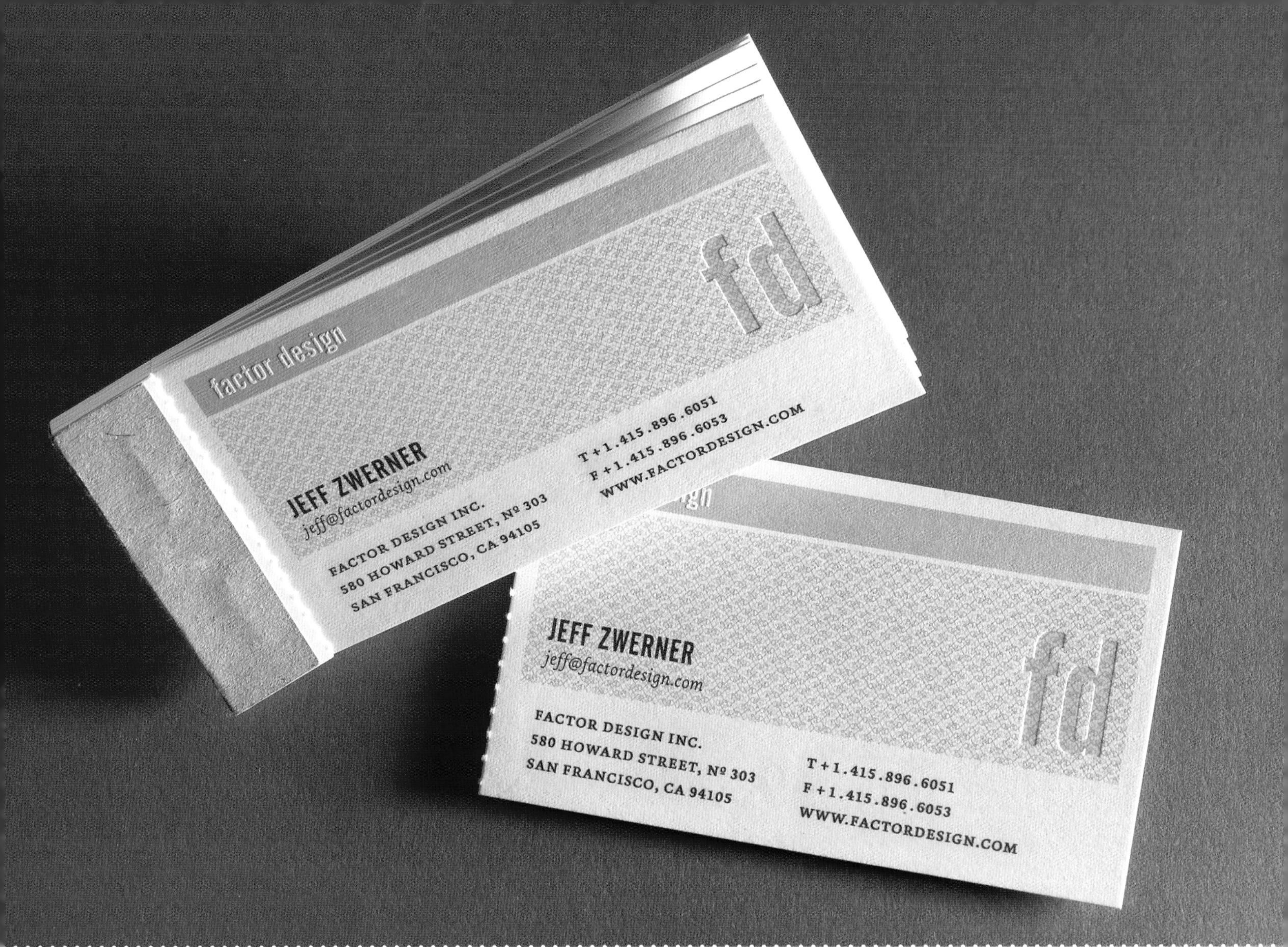

IDENTITY +
SELF-PROMOTION

Factor Design

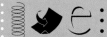

PROJECT FACTOR DESIGN BUSINESS CARDS
DESIGNER FACTOR DESIGN
CREATIVE DIRECTOR JEFF ZWERNER
JUNIOR DESIGNER ALWIN MULYONO
CLIENT SELF-INITIATED

PAPER FACTS:
STOCK NEENAH CLASSIC CREST
SOLAR WHITE SMOOTH FINISH 110lb
SIZE 2 × 3½in (51 × 83mm)
PRINT TECHNIQUE OFFSET (TRADITIONAL AND SPLIT FOUNTAIN)

ADDITIONAL TECHNIQUES FOIL STAMPING, ENGRAVING, PERFORATION, STAPLING
PRINTER DIGITAL ENGRAVING

Each Factor Design employee receives a set of cards as individually bound booklets. The simple composition of type and color is rendered through an abundance of tactile techniques: the "fd" is hot-foil stamped; the company logo uses white engraving; the address uses colored engraving. The fine patterns shade from red/pink to blue/purple using a split-fountain printing technique. A contrasting paper stock is used for the binding to accentuate its functionality.

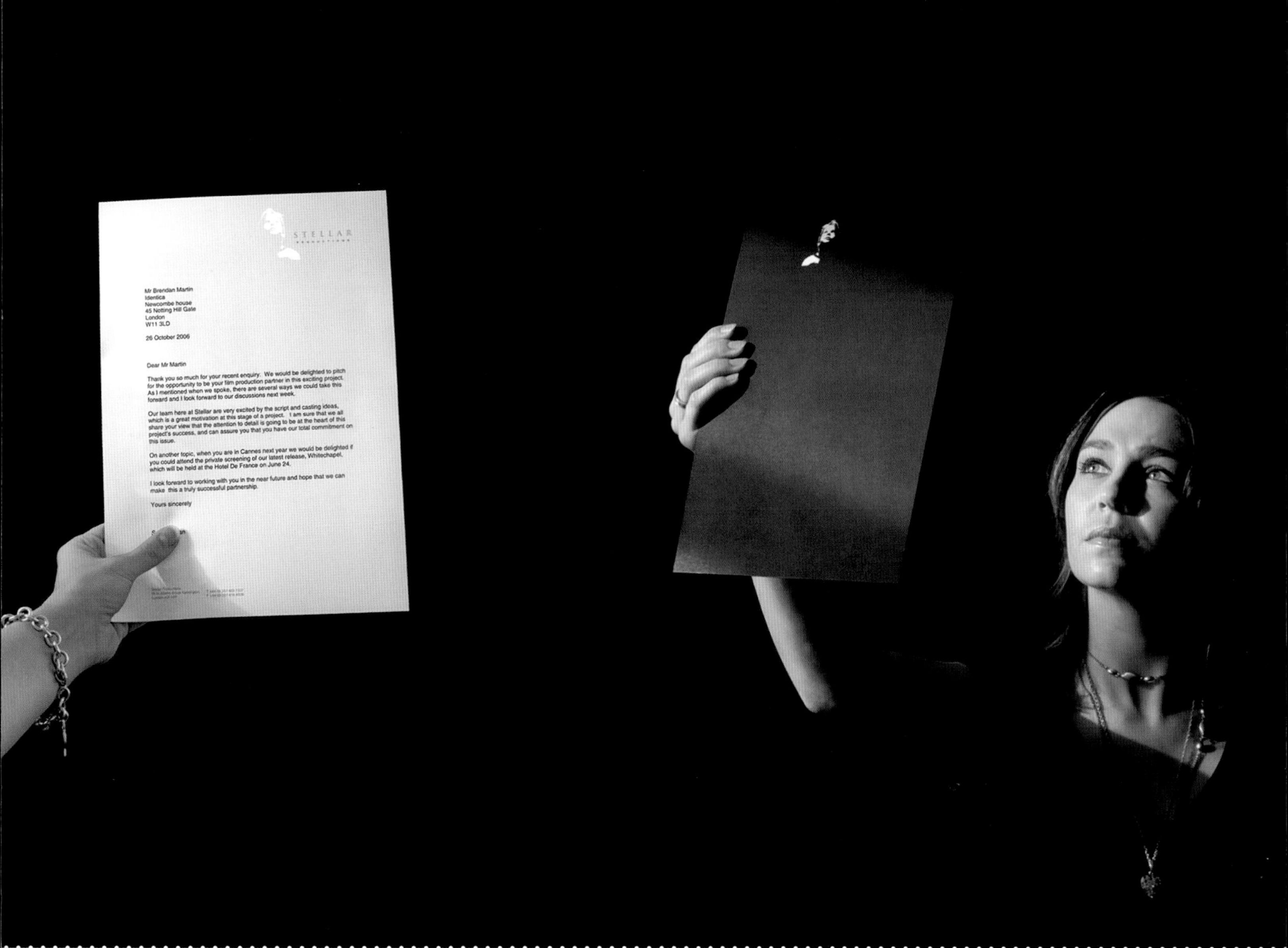

Tango

PROJECT STELLAR PRODUCTIONS STATIONERY
DESIGNER DAN CALDERWOOD at TANGO
CREATIVE DIRECTOR DANA ROBERTSON
CLIENT STELLAR PRODUCTIONS

PAPER FACTS:
STOCK MCNAUGHTON CHALLENGER OFFSET 100gsm
SIZE A4 (210 × 297mm; 8¼ × 11¾in)
PRINT TECHNIQUE OFFSET LITHO
ADDITIONAL TECHNIQUES TWO SPECIALS, BLACK AND SILVER TO FACE, SINGLE-COLOR PRINT TO REVERSE
PRINTER LNS PRINT

Tango created a unique and emotive brand identity for film-production company Stellar Productions, featuring a child's face illuminated by starlight. The natural translucency of paper offered a simple yet magical solution for the company's stationery. The back of the letterhead is printed black with the child's face reversed out so that the light coming through the page illuminates the icon. The receiver is compelled to emulate the logo by holding the page up to the light to get the full effect.

IDENTITY +
SELF-PROMOTION

Egelnick and Webb

PROJECT LOVE YOUR WORK
DESIGNER EGELNICK AND WEBB
CLIENT SELF-INITIATED

PAPER FACTS:
STOCK INK-JET PAPER
SIZE A5 (148 × 210mm; 5$^{13}/_{16}$ × 8$^{1}/_{4}$in)
PRINT TECHNIQUE INK-JET PRINTED IN-HOUSE
ADDITIONAL TECHNIQUE FRENCH-FOLDED
BINDING HANDBOUND BY BOOKMAKERS

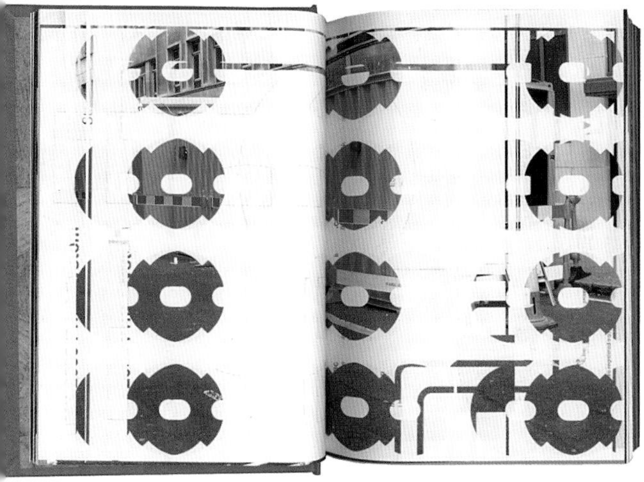

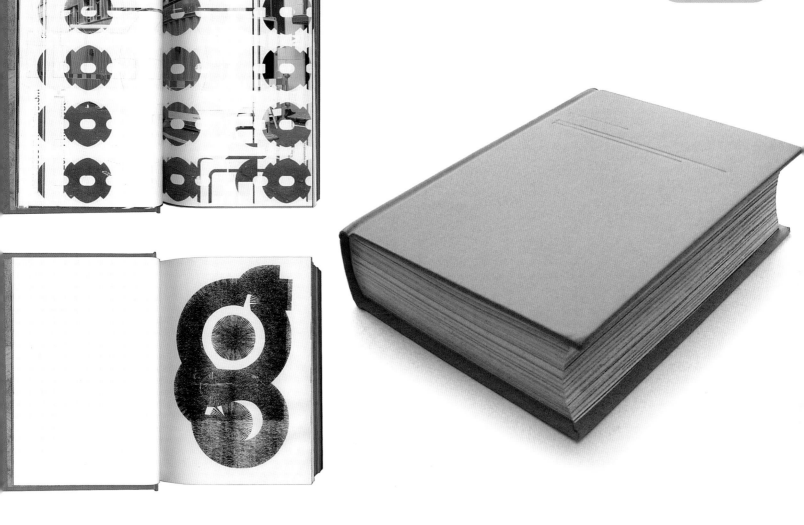

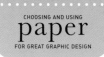

Love Your Work is a self-promotional book, conceived to show the range and depth of UK design studio Egelnick and Webb's thinking and imagemaking. They realized they had lots of interesting "starting points and happy accidents" that never made it into their portfolio of finished projects. So, rather than see them "wallow in archive purgatory," they decided to compile them in a sketchbook style in the hope that they might spark an idea for a project and be developed fully.

The decision to self-produce the piece dictated the choice of standard ink-jet paper. Three days' worth of ink-jet printouts made up one individual book, which was French-folded and handbound by book finishers. The studio measures the effectiveness of the piece by a high degree positive feedback—and the fact that one was stolen.

IDENTITY +
SELF-PROMOTION

konnectDesign

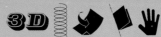

PROJECT CAYENNE
DESIGNERS KAREN KNECHT, JOYCE PENNELL at konnectDESIGN
CREATIVE DIRECTOR KAREN KNECHT
CLIENT DAMON PRODUCTIONS

PAPER FACTS:
STOCK TEXT: FINCH FINE SMOOTH COVER 100# COVER: TOPKOTE COVER 78lb, MOUNTED TO 90pt BLACK CHIPBOARD AND 1.5mm (1/16in) GLOSS LAMINATION
SIZE 9½ × 9½in (241 × 241mm)

PRINT TECHNIQUES BOOK: FOUR-COLOR PROCESS, STOCHASTIC PRINTING ON UNCOATED STOCK, PMS 877 SILVER OVERPRINTING AND UNDERPRINTING, FOUR-COLOR AND TWO-COLOR PROCESS IMAGES
ADDITIONAL TECHNIQUES PAGE EDGES GILDED WITH SILVER; HAND-APPLIED LAMINATED COVERS; SLIPCASE: ROUGH WOODEN BOXES, SPRAY-PAINTED AND HAND-ASSEMBLED, COVERED WITH INK-JET PRINTS; CD: FOUR-COLOR SILKSCREEN
PRINTER PRIMARY COLOR
BINDING BOOK: SMYTH-SEWN, CLOTH BINDING BY ROSWELL BOOKBINDING; SLIPCASES: DAMON PRODUCTIONS, konnectDESIGN

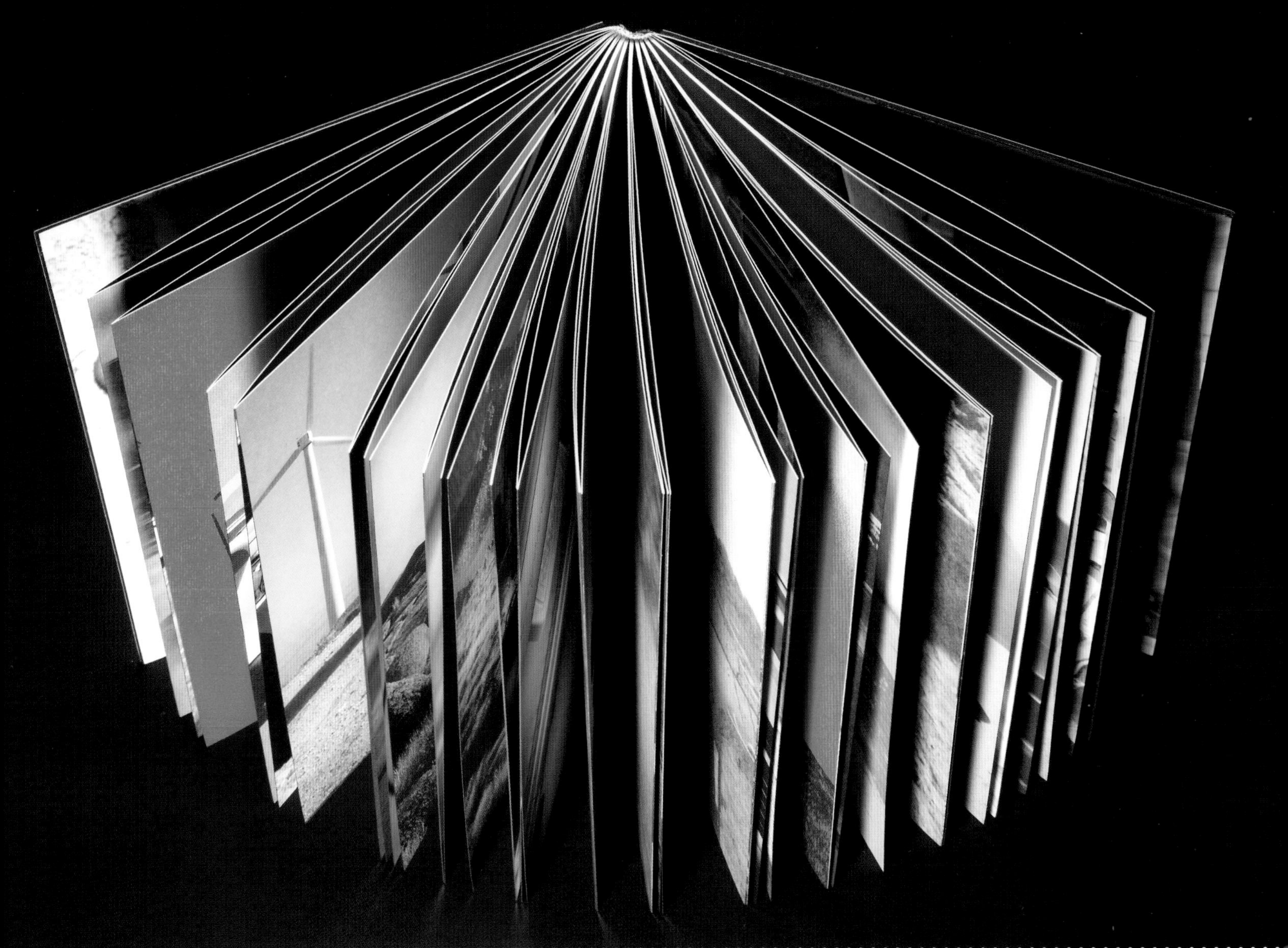

ABOVE: TIM DAMON'S CAYENNE BOOK
Photography: JoDean Bifoss for konnectDesign

Photographer Tim Damon packed up his cameras and set out on an adventure in a Porsche Cayenne. The result was a 90-page, image-driven journey that begins in Los Angeles and ends at a Mexican car wash. The intent of designers konnectDesign was to convey the grittiness of the journey with an "Hecho En México" sensibility. The book emphasizes the visual and tactile through big pictures, minimal text, uncoated paper, rough binding, visible stitching, lamination, washes of silver, and handmade wooden slipcases.

A heavy stock provided the desired weight and feel. The use of silver PMS and stochastic screen—unconventionally printed on uncoated stock—gave the images an experimental quality. The inside back cover carried a CD of the classic song "Car Wash" in Spanish. The final book was hand-delivered to advertising agencies around the world—occasionally accompanied by a bartender serving margaritas for the full sensory experience. Damon's response couldn't be more positive. "It's brought me jobs I wasn't being considered for before. It kicks ass."

IDENTITY + SELF-PROMOTION

theFarm

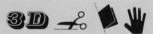

PROJECT SOMEWHERELSE
DESIGNER theFARM
CLIENT SELF-INITIATED

PAPER FACTS:
STOCK INVITATIONS: COLORPLAN PRISTINE WHITE 350gsm; FLY-POSTERS: COLORPLAN PRISTINE WHITE 120gsm; GIVEAWAY POSTERS: COLORPLAN PRISTINE WHITE 135gsm; RESPONSE CARDS: COLORPLAN PRISTINE WHITE 350gsm

SIZE INVITATIONS: 148.5 × 230mm (5¹³⁄₁₆ × 9in); FLY-POSTERS: A1 (594 × 840mm; 23³⁄₈ × 33in); GIVEAWAY POSTERS: A3 (297 × 420mm; 11³⁄₄ × 16¹⁄₂in); RESPONSE CARDS: SQUIRREL DIE-CUT FROM A5 (148 × 210mm; 5¹³⁄₁₆ × 8¹⁄₄in) CARD
PRINT TECHNIQUE SINGLE-COLOR (BLACK) OFFSET LITHO
ADDITIONAL TECHNIQUES TWO DIE-CUT HOLES IN INVITATION CARD TO ATTACH PAINTBRUSHES
PRINTER PUSH

theFarm were approached by the London Design Festival to create an installation within the heart of the show. The opportunity was used to launch theFarm's marketing campaign Somewherelse. This interactive installation was designed to be a talking point that would spread awareness of the agency and provoke a response. Promoted with invitations and flyers, visitors were encouraged to take away posters and response cards. All print items were harmonized by printing in black only on the same stock, in different weights as appropriate.

The 2D print items were conceived as representations of the 3D content of the installation; so the response card was die-cut to represent a squirrel, while the invitation card had two die-cut holes that allowed paintbrushes to be attached, reflecting the "painting-by-numbers" theme.

Originally set to run for three days, the overwhelmingly positive response to the installation prompted the organizers to ask theFarm to leave it running for the entire two weeks of the festival.

FLORA GRUBB
GARDENS
PALM BROKER, EXCEPTIONAL PLANTS & FURNISHINGS
I'm Laura Stratton
Swing by our garden at 1634 Jerrold Ave. San Francisco, California 94124. Ring me at 415 694 6453 or call the store at 415 648 2670. Fax us at 415 648 2674 or drop me a line at laura@floragrubb.com.
I'm Saul Nadler
Swing by our garden at 1634 Jerrold Ave. San Francisco, California 94124. Ring me at 415 694 6440 or call the store at 415 648 2670. Fax us at 415 648 0777 or drop me a line at saul@floragrubb.com.
FLORA GRUBB
GARDENS
PALM BROKER, EXCEPTIONAL PLANTS & FURNISHINGS

IDENTITY +
SELF-PROMOTION

Volume Inc.

PROJECT FLORA GRUBB GARDENS BUSINESS CARDS
DESIGNER VOLUME INC.
CLIENT FLORA GRUBB GARDENS

PAPER FACTS:
STOCK CRANE & CO. NATURAL WHITE 134lb
SIZE 2 × 3½in (51 × 83mm)
PRINT TECHNIQUE TWO-COLOR, TWO-SIDED LETTERPRESS
PRINTER DIGITAL ENGRAVING

SPECIAL CONSIDERATIONS:
"The logo had to go through multiple adjustments for its letterpress debut, since holding very fine detail can be an issue when using this process."

Eric Heiman
Volume Inc., US

Flora Grubb Gardens is an exotic-plant nursery in San Francisco that had been operating under two separate names. The identity redesign sought to combine these disparate entities under one design roof and focus the brand around its owner, Flora Grubb, to capture the unique aspects of her business and personality: exotic product selection; friendly, down-to-earth service; and a proactive educational approach to talking about plants and gardening.

The logo fuses clean, unfussy typography with the exoticism of the agave imagery. The letterpress process was chosen to give the business cards an elegant, tactile quality that would communicate that Flora Grubb Gardens is as established and reliable as it is friendly and knowledgeable. The cards are printed on a slightly textured, thick stock, chosen for its look, feel, and ability to withstand deep letterpress on both sides. The result has a vintage quality that works in harmony with the visual identity and reflects the personable language used to impart company information.

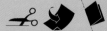

IDENTITY +
SELF-PROMOTION

nextbigthing

PROJECT CHRISTMAS CARDS
DESIGNER NEXTBIGTHING
CLIENT SELF-INITIATED

PAPER FACTS: DONKEY
STOCK CHALLENGER LASER MATT 80gsm
SIZE A5 (148 × 210mm; 5¹³⁄₁₆ × 8¼in) UNFOLDING TO A1 (594 × 841mm; 23⅜ × 33in)
PRINT TECHNIQUES FOUR-COLOR OFFSET LITHO, SPECIAL METALLIC SILVER
ADDITIONAL TECHNIQUE FOLDING
PRINTER BAXTERS

PAPER FACTS: CHRISTMAS CARD 2004
STOCK PRINTER'S HOUSE SILK, 300gsm
SIZE FINISHED SIZE A4 (210 × 297mm; 8¼ × 11¾in)
PRINT TECHNIQUES FOUR-COLOR OFFSET LITHO + PMS 877 SILVER
ADDITIONAL TECHNIQUES SPOT UV VARNISH, MATTE LAMINATION, DIE-CUTTING
PRINTER ELITE PRINT

Maria
Kristy
emily
Howard
This bit of festive fun has been brought to you by:
Nextbigthing
7th floor, Wellington House
8 Upper St Martins Lane
London WC2H 9DL
T: +44 (0)20 7379 1001
www.nextbigthingcreative.co.uk
...sorry about the mess

BIG FUN*
* Every snowflake has six sides, yet no two are alike. Each flake is beautifully individual. Pop out the circles to create your very own unique snowflake, making a small snow shower at the same time. You'll find some we did earlier on the back of this card. Have fun.

A Christmas card says a lot about the sender. When the sender is a design consultancy, it becomes a showcase for creativity. Nextbigthing conceived an irreverent take on the old parlor game, pin the tail on the donkey. An A5 (148 × 210mm; 5¹³⁄₁₆ × 8¼in) leaflet unfolds to A1 (594 × 841mm; 23⅜ × 33in), revealing the game on one side with information and instructions on the reverse. Witty and unexpected, the large poster format has great impact that is enhanced by the choice of a matte stock with a retro feel.

It was a hard act to follow. The following Christmas saw a card with the same degree of interactivity, but a change of design direction. The inclusion of 431 die-cut holes allowed the recipient to customize the card by creating his or her own snowflake pattern, inspired by spot-varnished designs already on the card signed by each designer. The greatest production challenge was sourcing a printer willing to make such a dense, complicated die and then to die-cut hundreds of circles that would remain in place until the recipient came to push them out.

IDENTITY +
SELF-PROMOTION

Egg

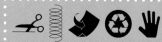

PROJECT 7-70 SWATCH BOOK
DESIGNER KRIS DELANEY at EGG
CREATIVE DIRECTOR MARTY MCDONALD
CLIENT SELF-INITIATED

PAPER FACTS:
STOCK REINCARNATION MATTE COVER
(100% RECYCLED; 50% POSTCONSUMER WASTE) 95lb
SIZE 7¾ × 2in (197 × 51mm)

PRINT TECHNIQUES SOY INKS, GLOSS VARNISH
ADDITIONAL TECHNIQUES DIE-CUT, DRILLED, COLLATED, HAND-ASSEMBLED
PRINTER PRINCETON PRESS

egg created this swatch book to communicate what its research findings discovered: that there are different shades of green consumer. As egg work with sustainable brands, the piece needed to have a high recycled content and use environmentally friendly soy inks. A varnish offered the glossy effect of a paint swatch book. As a result, egg's new-business revenues increased 600%.

Squires & Company

PROJECT PULP IMAGE PROMO
DESIGNER SQUIRES & COMPANY
CLIENT JAMES BLAND PHOTOGRAPHY

PAPER FACTS:
STOCK MAILER: FRENCH SMART WHITE 100lb CARDBOARD; ENVELOPE: GLASSINE
SIZE 4 × 6in (102 × 152mm) UNFOLDING TO 24 × 6in (610 × 152mm)
PRINT TECHNIQUE PHOTOGRAPHY PRINTED ON A UV PRESS, WITH A TOUCH PLATE OF RED

ADDITIONAL TECHNIQUES ACCORDIAN-FOLDED, HAND-STAMPED
PRINTER WILLIAMSON PRINTING CORP.

This photographer's promotion needed to show his talent for complex studio photoshoots, and it was aimed at magazines and the music industry. All of the imagery for the Pulp Image concept was shot in-camera; the typography was textured using a Xerox machine and Scotch tape, then merged into the imagery. The interior glassine envelope and exterior mailing cardboard were hand-stamped to add to the overall antiqued look.

IDENTITY +
SELF-PROMOTION

B&W Studio

PROJECT BRICK WALL
DESIGNERS LEE BRADLEY, STEVE WILLS, ANDREW DROOG at B&W STUDIO
CLIENT MACHELL BUILDING CONTRACTORS

PAPER FACTS:
STOCK COLORPLAN MIST WITH A GRANULAR EMBOSSED EFFECT 350gsm
SIZE A2 LANDSCAPE (594 × 420mm; 23⅜ × 16½in)
PRINT TECHNIQUE SPECIAL SINGLE-COLOR
ADDITIONAL TECHNIQUES EMBOSSING, PERFORATION
PRINTER HARROGATE PRINTING LTD.

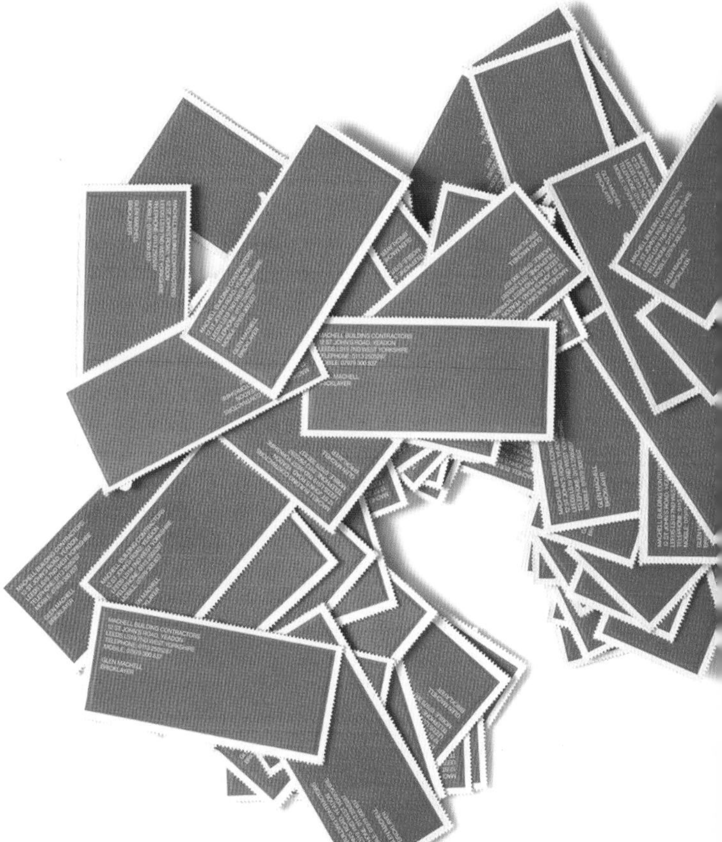

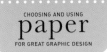

An uncharacteristically adventurous construction company approached B&W Studio to produce "something different" for its business cards. Buoyed by the challenge, the designers' response is brilliant in its simplicity: a brick wall business-card sheet, perforated so that each "brick" card could be torn off as needed. Typography was kept deliberately simple so as not to detract from the concept.

The embossed Colorplan stock had a granular texture, in a Mist colorway that emulated the color of mortar. A2 (594 × 420mm; 23⅜ × 16½in) sheets were printed with one special for the brick color, perforated across the entire sheet and embossed with a specially commissioned tool to give the impression of raised bricks. The project won Gold in the 2006 Roses Design Awards and was nominated for the 2007 Design Week Awards.

Aloof Design

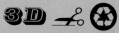

PROJECT ELIAS & GRACE IDENTITY
DESIGNER LEIGH SIMPSON at ALOOF DESIGN
CLIENT ELIAS & GRACE

PAPER FACTS:
STOCK VERUS OMAR AND NATURAL KRAFT IN VARIOUS WEIGHTS 300–600gsm
SIZE VARIOUS
PRINT TECHNIQUE OFFSET LITHO
ADDITIONAL TECHNIQUES DIE-CUTTING, SHEET-TO-SHEET LAMINATION
PRINTER LONGRIDGE

The Elias & Grace store in London's Primrose Hill provides a modern approach to maternity and children's clothing. Aloof Design created the brand identity, stationery, and website as well as a range of playful packaging and garment labeling to appeal to both parent and child as well as unifying independent designers' collections under the Elias & Grace brand. The concept of the baby-ticket die-cut within a larger ticket mirrors the mother-and-child clientele. The tickets are adorned with colored-glass beads and metal bells strung with brown linen thread.

Aloof sourced from a broad palette of natural, recycled papers and chose an affordable heavyweight kraft material for the swing-tickets with a complementary shade of paper for the bags. The chosen material, which was only available in a 310gsm weight, was litho printed with the brand identity before being duplexed to form the heavyweight board. They developed unique ink mixes to ensure print color stood out and remained consistent on the various uncoated paper stocks, a process that required many proofs and constant communication with the bag manufacturer.

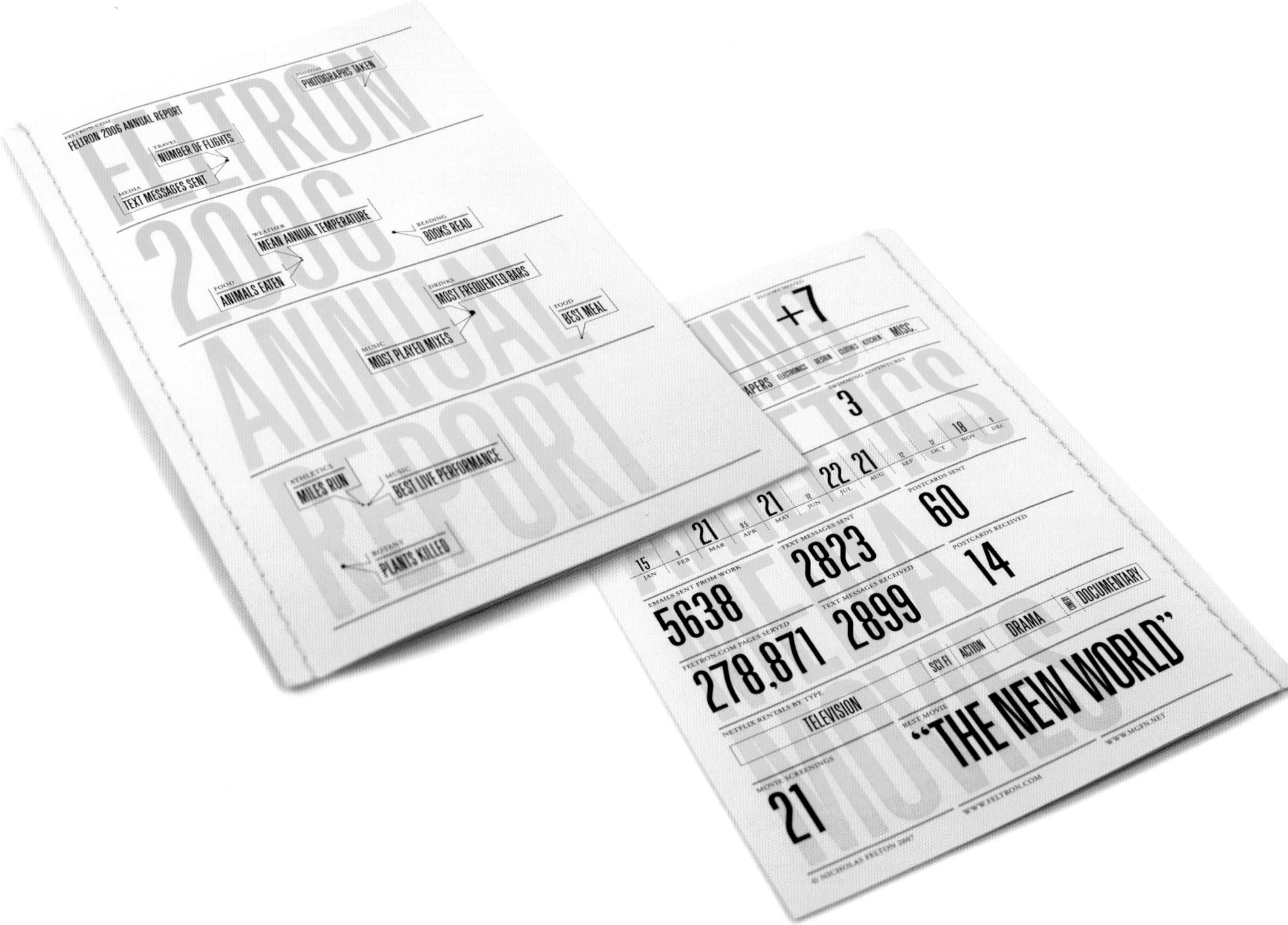

IDENTITY +
SELF-PROMOTION

Nicholas Felton

PROJECT FELTRON ANNUAL REPORT
DESIGNER NICHOLAS FELTON
CLIENT SELF-INITIATED

PAPER FACTS:
STOCK REPORT: NEENAH CLASSIC CREST 80lb; NOTE CARD: 100lb
SIZE REPORT: 6 × 9in (152 × 229mm); NOTE CARD: 6 × 9in (152 × 229mm); ENVELOPE: 6¼ × 9¼in (159 × 235mm)

PRINT TECHNIQUE TWO-COLOR OFFSET LITHO
ADDITIONAL TECHNIQUE BLACK OVERPRINT ON YELLOW
PRINTER HANDSOME PRINTING COMPANY
PRODUCTION MANAGER DANIELLE HUTHART at WHITESPACE.HK
BINDING REPORT: SEWN-STITCHED

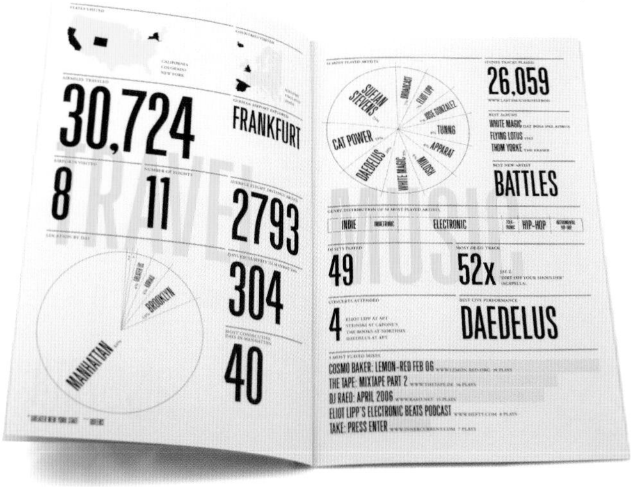

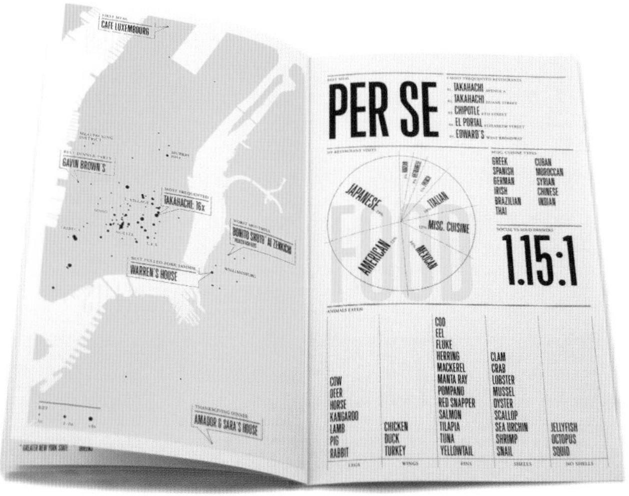

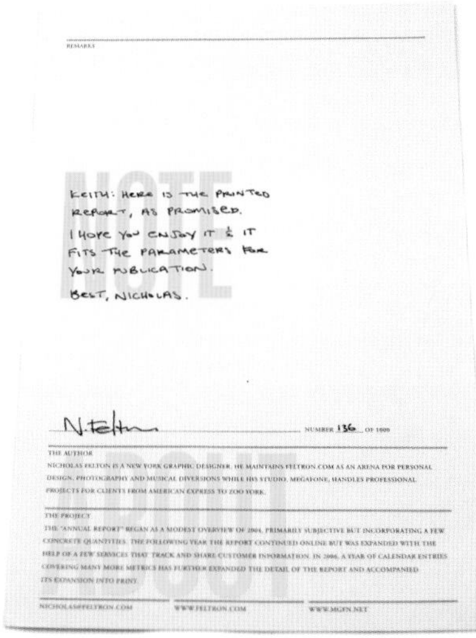

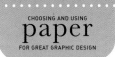

Founder of New York design studio Megafone, Nick Felton produces a personal annual report that plays with the conventions of this corporate staple to create a witty form of self-promotion. Under the pseudocorporate guise of Feltron, the 2006 offering uses print to deliver gravitas to the lighthearted communication, offering information as diverse as the number of emails sent in the year and a breakdown of which animals he consumed. The design takes a strictly typographic approach, striving for transparency and consistency of communication.

The envelope, notecard, and report use bold yellow and black type on an uncoated gray stock, chosen both for its esthetic qualities and its availability in Hong Kong, where the piece was produced. A yellow thread-stitch binding displays impeccable attention to detail.

The result garnered praise from Khoi Vinh, Design Director at NYTimes.com: “This is a work of delightful inventiveness, executed in the kind of highly detailed diagrammatic vernacular that designers tend to fetishize—‘info-porn’ is the term—and with Felton’s precise, disciplined, and nearly unfailing esthetic eye.”

CHAPTER 6

packaging + products

Robin Day
Tricorne tray
designed by Robin Day
twentytwentyone

PACKAGING + PRODUCTS

Charles S. Anderson

PROJECT POP INK PAPER PRODUCTS, GIFT WRAP, NOTE CARDS, GREETINGS-STAMP SHEETS
DESIGNER CHARLES S. ANDERSON DESIGN PRODUCED IN COLLABORATION WITH FRENCH PAPER AND LAURIE DEMARTINO DESIGN
CLIENT SELF-INITIATED

PAPER FACTS:
STOCK GIFT WRAP TEXT: FRENCH SMART WHITE 70lb; NOTE CARDS: FRENCH SMART WHITE 70lb; NOTE CARD ENVELOPES: VARIOUS FRENCH PAPER 80lb

SIZE GIFT WRAP: $19\frac{1}{2} \times 27$in (495 × 686mm); NOTE CARDS: $4\frac{1}{2} \times 6$in (114 × 152mm); NOTE CARD ENVELOPES: A6 (105 × 148mm; $4\frac{1}{8} \times 5\frac{13}{16}$in)
PRINT TECHNIQUE FOUR-COLOR OFFSET LITHO
ADDITIONAL TECHNIQUE STICKERS USED TO PERSONALIZE NOTE CARDS
PRINTER DOWAGIAC COMMERCIAL PRESS

King OF ALL YOU SURVEY. WHICH ISN'T MUCH.
Congratulations ON DOING WHATEVER IT WAS YOU DID
THINKING OF YOU
AND ODDLY, SCOTT BAIO
SPEEDY RECOVERY
HAPPY ANNIVERSARY
TO YOU AND WHAT'S HIS NAME
happy ANNIVERSARY again
GET WELL SOON
YOU'LL SAVE A FORTUNE IN MEDICINE!
Happy Birthday
Happy Birthday
TO MY DEAR:
SON DAUGHTER HUSBAND WIFE COUSIN BUTCHER
(PLEASE CHECK ONE)
LOVE
VOTED ONE OF THE WORLD'S TOP EMOTIONS (RIGHT BEHIND "RAGE")
YOU SHINE LIKE THE STARS!
SPECIFICALLY, LIKE STAR #NC485 IN THE CRAB NEBULA
Happy Birthday
I DON'T KNOW WHY YOU SAY GOODBYE, I SAY... Hello

SPECIAL CONSIDERATIONS:

"French Paper manufactures such high-quality paper that these products didn't require any innovative print or finishing techniques: 98-bright French Smart White makes even standard four-color-process printing look extraordinary."

Sheraton Green, Charles S. Anderson Design, US

Established in 1989, Charles S. Anderson Design produces award-winning art, packaging, identity, and product design for a diverse list of clients, including Barneys New York, Target, Urban Outfitters, Coca-Cola, Levi's, and Warner Brothers. Produced in collaboration with French Paper and Laurie DeMartino Design, their range of Pop Ink products includes a line of stationery that combines sophisticated repeat patterns in muted colors with pop elements and witty messages. The high-quality paper ensures that from gift wrap to greetings cards every product feels as good as it looks.

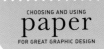

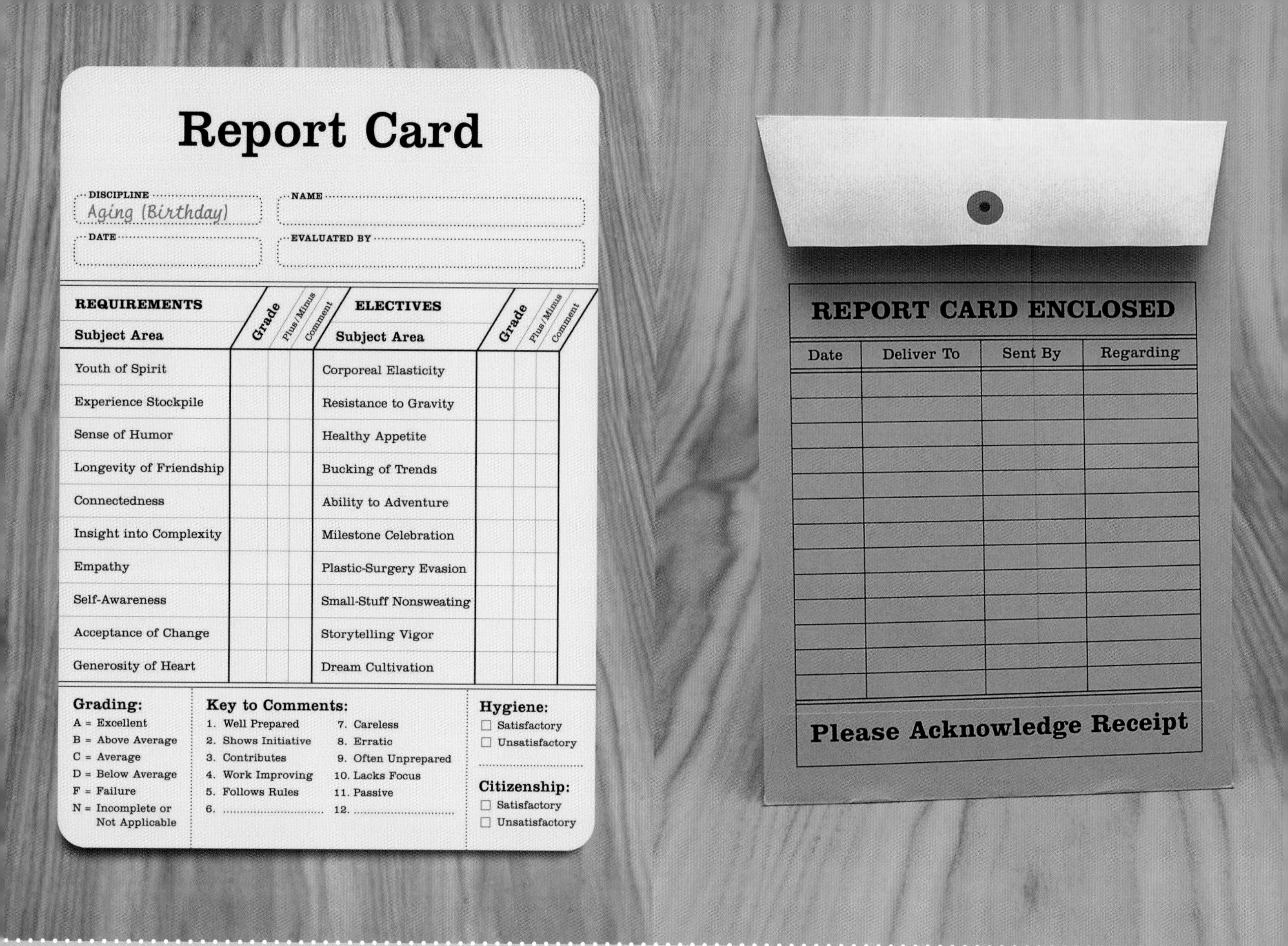

Report Card
DISCIPLINE
Aging (Birthday)
NAME
DATE
EVALUATED BY
REQUIREMENTS
Subject Area
Grade
Plus/Minus
Comment
Youth of Spirit
Experience Stockpile
Sense of Humor
Longevity of Friendship
Connectedness
Insight into Complexity
Empathy
Self-Awareness
Acceptance of Change
Generosity of Heart
ELECTIVES
Subject Area
Grade
Plus/Minus
Comment
Corporeal Elasticity
Resistance to Gravity
Healthy Appetite
Bucking of Trends
Ability to Adventure
Milestone Celebration
Plastic-Surgery Evasion
Small-Stuff Nonsweating
Storytelling Vigor
Dream Cultivation
Grading:
A = Excellent
B = Above Average
C = Average
D = Below Average
F = Failure
N = Incomplete or Not Applicable
Key to Comments:
1. Well Prepared
2. Shows Initiative
3. Contributes
4. Work Improving
5. Follows Rules
6.
7. Careless
8. Erratic
9. Often Unprepared
10. Lacks Focus
11. Passive
12.
Hygiene:
Satisfactory
Unsatisfactory
Citizenship:
Satisfactory
Unsatisfactory
REPORT CARD ENCLOSED
Date
Deliver To
Sent By
Regarding
Please Acknowledge Receipt

PACKAGING + PRODUCTS

Knock Knock

PROJECT REPORT CARDS FOR GROWNUPS
DESIGNER KNOCK KNOCK
CLIENT SELF-INITIATED

PAPER FACTS:
STOCK CARD: CORONADO BRIGHT WHITE SUPER SMOOTH COVER 100lb
SIZE 5 × 7in (127 × 178mm)
PRINT TECHNIQUE OFFSET LITHO
PRINTER PRINTUP GRAPHICS

Report Card

DISCIPLINE						
Staying in Touch			NAME			
DATE			ALBERT KLEZMER			
01/01/04			EVALUATED BY			
			SALLY ENSENADA			

REQUIREMENTS				ELECTIVES			
Subject Area	Grade	Plus/Minus	Comment	**Subject Area**	Grade	Plus/Minus	Comment
Live Telephone Pickups	B	−	8	Phone-Number Quantity	B	+	3
Speed of Callback	A	+	1	E-Mail Response Rate	C	−	4
Penmanship	C	−	3	Effective Emoticon Use	A	−	8
Plan-Making Availability	D	−	8	Cellular Programming	F	+	11
Punctuality	A	+	4	Social Inclusion	D	+	12
Cancellation Notification	B	−	2	Spontaneous Invitation	C	−	6
RSVP Execution	F	+	6	Birthday Remembrance	A	+	5
Thank-You Etiquette	A	−	11	Holiday Newsletters	A	−	1
Gossip Sharing	B	−	5	Gift-Giving Acumen	B	−	2
Funny Story Relay	A	+	3	Psychic Connection	C	+	3

Grading:
A = Excellent
B = Above Average
C = Average
D = Below Average
F = Failure
N = Incomplete or Not Applicable

Key to Comments:
1. Well Prepared
2. Shows Initiative
3. Contributes
4. Work Improving
5. Follows Rules
6. _____
7. Careless
8. Erratic
9. Often Unprepared
10. Lacks Focus
11. Passive
12. _____

Hygiene:
☑ Satisfactory
☐ Unsatisfactory

Citizenship:
☑ Satisfactory
☐ Unsatisfactory

Based in Venice, California, Knock Knock was founded by Jen Bilik to create interesting, smart, well-designed gift and stationery products. Their Report Cards for Grownups have proved perennial best-sellers and, with their combination of vintage styling, tactile materials, and witty messages, it's easy to see why. While production is simple ink on paper, this product is a great example of how straightforward printing techniques on readily available stock combined with an off-the-shelf envelope can all be given a twist to make a concept really stand out.

The designs evoke childhood nostalgia through report-card esthetics, content, and structure. Inspiration came from real vintage report cards dating from between 1850 and 1950, purchased as research material through eBay. Retro fonts, colors, and rounded corners give the cards an authentic feel. The addition of a side-loading manila envelope, styled to resemble interoffice communication, creates an ironic touch, that of the idea of expressing affection in the guise of a bureaucratic form. The sender is encouraged to grade the recipient in real-life subjects such as friendship, self-awareness, or sex.

Paperpod

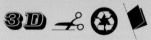

PROJECTS TOYS, FURNITURE
DESIGNER PAPERPOD
CLIENT SELF-INITIATED

PAPER FACTS:
STOCK CARDBOARD
SIZE VARIOUS
ADDITIONAL TECHNIQUES DIE-CUTTING, FOLDING

Children often have as much fun with the packaging as with the gift inside. With over 20 years' experience in the packaging industry, the designer of Paperpod has created products to bridge the gap between plastic and wooden toys. Organic shapes, child-friendly designs, and basic assembly make these products great for children, parents, and playworkers. They can be folded flat for easy storage and the unfinished surfaces act as a blank canvas for children to decorate, so they stimulate the imagination too.

Cardboard is a natural product, which, in its raw (brown) state, is free from bleaching chemicals, free from plastics, and sourced from recycled materials. Long recognized in the packaging and promotional industries as a tough, durable yet biodegradable product, cardboard is ideally suited for products aimed at socially and environmentally aware parents. The versatility of cardboard means that a doll's house can be folded up and stored under the bed and a rocket tucked away at the back of the shed.

PACKAGING + PRODUCTS

Art Meets Matter

PROJECT FACTUM® PAPERBOARD FURNITURE
DESIGNERS TONY DAVIS, DAVID STANNARD at ART MEETS MATTER
CLIENT SELF-INITIATED

PAPER FACTS:
STOCK COATED, RECYCLED EB FLUTE BOARD
SIZE CHAIR: 830 × 380 × 510mm ($23\frac{11}{16}$ × 15 × 20in); CUBE: 435 × 390 × 390mm ($17\frac{1}{8}$ × $15\frac{11}{32}$ × $15\frac{11}{32}$in)
PRINT TECHNIQUE FOUR-COLOR SCREENPRINTING ONTO PLAIN PAPERBOARD
ADDITIONAL TECHNIQUES DIE-CUTTING, HAND-GLUING

SPECIAL CONSIDERATIONS:
"The fluting of the board runs vertically providing maximum strength for loads up to 100kg (220lb). The sides of the Factum Chair and Cube fold in underneath the seat in a triangular shape. This, as well as the direction of the fluting, is an essential design detail that makes Factum furniture so strong and supportive."

Tony Davis, Art Meets Matter, UK

Factum won Most On-trend Product at London's Pulse 2006. "Cardboard furniture that comes flatpack in the post—genius."

Factum is designed as ecofriendly flexible furniture. Origami informed the initial design development. Factum can be folded in on itself to create a flat package and sent to customers through the post. Each piece comes in its own suitcase-shaped box and unfolds into Cube or Chair in seconds with no need for instructions. It can be folded away or hung on the wall using its polyprop display case to make a functional design statement. The design and manufacturing process makes clever use of existing materials and industrial processes.

Sheets of plain paperboard are industrially screenprinted with a surface design using the same technique that shops use to print large advertising banners and displays. Arranged to create the least amount of material wastage, the printed board is then fed into an industrial die-cutting machine that cuts out the pieces and scores the fold lines. These pieces are then folded to shape and hand-glued together to create the finished piece. Strength comes from ecofriendly recycled and recyclable EB flute board, sourced from the industrial-packaging industry.

Carter Wong Tomlin

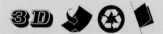

PROJECT howies PACKAGING
DESIGNER CARTER WONG TOMLIN
CLIENT howies

PAPER FACTS: 100% ORGANIC T-SHIRT
STOCK BROWN KRAFT RECYCLED PAPER TULIP-BULB BAG
SIZE 210 × 297mm (8¼ × 11¾in)
PRINT TECHNIQUE TWO-COLOR PRINT ON RECYCLED PAPER
PRINTER FIORINI PRINTERS

PAPER FACTS: BASE LAYER
STOCK ROBERT HORNE TRIPLEX 450gsm BOARD
PRINT TECHNIQUES WATER-BASED VEGETABLE INKS, FOUR-COLOR PRINT
PRINTER BEACON PRESS

The search for a distinctive and environmentally friendly solution to howies' T-shirt packaging led Carter Wong Tomlin to Italy, where they sourced a recycled tulip-bulb pack. Everything about it was right. The brown kraft stock had the right feel and character for the product: 100% organic-cotton T-shirts. The idea of adapting an existing bag rather than simply sourcing recycled stock was in keeping with howies' ethics and attitude.

And for a quirky yet practical touch, the mesh window, designed to allow the bulbs to breathe, proved an excellent way of displaying the product within. A 40% increase in T-shirt sales confirmed the effectiveness of the design.

Turning to howies' performance base-layer garments, a more straightforward solution was required to reflect the products' technical edge. This was achieved without compromising the brand's environmental stance by printing the boxes on 95% recycled Horne Triplex board using water-based vegetable inks.

Stanley Donwood

PROJECT THOM YORKE: THE ERASER
DESIGNER STANLEY DONWOOD
CLIENT XL RECORDINGS

PAPER FACTS:
STOCK UPM FINE 300gsm
SIZE 125 × 125mm ($4\frac{15}{16}$ × $4\frac{15}{16}$in) UNFOLDING TO 625 × 125mm ($24\frac{5}{8}$ × $4\frac{15}{16}$in)
PRINTER THINK TANK MEDIA

The artwork for Thom Yorke's album *The Eraser* provided the key to Think Tank's packaging concept. The iconic montage of London architecture, produced by Yorke's long-term collaborator Stanley Donwood, needed packaging that acted as a canvas to display the continuous flow of the design. The solution was a ten-panel CD pack printed on 300gsm UPM fine and concertina-folded, while the vinyl-record packaging was printed onto the reverse of a 350gsm board with all black areas blind debossed for maximum effect.

B&W Studio

PROJECT SOUL CAL CLOTHING
DESIGNER LEE BRADLEY, ANDREW DROOG at B&W STUDIO
CLIENT REPUBLIC

PAPER FACTS:
STOCK CARDBOARD
SIZE 125 × 85mm (4 15/16 × 3 5/16in)

Looking to up its street cred, clothing brand Soul Cal approached B&W Studio for a new identity and new clothing swing-tags. The designers took graffiti art as their inspiration, and the logo artwork was created authentically with spray paint and a cardboard stencil. The swing-tags reinforce the stencil feel: the bespoke logo was die-cut from raw cardboard, stickers applied, and a hole drilled to take the unusual touch of an elastic band. The branding was screenprinted on to garments.

PACKAGING +
PRODUCTS

Pearlfisher

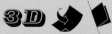

PROJECT SPOYLT IDENTITY AND PACKAGING
DESIGNER KAREN WELMAN, DARREN FOLEY at PEARLFISHER
CLIENT BARBARA BRUDENELL-BRUCE

PAPER FACTS:
STOCK CELLOGLAS MIRRI H PINK 370gsm, 100gsm
SIZE 450 × 300 × 150mm ($17\frac{11}{16}$ × $11\frac{13}{16}$ × $5\frac{7}{8}$in), 200 × 200 × 120mm ($7\frac{7}{8}$ × $7\frac{7}{8}$ × $4\frac{3}{4}$in)
ADDITIONAL TECHNIQUES LAMINATION, FOIL BLOCKING, FLAT FOLD TO RIGID-3D FOLD
PRINTER COSIFIBELGROUP.COM

For the upmarket lingerie brand Spoylt, Pearlfisher came up with a packaging solution that is both practical and luxurious. To solve the client's problem of stocking hundreds of boxes in a limited space, an ingenious flat fold to rigid-3D fold cardboard construction was designed, allowing the boxes to be stored flat and made up as required. A sophisticated metallic stock was chosen in a brand-complementary colorway. Lamination and foil blocking gave the packaging a suitably luxurious feel.

37°
cool when warm & warm when cool

Pearlfisher

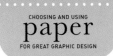

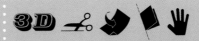

PROJECT 37° IDENTITY AND PACKAGING
DESIGNER KAREN WELMAN, DARREN FOLEY at PEARLFISHER
PHOTOGRAPHER ALAN NEWNHAM
CLIENT 37°

PAPER FACTS:
STOCK CARD, 3M RADIANT FILM
SIZE 250 × 250 × 120mm (9 27/32 × 9 27/32 × 4 3/4in), 180 × 180 × 120mm (7 × 7 × 4 3/4in)
ADDITIONAL TECHNIQUES DOUBLE-WALLED CARDBOARD ENGINEERING, DIE-CUTTING, HAND-TIED RIBBON
PRINTER ARGENT LITHO

For this range of baby clothing, which uses smart textiles to maintain a baby's body temperature at 37°C, Pearlfisher were briefed to create packaging that would express the innovation of the product without losing the "soft" values of the baby market. Double-walled cardboard engineering ensured the product was protected, while 3M Radiant Film was used to give a hot-and-cold color range that emphasized the product's temperature-regulating properties.

Christmas Charms
Designed by VIVI & illustrated by LUCY JANE BATCHELOR
www.vividesigns.com www.lucyjanebatchelor.co.uk

ROBIN CAKE DECORATION
For a very splendid cake!
Designed by VIVI & illustrated by LUCY JANE BATCHELOR
www.vividesigns.com www.lucyjanebatchelor.co.uk

Lucy Jane Batchelor

PROJECT THE VIVI WINTER RANGE
DESIGNER LUCY JANE BATCHELOR
CLIENT VIVI

PAPER FACTS:
STOCK CYCLUS OFFSET (100% DE-INKED RECYCLED, 60% MINIMUM POSTCONSUMER WASTE, PROCESSED CHLORINE-FREE, ACID-FREE) 350gsm
SIZE 159 × 112mm (6¼ × 4¹³⁄₃₂in)
PRINT TECHNIQUE PRINTED WITH SOY-OIL INKS (THE SOFT PAPER FINISH GIVES A MUTED COLOR)
PRINTER SEVERNPRINT (AWARD-WINNING ENVIRONMENTAL PRINTERS)

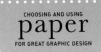

VIVI, aka UK jewelry designer Viviana de Gallegos, produces silver gifts for special occasions. For her range of festive tableware and charms she approached designer and illustrator Lucy Jane Batchelor to create packaging that would emphasize the keepsake nature of the products. Lucy's ecologically aware design principles were also considered appealing to Vivi's audience—all her work is produced on 100% recycled stock using vegetable-based inks. The combination of product and packaging has a charmingly nostalgic quality.

Simple paper construction offers the packaging flexibility to adapt as the range expands. The Robin Tree Decoration card, therefore, has six punched holes, which allow it to double up as the Christmas Charms packaging, with a blank space left top right to accommodate the name. Various paper constructions were used to hold the silver pieces: the Party Cake Candle Holders set is a box construction, while the Robin Cake Decoration card has a fold-down shelf with a hole to hold the decoration. The holes are backed with foam pads to secure the trinkets in place during handling.

PACKAGING + PRODUCTS

Egelnick and Webb

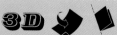

PROJECT LUMINO COFFRET
DESIGNER EGELNICK AND WEBB
CLIENT L'ORÉAL PROFESSIONNEL

PAPER FACTS:
STOCK PAPER WRAPAROUND 1.5mm (1/16in) BOARD 140gsm, PEARLIZED TRACING PAPER 90gsm
SIZE 190 × 90 × 245mm (7½ × 3½ × 7⅝in)
PRINT TECHNIQUE OFFSET LITHO PRINT ON PAPER WRAPPED AROUND FOLDING BOXBOARD
ADDITIONAL TECHNIQUES MATTE LAMINATION, SILVER-FOILED LOGO
PRINTER KEENPAC

For the launch of the Lumino range, L'Oréal needed a gift box that would raise product awareness and drive sales. Egelnick and Webb developed a coffret constructed from board wrapped with a matte-laminated paper for a silky, premium feel. A pearlized tracing paper was chosen for the overlapping leaves—its showthrough inventively used with the graphic printed on the reverse of the bottom leaf and type on the front of each one, offering a slow reveal of the information before reaching the products inside. The lid was tied with a white silk ribbon and folded back on itself to provide a platform.

Absolute Zero°

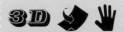

PROJECT SPOIL ME SENSELESS AND SHOW ME LOVE PACKAGING
DESIGNER ABSOLUTE ZERO°
CREATIVE DIRECTOR CHANTAL LAREN at POUT
CARD ENGINEER SWALLOWFIELD PLC
CLIENT POUT

PAPER FACTS:
STOCK ART PAPER 157gsm, 128gsm, 2mm (5/64in) GRAY BOARD
ADDITIONAL TECHNIQUES FOILED LOGO, FLOCKED ICONS
PRINTER SWALLOWFIELD PLC

Pout is an innovative cosmetics brand whose customers delight as much in the playful detailing of their packaging as their "five minutes to fabulous" formulations. Each season they group products together under a gift-inspired theme. For Christmas gifts, special boxes covered in a metallic pearlized paper were sourced. A gold-foiled logo and bespoke flocked pattern added to the feel of luxury, while hand-tied ribbons offered the ultimate Pout detail.

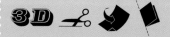

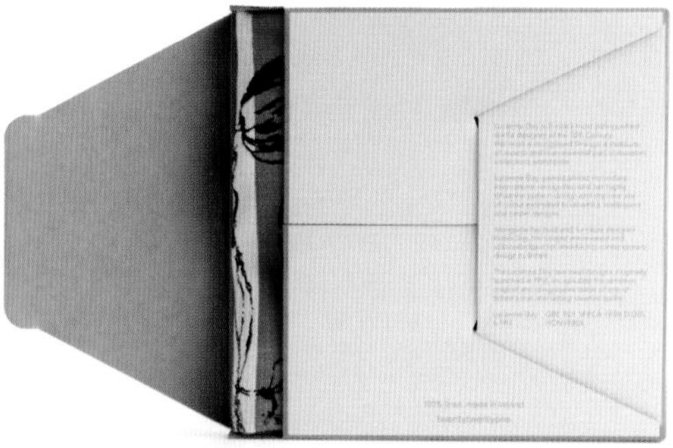

PACKAGING +
PRODUCTS

Aloof Design

PROJECT PACKAGING FOR LUCIENNE AND ROBIN DAY
DESIGNER LEIGH SIMPSON at ALOOF DESIGN
CLIENT TWENTYTWENTYONE

PAPER FACTS:
STOCK E FLUTE KRAFT, KRAFT TEST LINER
PRINT TECHNIQUE SILKSCREEN
ADDITIONAL TECHNIQUE DIE-CUTTING
PRINTER CREST DISPLAYS

SPECIAL CONSIDERATIONS:
"By developing a self-forming locking mechanism, all packs could be delivered flat and assembled before use without the use of glue. When creating the net shapes, our team were mindful of ensuring as little wastage from the sheet as possible, and this is reflected in the final designs."

Michelle Kostyrka, Aloof Design, UK

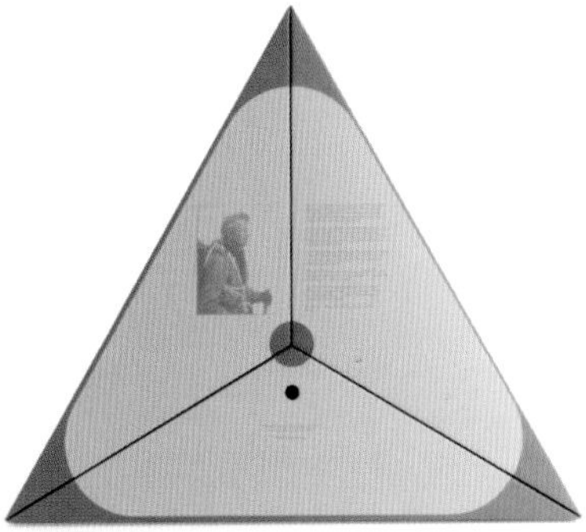

Aloof Design encourage consumers to see packaging as an integral and enjoyable part of the product experience. They designed and produced a range of branded packaging for furniture retailer twentytwentyone to celebrate reissued works by internationally distinguished 20th-century designers Lucienne and Robin Day. The collection launched with a series of silkscreen-printed Irish-linen tea towels selected from Lucienne's archive—which dates from 1954 onward—and the Tricorne tray manufactured in plywood with birch or walnut veneer designed by Robin in 1955.

Recycled kraft packaging, hand-printed with silkscreened graphics, complements the natural materials. The pack designs are carefully detailed constructions, assembled without glue, and they function as effective point-of-sale devices. Graphics have been kept to a minimum, with die-cut apertures allowing the products to be seen and touched. Since industrial kraft materials are hard to get hold of in small quantities—minimum purchase is 1,000 sheets—mock-ups were done in a substitute material. Not until full machine proofing were the designers finally able to test the design.

PACKAGING +
PRODUCTS

basic packaging structures

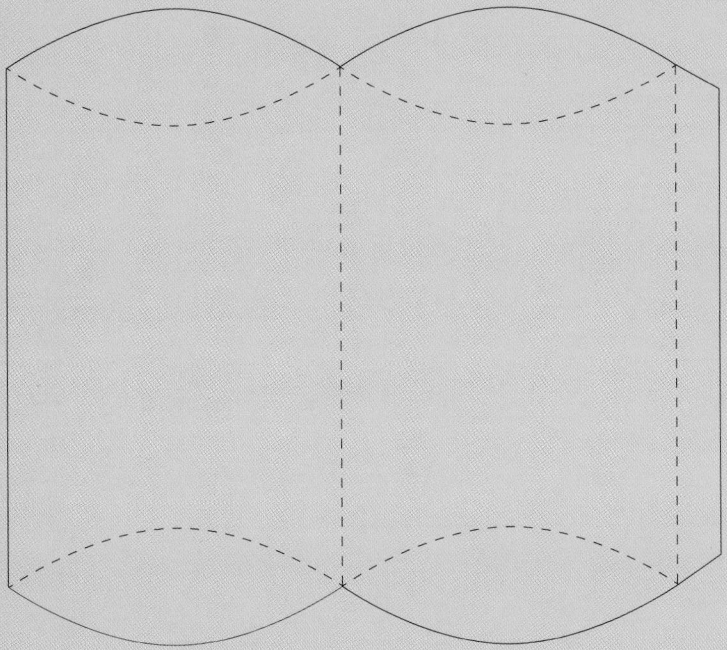

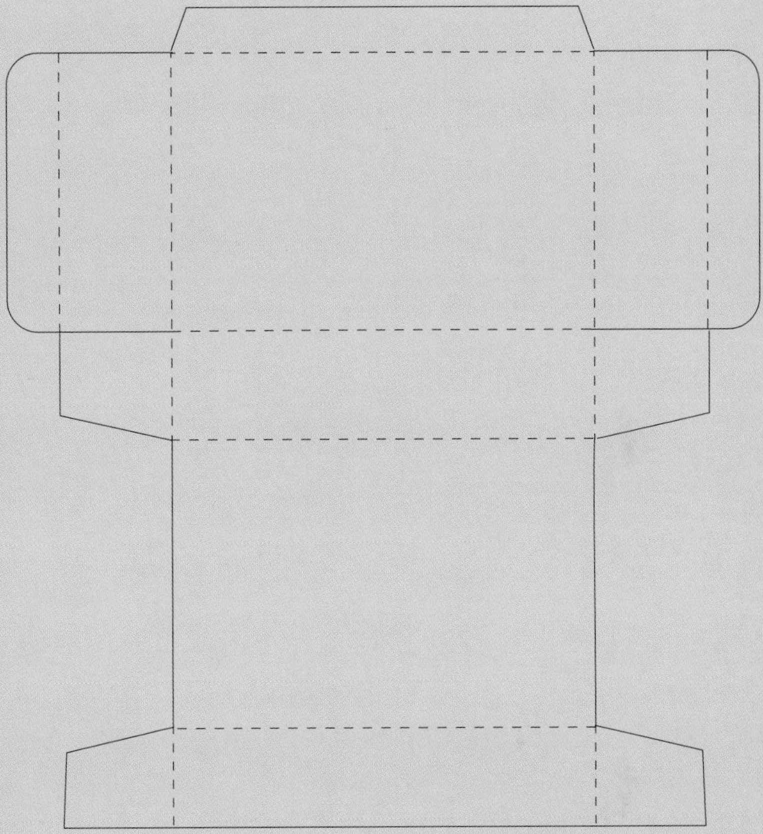

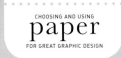

PILLOW PACK

STRAIGHT TUCK

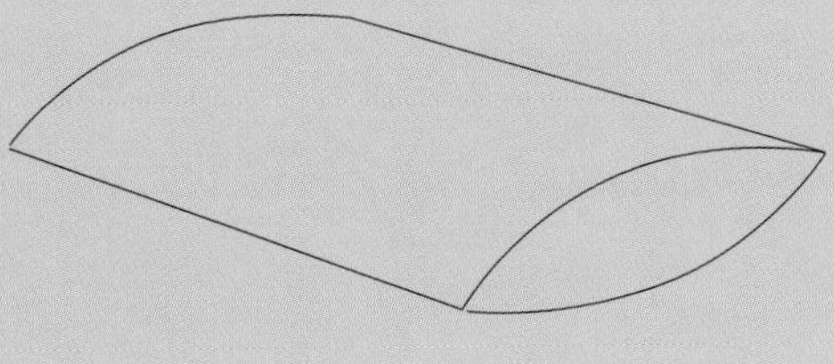

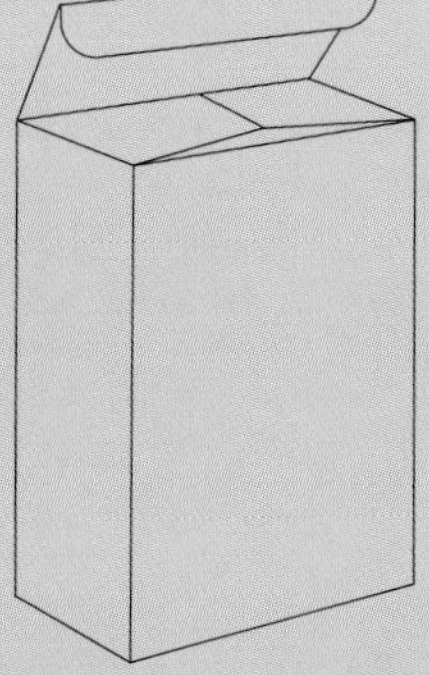

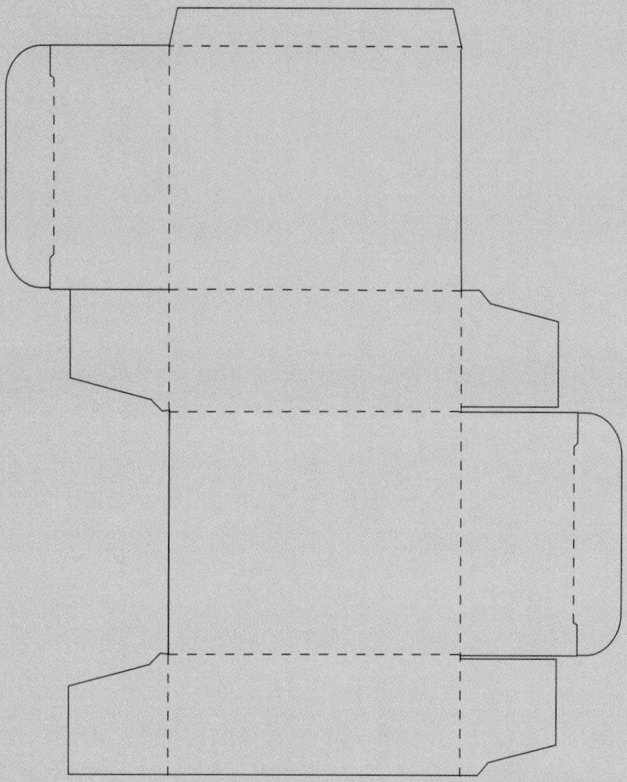

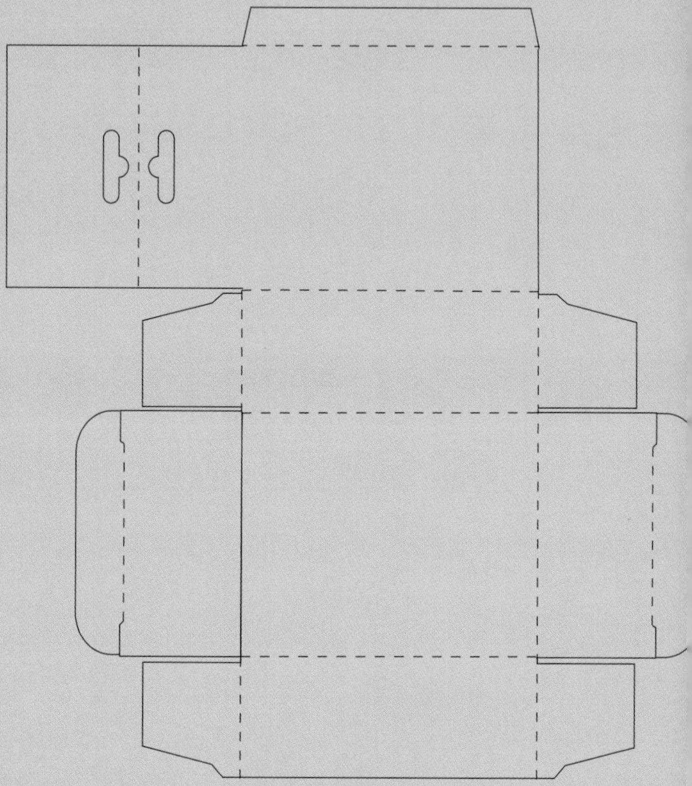

PACKAGING +
PRODUCTS

REVERSE TUCK

**STRAIGHT TUCK
WITH HANGING PANEL**

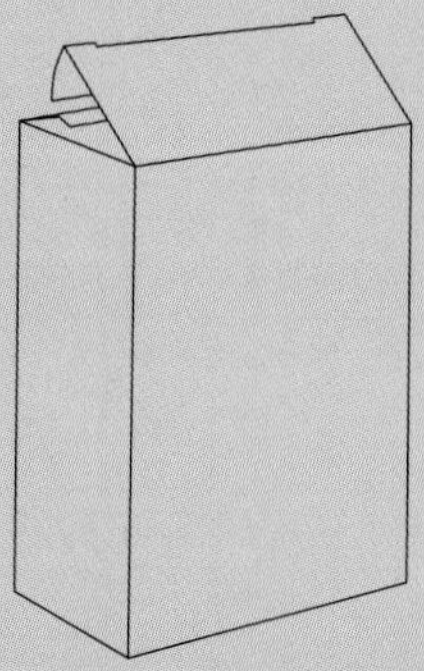

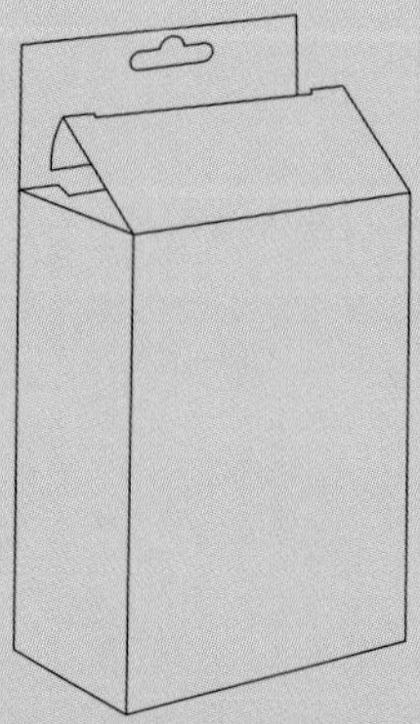

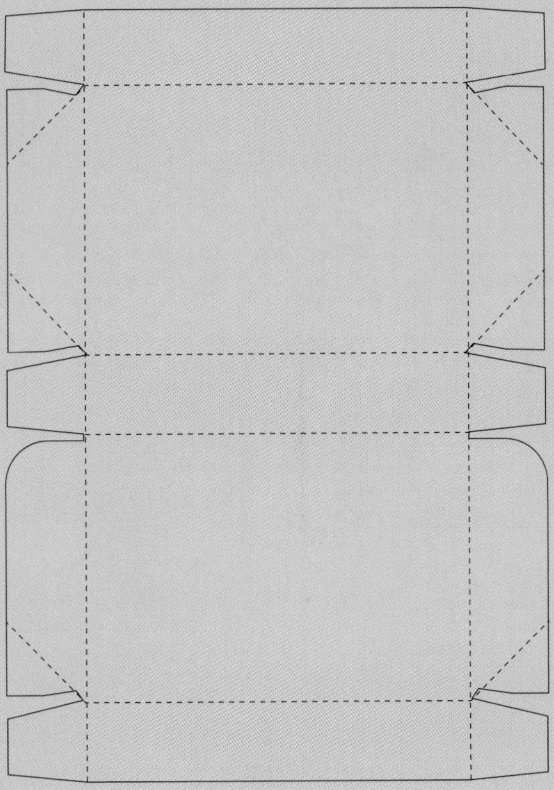

ONE-PIECE TRAY WITH INTEGRATED LID

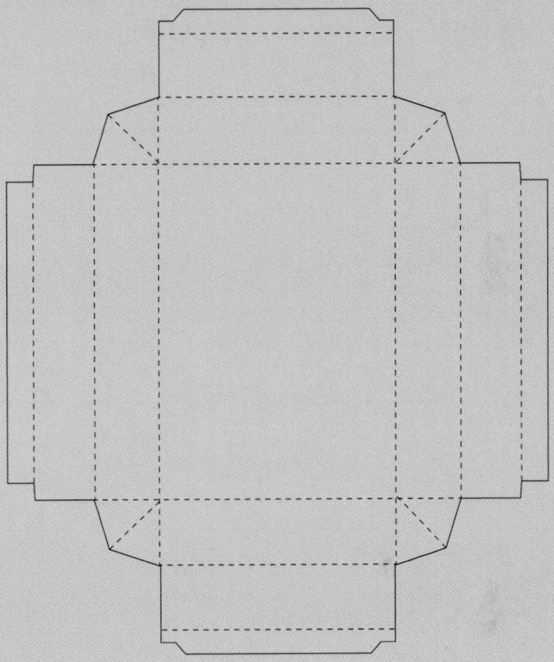

NONGLUE WEB CORNER TRAY

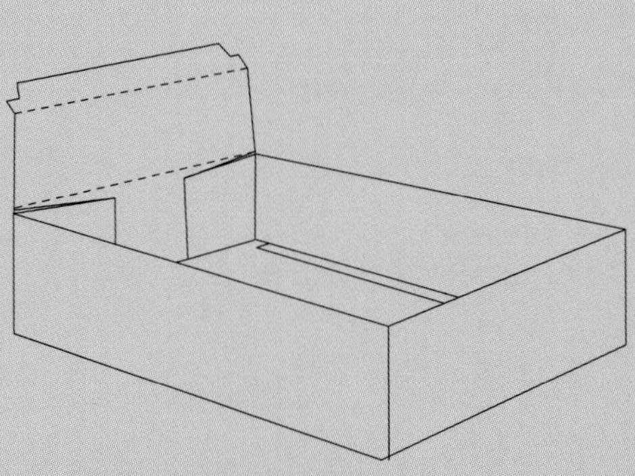

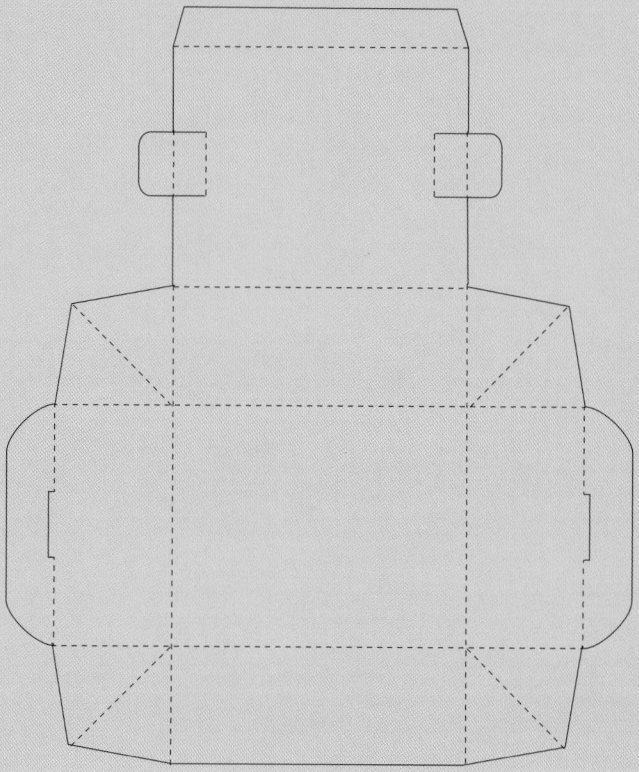

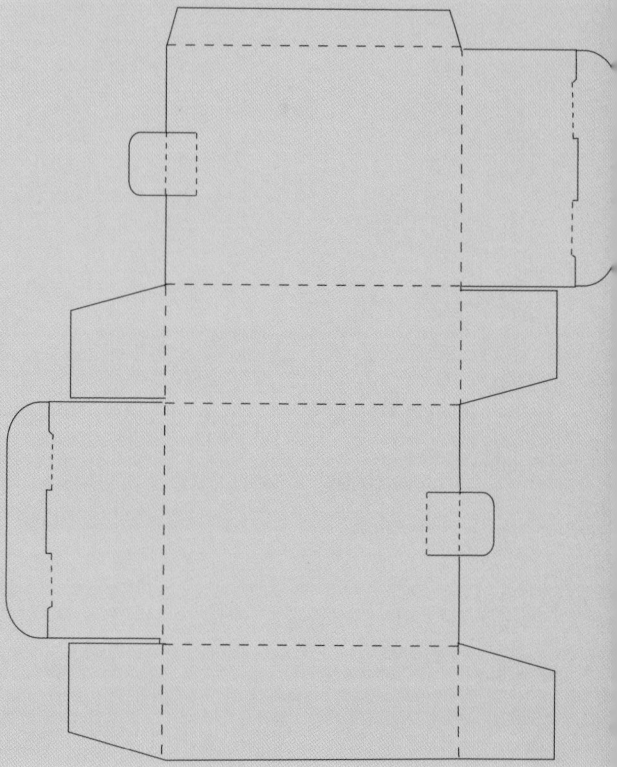

TUCK AND TONGUE WITH GUSSET DUST FLAP

TUCK AND TONGUE

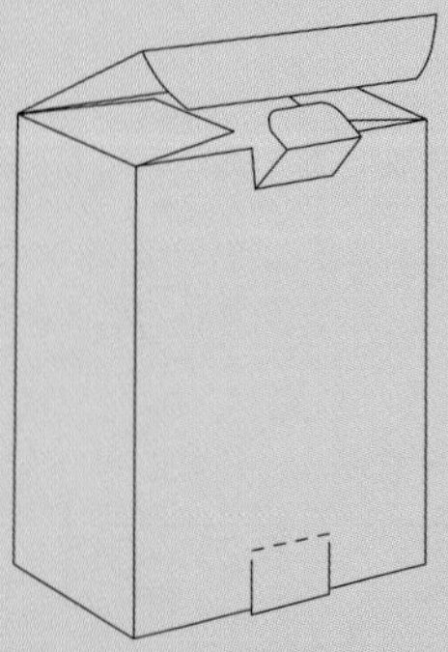

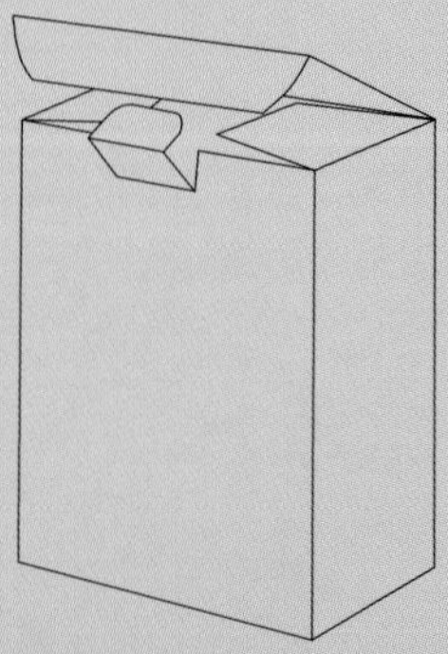

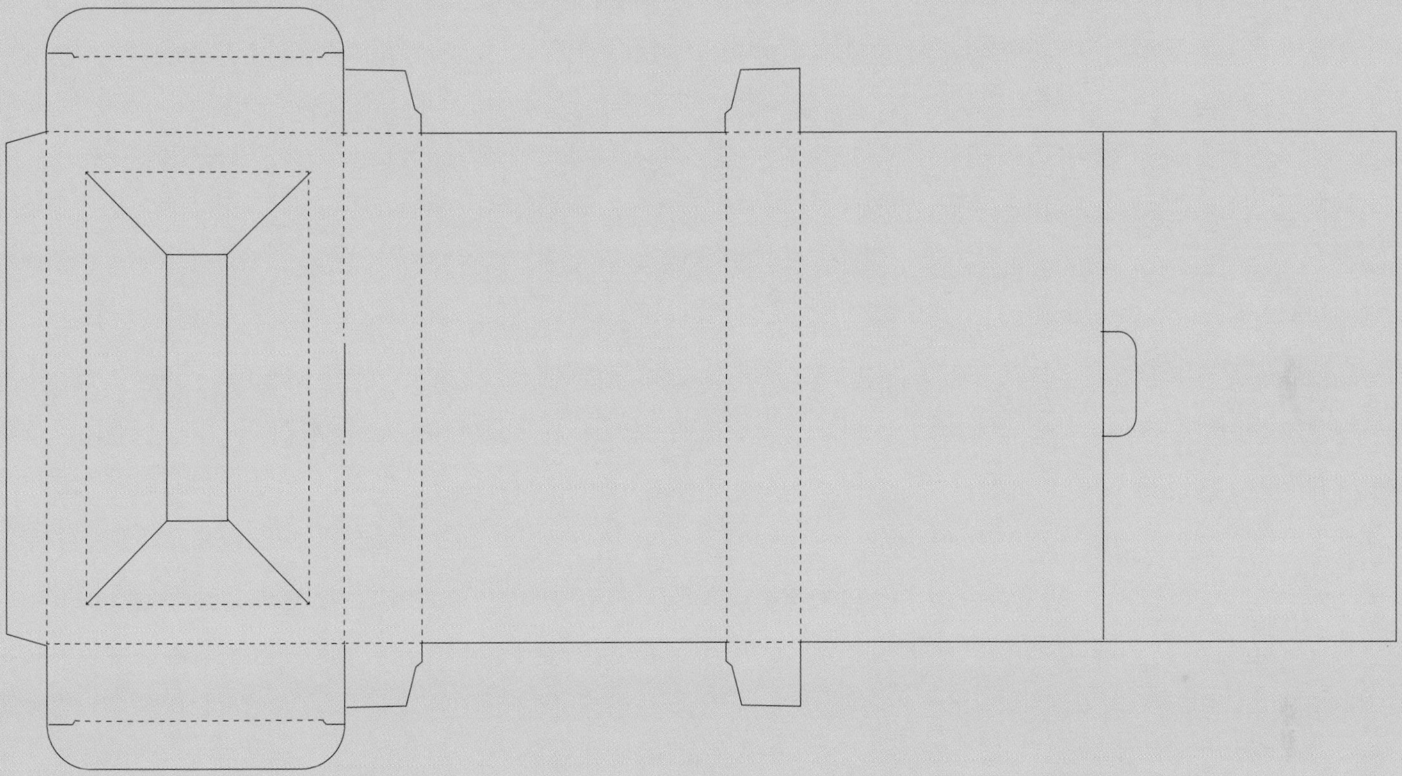

DISPLAY CARTON

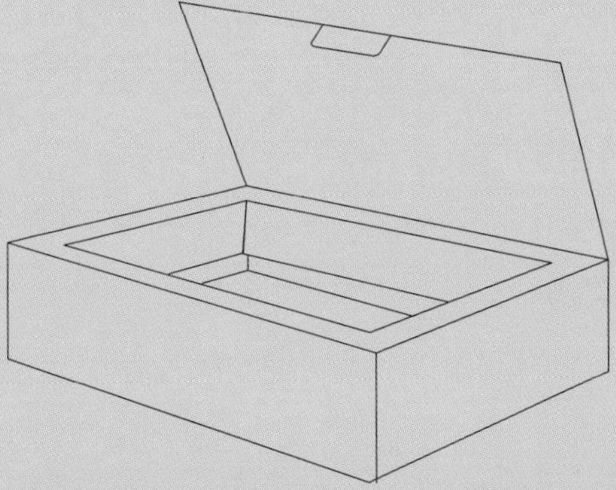

CHAPTER 7

one-off creations

BUYME
BUYME

craig kirk

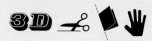

PROJECT MATCHBOXES
DESIGNER CRAIG KIRK
CLIENT SELF-INITIATED

PAPER FACTS:
STOCK VARIOUS UNCOATED PAPERS RANGING FROM 100–200gsm
SIZE VARIOUS
PRINT TECHNIQUE FOUR-COLOR INK-JET
ADDITIONAL TECHNIQUE HANDMADE

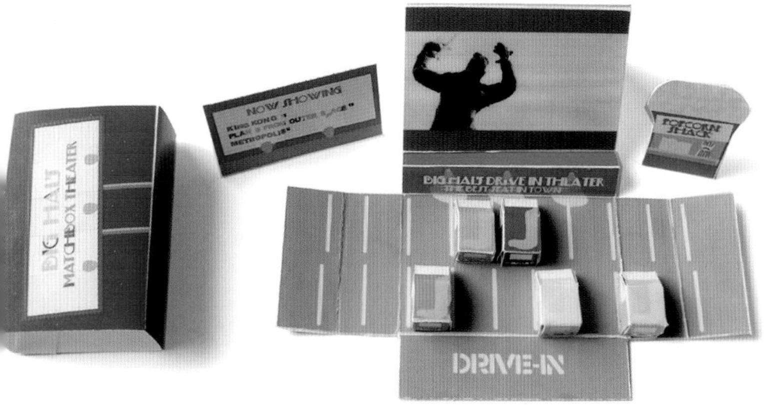

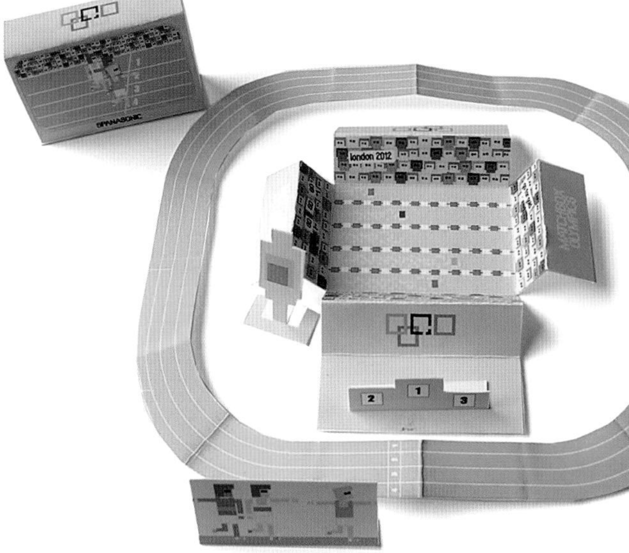

Craig Kirk's matchboxes are playful, intriguing curiosities. Stemming from an interest in paper folding, Craig's hands-on approach to graphics and love of lo-tech materials gave rise to his first creation: the Glastonbury matchbox. Conceived as a way of communicating and reflecting the Glastonbury Festival (an outdoor music festival) in a compact and inexpensive way, the matchbox designs rolled off from there, with new matchboxes being created all the time.

Every matchbox is exactly the same size—35 × 55mm ($1\frac{3}{8} \times 2\frac{3}{16}$in)—but each contains something completely unique. Once delicately opened and assembled, they form a vast array of original environments and installations. The miniature scenes and props are created from various uncoated papers with nothing more sophisticated than an ink-jet printer. Craig sees the matchbox less as a container and more as an opportunity: "It's not about things in matchboxes, it's about things coming out of them. Surprise, inspire, smile."

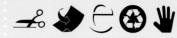

Doshi Levien

PROJECT BEST QUALITY
DESIGNER DOSHI LEVIEN
CLIENT SELF-INITIATED

PAPER FACTS:
STOCK RECYCLED ADVERTISING PAPER
SIZE FINAL ENVELOPE SIZE 222 × 110mm ($8\frac{3}{4} \times 4\frac{1}{3}$in)
PRINT TECHNIQUE STAMPED
ADDITIONAL TECHNIQUES EMBOSSING, DIE-CUTTING, FOLDED, AND GLUED

SPECIAL CONSIDERATIONS:
"We are supposed to pick out these envelopes at random, but instead find ourselves choosing envelopes to match the character of the intended recipient. We are sending quite a few Coca-Cola envelopes to the USA. Some of the envelopes are a bit grubby, so we pay our bills with these! In any case, people forgive the odd crease and blemish when they see what we're up to."

Jonathan Levien, Doshi Levien, UK

A chance encounter with a paper-recycling factory in New Delhi gave Nipa Doshi and Jonathan Levien an idea for a set of company envelopes that would perfectly communicate the duality of their studio's personality. Misprinted or overprinted advertisements for Western and Indian brands are hand-sorted for diversity of designs and suitability for ink-jet printing. The papers are die-cut, stamped, embossed with the company logo, folded, and glued to create the envelopes—each one unique.

The appeal of the envelopes lies in the contrast of the white exterior and random colorful interiors, selected on the whim of whoever sorts the paper. The scalloped flap has a contemporary Indian feel. The "Best Quality Since 2000" legend is another Anglo-Indian touch: many Indian products have "Best Quality" stamped on them, while "Since 2000" references the British tradition of implying quality through length of establishment.

ONE-OFF CREATIONS

Laura Cooperman

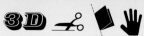

PROJECT VARIOUS ARTWORKS
ARTIST LAURA COOPERMAN
CLIENT SELF-INITIATED

PAPER FACTS:
STOCK ARCHES WATERCOLOR PAPER, ARJOMARI MOLD-MADE VARIOUS WEIGHTS
SIZE VARIOUS

SPECIAL CONSIDERATIONS:
"I like the simplicity of creating my work: just an X-ACTO knife and paper. I prefer Arches paper because of its weight and texture. Everything I arrive at is due to a failure, but failure in a constructive way."

Laura Cooperman, US

After graduating from the Maryland Institute of Art, Laura Cooperman studied in New York and worked for the artist Nancy Spero, meticulously cutting out a several-hundred-foot-long frieze of Nancy's artwork *Mourning Women*. Laura became engrossed in the delicate, methodical process of paper cutting and began experimenting with light, depth, and movement. Awarded the Grainger Marburg travel grant, Laura traveled to China to study traditional Chinese paper cutting and to document and interpret the effects of Beijing's urban renewal through her cut-paper overlays.

Laura works from her own photographs or images found in reference books, sketching in pencil on the paper and then proceeding directly to cut. Arches paper offers her the right balance of weight and texture. She assembles the cut pieces, then pins them to the wall with thin metal rods, setting individual sections at varying distances from the wall to create depth. For her mechanical pieces, Laura plays around with various found machines and gears, taking apart objects and welding things together, adding paper or metal until she is satisfied with the results.

cat chow

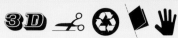

PROJECT NOT FOR SALE, DOWN COAT, DISTRESSED
ARTIST CAT CHOW
CLIENT SELF-INITIATED

PAPER FACTS:
STOCK NOT FOR SALE: 1,000 US ONE-DOLLAR BILLS, EACH BILL SHREDDED INTO AROUND 25 STRIPS; DOWN COAT: QUILTED BLUE KLEENEX TISSUES; DISTRESSED: SANDPAPER

SPECIAL CONSIDERATIONS:
"I wanted people to contemplate the value of a dress that was made from $1,000-worth of shredded money. Is it worth the same, nothing, or much more than the amount it had originally started with? Ironically the dress will never be sold—as the name implies."

Cat Chow, US

Chicago-based artist Cat Chow asked friends, acquaintances, and strangers to donate one dollar each toward Not For Sale, a dress constructed from a thousand shredded dollar bills. The donations were exchanged for brand-new bills in order to keep the uniformity of the piece. Each bill was shredded into approximately 25 strips, then stitched with invisible thread to make rings that were connected up in a chain-mail pattern. When exhibited, the dress stands like a memorial in front of a wall bearing the names of the thousand sponsors.

The material and concept of Not For Sale are inextricably linked. Originally, the half-finished knee-length dress was shown in an art fair. When the remaining bills were attached, the dress puddled to the ground as a floor-length couture-style evening gown, referencing the value placed on designer clothing, just as the art world bestows value on work by big-name artists. Further paper-based projects include Down Coat, which derives its comforting quality from quilted blue Kleenex tissues, and Distressed, which, by contrast, is constructed from sandpaper.

Mark Bolitho

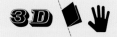

PROJECT TUMBLING SALARYMAN
ARTIST MARK BOLITHO
ART DIRECTOR SARAH HABERSHON
CLIENT THE GUARDIAN NEWSPAPER

PAPER FACTS:
STOCK JAPANESE-PRINT CHIYOGAMI PAPER 80gsm

SPECIAL CONSIDERATIONS:
"Technically, chiyogami does not fold very well as a result of its malleability. This was overcome by using a strengthening aluminum foil to hold some of the paper's shape."

Mark Bolitho, Creaselightning, UK

the guardian Saturday 13.01.07 guardian.co.uk — Graduate career section » From the back page

work

'We go out like friends and have a lovely evening. The only difference is they pay for it' » The sex worker, page 3

Death by overtime

Japan's economy is looking healthy again – but the country's corporate warriors are not. Justin McCurry in Tokyo reports on why the salarymen are working themselves sick

His is the ordinary face behind an extraordinary economic success story. But with his ill-fitting polyester suit, battered briefcase and air of fatigued despondency on the morning commute, the Japanese salaryman, once hailed as the driving force behind Japan's postwar growth, cuts a rather despondent figure these days.

Japan's corporate warriors are victims of their own success. After more than a decade in the doldrums, Japan's economy is in the midst of its most sustained economic recovery since the bubble burst in the early 1990s. Confidence is up, but so are the demands on the salaryman's time and energy.

Japan's renaissance, far from offering its workers any respite, has them confronting a hangover from the bubble years of the 1980s: long working hours, estrangement from family and friends, ill health, and even suicide.

The victims are men such as Naohiro Nishitani (not his real name), for whom relief from the daily slog as an office manager in central Tokyo comes with a long drag on his cigarette and a gulp of beer. It is only now, at the end of a 12-hour working day, that he can loosen his tie, let out a sigh, and relax.

Just a few months ago Nishitani could barely drag himself out of bed, let alone work and socialise. He took to sleeping through entire weekends and was regularly late for work. He lost interest in simple pleasures; thinking about the future brought him out in a cold sweat.

"I realised that I had been under a lot of pressure at work," says the 42-year-old divorcee. "I was working from early morning until 10 at night and clashing regularly with a colleague. One argument in particular just pushed me over the edge."

It took a visit to a psychiatrist for Mr Nishitani to discover that he was suffering from stress through overwork, a condition that is making life a misery for countless other salarymen like him.

A poll by the Research Institute for the Advancement of Living Standards found that almost a third of men working for private companies in Tokyo and Osaka spent more than 12 hours a day at the office. Only half were paid proper overtime, and the other half complained that unsympathetic bosses and the "atmosphere" of their workplace prevented them from claiming their legal entitlements.

About a quarter of men in their 30s work more than 60 hours a week, according to official figures, although the actual number is thought to be much higher. But it would be wrong to describe the Japanese salaryman as a workaholic. There is no compulsion involved: indeed, surveys show that, on the contrary, many would rather spend their evenings anywhere but the office: playing sports, spending time with friends and family.

Working hours have been rising in Japan since the 1990s, as workers who held on to their jobs during the lean years of restructuring were forced to take on the workloads of colleagues who were made redundant. Better days for Japan's economy have done little to ease the pressure. Instead, it has driven men into working longer hours, at a cost to their family life and health.

The longer married men spend at the office, for instance, the less likely they are to have the time, or energy, to start a family. Last year, Japan's population decreased for the first time since the end of the second world war. A Japanese woman can now be expected to produce 1.4 children in her lifetime, well below the 2.1 children experts say are needed to keep the economy ticking over.

'The idea that you perform well, go home and relax still isn't understood'

After years of complacency, the government has been forced to act. Earlier this month it approved a white paper that calls for shorter working hours for fathers to give them more time with their families.

Regardless of how their working day is arranged, salarymen know that the job doesn't end when the office lights go off. They are then expected to join their bosses on afterwork drinking sessions – rare opportunities, at least, to bare their souls about office politics in a haze of booze without fear of repercussions the following morning.

Karoshi, death from overwork, entered the Japanese public consciousness in the late 1980s at the height of the bubble era, when the labour ministry started keeping statistics on apparently healthy men, some still in their 20s, who had dropped dead from heart attacks and strokes brought on by work-related stress.

The difficulty in determining whether a heart attack or stroke has been caused directly by overwork makes it almost impossible to keep accurate *karoshi* figures. The official number is several hundred a year, but counsellors believe the real total could run in to the thousands.

For many salarymen, the pressures of the office continue to loom large even when they stop working altogether.

With millions of baby boomers expected to retire next year, Japan is bracing itself for a dramatic rise in divorces among middle-aged couples, as men who have devoted every waking moment to their company are shunned by their long-suffering wives.

"Silver divorces" are expected to rise again when a new law entitling women to up to half their husband's pension after a breakup goes into force next spring.

That is, of course, if their overworked husbands make it as far as retirement. Men in their 40s and 50 make up the biggest group among the 30,000 Japanese who kill themselves every year. More than two-thirds of men who left a will cited financial worries or problems at work as the cause of their suicide.

In an attempt to improve the lot of the salaryman, the government is mulling a proposal »2

With 100s of jobs including 5 Management | 5 General | 7 Sales | 8 HR | 8 Marketing & PR | 21 Creative & Media | 22 New Media | 32 Secretarial | 35 IT & T | 36 Science & Technology | 36 Courses | 37 TEFL | 37 Education | 37 Public | 39 Social Care | 39 Tenders | plus graduate **guardian.co.uk/jobs**

Paper can offer unexpected design solutions. The *Guardian*'s Saturday "Work" section was leading with an article on the health problems caused by overwork experienced by Japanese businessmen. Rather than commissioning illustrations or photography, Art Director Sarah Habershon approached paper-folding expert Mark Bolitho to create an origami man, thrown to the floor by the pressures of work. The brief specified that the model should look like a classic origami piece and have the key features of a Japanese salaryman, such as a briefcase.

The choice of a brightly colored, woodblock-printed chiyogami paper meant that the model was immediately recognizable as Japanese, which was restated by the association of origami with Japan. The model was shaped using the tension of the paper, with the bend at the waist strengthened by aluminum foil placed inside the model. The model was then photographed, making a striking accompaniment to the article.

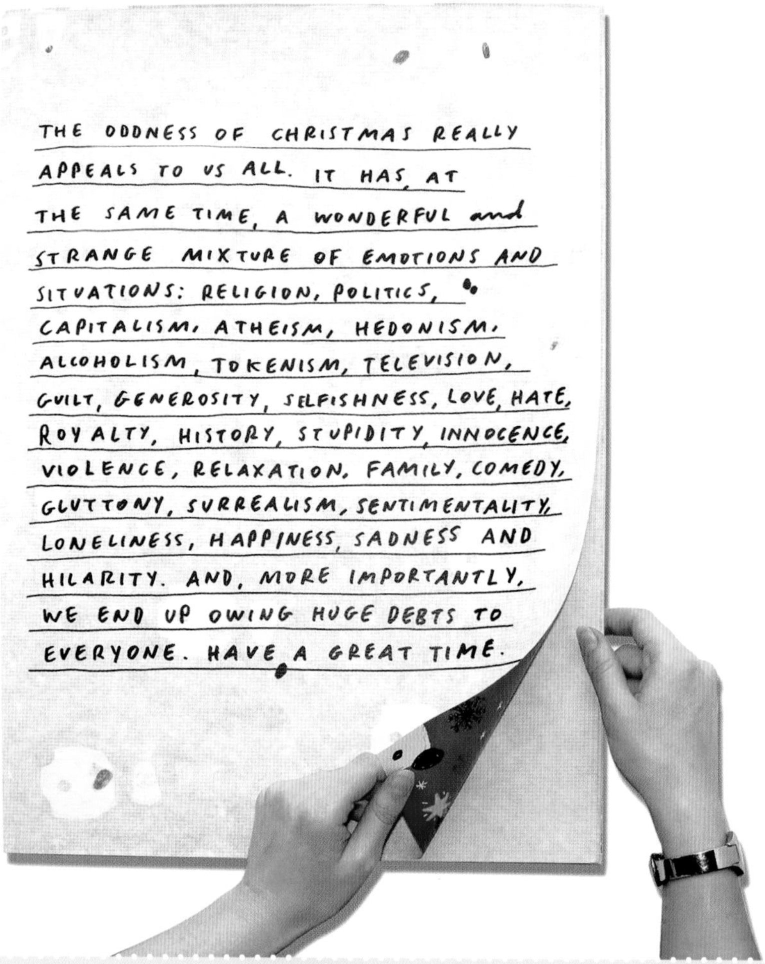

THE ODDNESS OF CHRISTMAS REALLY
APPEALS TO US ALL. IT HAS, AT
THE SAME TIME, A WONDERFUL and
STRANGE MIXTURE OF EMOTIONS AND
SITUATIONS: RELIGION, POLITICS,
CAPITALISM, ATHEISM, HEDONISM,
ALCOHOLISM, TOKENISM, TELEVISION,
GUILT, GENEROSITY, SELFISHNESS, LOVE, HATE,
ROYALTY, HISTORY, STUPIDITY, INNOCENCE,
VIOLENCE, RELAXATION, FAMILY, COMEDY,
GLUTTONY, SURREALISM, SENTIMENTALITY,
LONELINESS, HAPPINESS, SADNESS AND
HILARITY. AND, MORE IMPORTANTLY,
WE END UP OWING HUGE DEBTS TO
EVERYONE. HAVE A GREAT TIME.

tango

PROJECT CHRISTMAS BROADSHEET
DESIGNER DANA ROBERTSON at TANGO
CLIENT SELF-INITIATED

PAPER FACTS:
STOCK END RUNS OF CHRISTMAS WRAPPING PAPER
SIZE 350 × 500mm ($13\frac{13}{16}$ × $19\frac{11}{16}$in)
PRINT TECHNIQUE ONE-COLOR OFFSET LITHO
ADDITIONAL TECHNIQUE FOLDING
PRINTER LNS PRINTERS

Tango is an award-winning design agency focused on branding, advertising, and retail. When it comes to their own promotions, they strive to reflect their ethos of delivering witty and intelligent communications. Clients are bombarded with "unusual" Christmas cards from design agencies, but few receive an irreverent Christmas-themed broadsheet printed on tacky wrapping paper.

The team sourced standard end-runs of wrapping paper, which were printed single-color litho on the reverse. Low-quality papers were sourced to achieve deliberate showthrough. The sheets were randomly selected and assembled so each version of the limited-run piece (150 maximum) is a one-off. The unbound loose sheets were simply folded to emulate a newspaper. Provocative copy and specially commissioned illustrations ensured that the content was as engaging as the format.

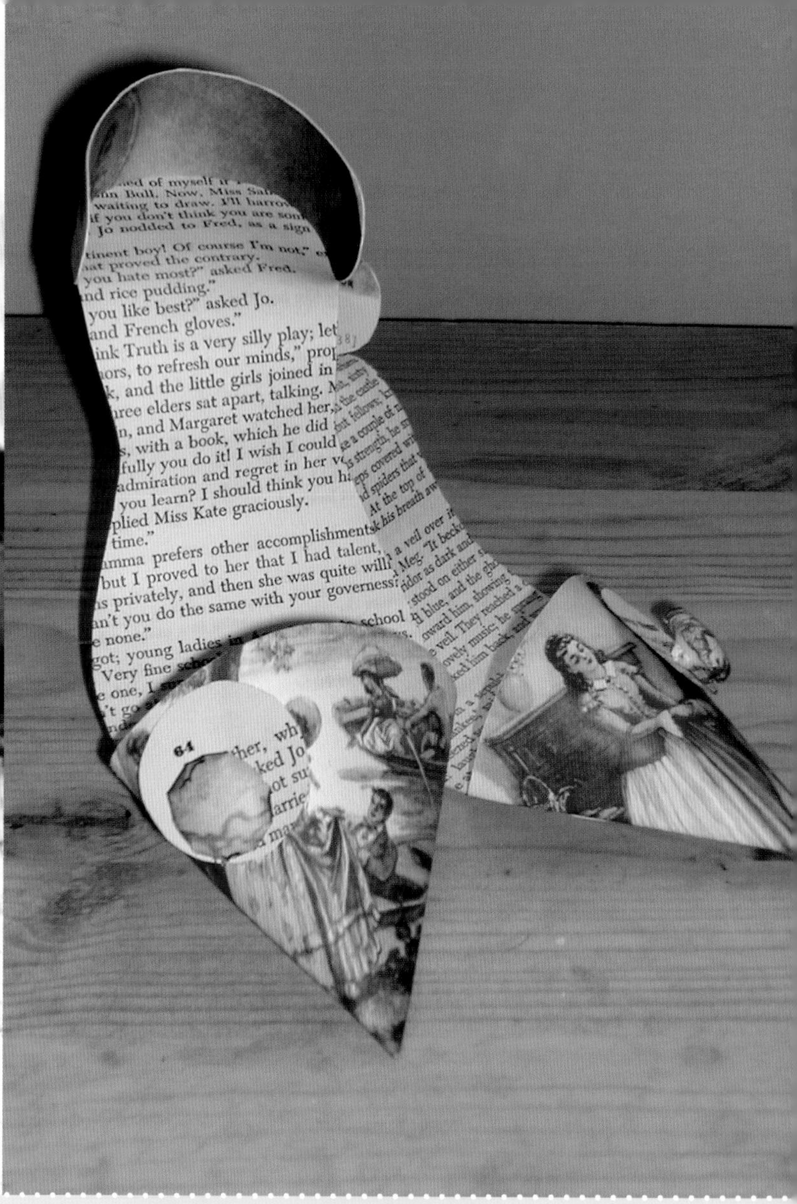

jennifer collier

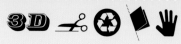

PROJECT SHOES
ARTIST JENNIFER COLLIER
CLIENT SELF-INITIATED

PAPER FACTS:
STOCK VARIOUS PAPERS, FOUND, RECYCLED, OR REUSED

Jennifer Collier creates innovative craft pieces using natural and found materials. The work is nonfunctional and aims to encourage people to speculate on the nature of value. She enjoys the idea of working with disposable organic materials that are transient in nature, imbuing them with worth and creating something intriguing and of great beauty. Found and recycled papers offer the perfect medium for a collection of one-off shoe creations.

Using vintage letters, envelopes, book papers, and maps, the artist explores themes of literature, memories, and recycling. The use of such a fragile material makes the viewer reassess the relationship between beauty and functionality and provokes thoughts about the fragility of the human body and the preciousness of the objects to which we attach value.

CHAPTER 8

limited budgets

www.elevatormoods
w.beck.com
www.gregwhite.tv
www.deviantart.com
TAKE OUT
AND SEE THINGS DIFFERENT
The spinning shafts of light
they turn yellow
THANK
HIGH

Think Tank Media

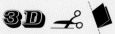

PROJECT FRANZ FERDINAND MEGAPHONES
DESIGNER THINK TANK MEDIA
CLIENT DOMINO RECORDING COMPANY

PAPER FACTS:
STOCK ONE-SIDED BOARD 300gsm
SIZE 315 × 390mm (12½ × 15⅜in)
PRINT TECHNIQUE OFFSET
ADDITIONAL TECHNIQUE FAN-SHAPE FOLDING
PRINTER THINK TANK MEDIA

Franz Ferdinand used iconic Constructivist-influenced cover art for their debut album. To promote the record, Domino Recordings called on Think Tank Media to produce a student survival kit for festivals, including branded condoms, T-shirts, and bottle-opener lighters. Perhaps the most ingenious promotional item was the low-cost megaphone, which brings the cover image to life in 3D through a simple folded-paper construction that was cheap enough to be produced and distributed in large quantities.

Volume Inc.

PROJECT LOCALMUSIC.COM BUSINESS CARDS
DESIGNER VOLUME INC.
CLIENT LOCALMUSIC.COM

PAPER FACTS:
STOCK PRINTER'S WHITE HOUSE STOCK 80lb
PRINT TECHNIQUE TWO-COLOR OFFSET LITHO, WITH THREE INK CHANGES
PRINTER SPEEDWAY PRINTING

Localmusic.com was an early online service designed to promote the local music scene in major US cities. San Francisco designers Volume Inc. produced an identity to reflect the esthetic and attitude of independent-music culture. The backs of the cards feature photographs of Localmusic.com stickers fly-posted around the city. With "zero money" for the job, they used the printer's house paper stock and made three ink changes in the same press run to maximize the color range of the cards without having to use a larger four- or six-color press or change printing plates.

Bob Milner

PROJECT MILK, TWO SUGARS
ARTISTS BOB MILNER, TOM SENIOR
CLIENT SELF-INITIATED

PAPER FACTS:
STOCK STANDARD 80gsm
SIZE A4 (210 × 297mm; 8¼ × 11¾in) FOLDED
PRINT TECHNIQUE PHOTOCOPY
PRINTER SELF-PRODUCED

SPECIAL CONSIDERATIONS:
"The availability and simplicity of photocopying is vital in our desire to make a new issue every month, as it offers a quick delivery of product. It is standard repro office paper—so probably not recycled. It is not an issue that Milk, Two Sugars has any interest in. We make the issues for reasons other than saving the planet. If all a publication has to boast is that it is recycled, it is likely the content will be dull. This is a fact. There are better ways to save the planet."

Bob Milner, Milk, Two Sugars, UK

Artists Bob Milner and Tom Senior founded Milk, Two Sugars as a platform to showcase their drawing. "Very early on we decided that it had to be free," explains Bob. "We did not want to be hindered by sponsors or funding. The content is determined by our approach to drawing and found imagery. The look is dictated by the necessity of cost. The format is lighter than a book, more substantial than a leaflet—ideal to be passed on. Broadly, the content is apolitical and nontopical so that the issues can exist beyond the present and still have relevance. We are serious in the desire to make a positive difference to people."

They draw the images on A4 paper (210 × 297mm; 8¼ × 11¾in) and then reduce them on a photocopier. The issue is assembled and a master copy is fed into a photocopier that copies, sorts, folds, and staples the copies. The headers for the free gifts are photocopied, cut to size, and hand-stapled to the filled plastic bags. The covers have been standard 80gsm colored paper to date, but they are looking at alternatives. For a future luxury edition they plan a screenprinted, hand-stitched cover with a 300gsm textured weave. Bob again: "It has a name in some fancy paper catalog. We managed to blag it."

SOFT BENCH

PK1

Aran Knitting
To fit 89cm x 118.5cm x 58.5cm

SOFT BENCH

Measurements and Materials

Overall dimensions of the featured Soft Bench are 89cm x 118.5cm x 58.5cm. Seat rungs are 30cm and are knitted in Moss Stitch. The backrest rungs are 28cm and are of various stitches. Length of seat and backrest are 112cm and are knitted in Moss Stitch. The arms and legs are knitted in Beryl's Honeycomb stitch. The yarn is Classic Aran by Wendy, Sage Heather (588).

Notes

This pattern is for the Soft Bench made in Glebe Farm, Birmingham, England in 2005 and was jointly knitted by ladies who have lived in the area for many years. The various stitches on the backrest rungs were the choice of the lady who knitted it: Beatrice Eagle, Beryl Pitt, Elaine Cook, Frances Johnson, June Rawlins, Margaret Morrison, Mary Wilson, Minnie Davis and Rose Cerrone.

[...]ou to wish to knit your own Soft Bench you can [...]pt the stitches featured below. However, Soft [...]ches do not have to be knitted; they can be [...] in all sorts of domestic crafts. The principles [...]king a Soft Bench are always the same.

[...] ill need to:-
[...] your bench
[...]stigate its history
[...]blish domestic craft skills in the area
[...]some people who have the skills and
[...] join you
[...] your pattern
[...]e pieces together

[...]ations

[...] = purl; st(s) = stitches; cm = centimetres; [...]her; beg = beginning; rep = repeat; [...]te; patt = pattern; cont = continue; [...]ng; approx = approximately

Moss Stitch

Over 15 sts. **1st row** K1, P1 to end. Rep every row.

Double Moss Stitch

Over 15 sts. **1st row** K1, P1 to end. **2nd row** K1, P1 to end. **3rd row** P1, K1 to end. **4th row** P1, K1 to end. These 4 rows make patt.

Beryl's Honeycomb

1st row K into 2nd st on left needle then K into 1st st, pull the 2 sts off tog. K into back of 2nd st on left needle then into 1st st and pull off tog. **2nd and alt row** P. **3rd row** K into back of 2nd st on left needle then into 1st st and pull off tog. K in 2nd st of left needle then into 1st st and pull off tog. These 4 rows form patt.

Beatrice and Rose's Squares

Over 20 sts. **1st row** K4, P4 to end. Rep for 3 rows. **5th row** P4, K4 to end. Rep for 3 rows. These 8 rows form the patt. You can increase and vary shapes of squares by varying number of stitches you K or P.

Frances' Cable

Cable over 8 sts with spare cable needle. **1st row** P4 sts with cable needle, slip 2 sts from left hand needle, hold at front. K2 sts from left needle. Rep to end. **2nd row** K4, P4 to end. **3rd row** K4, P4 to end.

Elaine's Rib

Over 16 sts. **1st row** K2, P2 to end. **2nd row** K2, P2 to end. Rep.

The Globe Farm Soft Bench is a project by Trevor Pitt.
Photographs by Dave Remes and Trevor Pitt. Designed with Absolute Zero°

Thanks to the ladies from Glebe Farm, Glebe Farm Library, Glebe Farm Community Centre, TB Ramsden Ltd (Bradford), Beryl Monica Pitt, Clare Thornton and Stina Hogkvirst

together we'll make it

THEpUBLIC

LIMITED BUDGETS

Trevor Pitt &c

PROJECT SOFT BENCH KNITTING PATTERN
DESIGNERS TREVOR PITT, ABSOLUTE ZERO°
CLIENT TREVOR PITT

STOCK ROBERT HORNE GO! SILK 115gsm
PRINT TECHNIQUE DIGITAL
PRINTER ADM IMAGING

A
SOFT BENCH
IN A HARD
LANDSCAPE

The inspiration for Soft Bench was a public bench on the housing estate where artist and curator Trevor Pitt grew up, now removed to make way for a parking lot. Trevor invited women from the Glebe Farm area of Birmingham, UK, to join him, using their amazing knitting skills to make the covering for a different kind of public seating. The literature to accompany the sculpture was integral to the artistic vision. Trevor devised a knitting pattern that offered all the information to create your own Soft Bench.

Key to success was for the piece to look and feel as close as possible to a vintage knitting pattern. London-based designers Absolute Zero° helped source a smooth, thin paper stock that had an authentic feel as well as designing the piece just the right side of pastiche. Original photography of the sculpture takes the place of models in knitwear. A flap reveals documentary photography of the piece on site. Full knitting instructions and a printed rule complete the knitting-pattern theme.

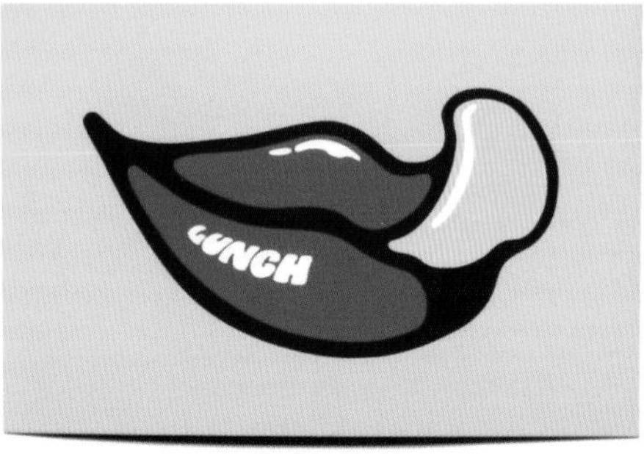

theFarm

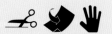

PROJECT LUNCH STATIONERY
DESIGNER theFARM
CLIENT NAKED COMMUNICATIONS

PAPER FACTS:
STOCK LETTERHEAD/COMPLIMENTS SLIPS: ARJOWIGGINS POP'SET 120gsm (IN FLAME ORANGE, OLD GOLD, SUNSHINE YELLOW, PISTACHIO, PINK, SHOCKING PINK); ENVELOPES: VIBRANT 11 100gsm (IN DEEP BLUE, ORANGE, CERISE, GOLD, LIME, RED)

SIZE LETTERHEAD: A4 (210 × 297mm; 8¼ × 11¾in)
ENVELOPES: DL (99 × 210mm; 3⅞ × 8¼in)
PRINT TECHNIQUE FOUR-COLOR OFFSET LITHO
PRINTER STICKERS: NATIONAL PRINT, UK

SPECIAL CONSIDERATIONS:
"We had to find suitable colored paper that was readily available and within budget. It was crucial that the colors and finishes of the stocks used did not look as though they came from an office stationery cupboard."

Chloe Franklin, theFarm, UK

ABOVE: LUNCH STATIONERY
Photography: Victoria Woolhead
© theFarm

theFarm were appointed to create an identity and corporate stationery for Lunch, an offshoot company of communications specialists Naked. The identity was intended to be unique, creative, and a bit anarchic, so theFarm created a vibrant-colored stationery system that allows each user to create personalized, unique letterheads, compliment slips, and envelopes. Blank sheets of colored stock can be individually "designed" by the Lunch team using four-color printed adhesive stickers.

As a start-up venture, budgets were tight. theFarm sourced colored paper that fitted with the brand identity. The blank paper was purchased in bulk and some was cut down to DL (99 × 210mm; 3⅞ × 8¼in) for the compliment slips. The stock paper was color matched for printed stickers, which were die-cut into branded shapes: the Lunch lips logo and the Lunch address as two boxes.

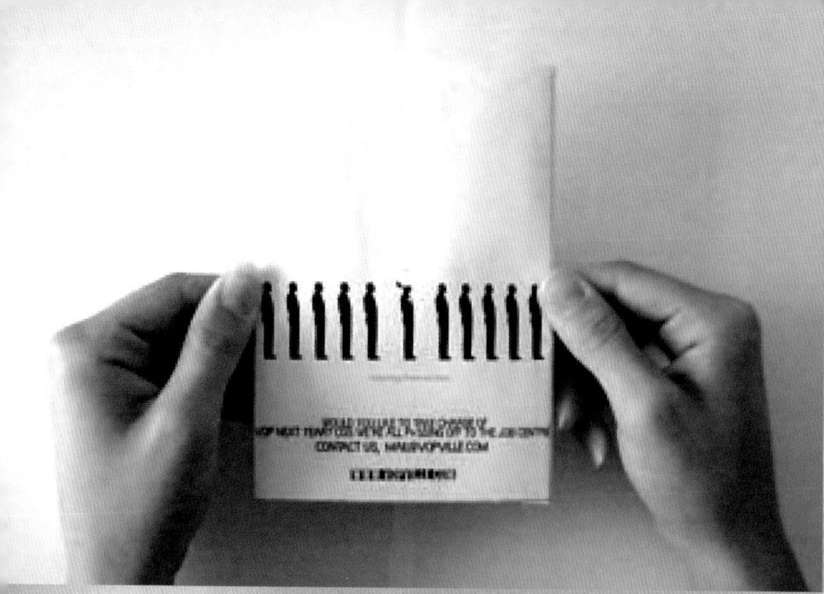

Craig Kirk

PROJECT VOP MAGAZINE
DESIGNER CRAIG KIRK
CLIENT UNIVERSITY OF GLOUCESTERSHIRE

PAPER FACTS:
STOCK STANDARD PHOTOCOPIER STOCK 140gsm
SIZE A3 (297 × 420mm; 11¾ × 16½in)

SPECIAL CONSIDERATIONS:
"All that content, plus the added bonus of a free foldout poster on the reverse of the A3 sheet. Now that's using a piece of paper for all its worth and giving the student folk a dandy poster to brighten their magnolia room walls with!"

Craig Kirk, UK

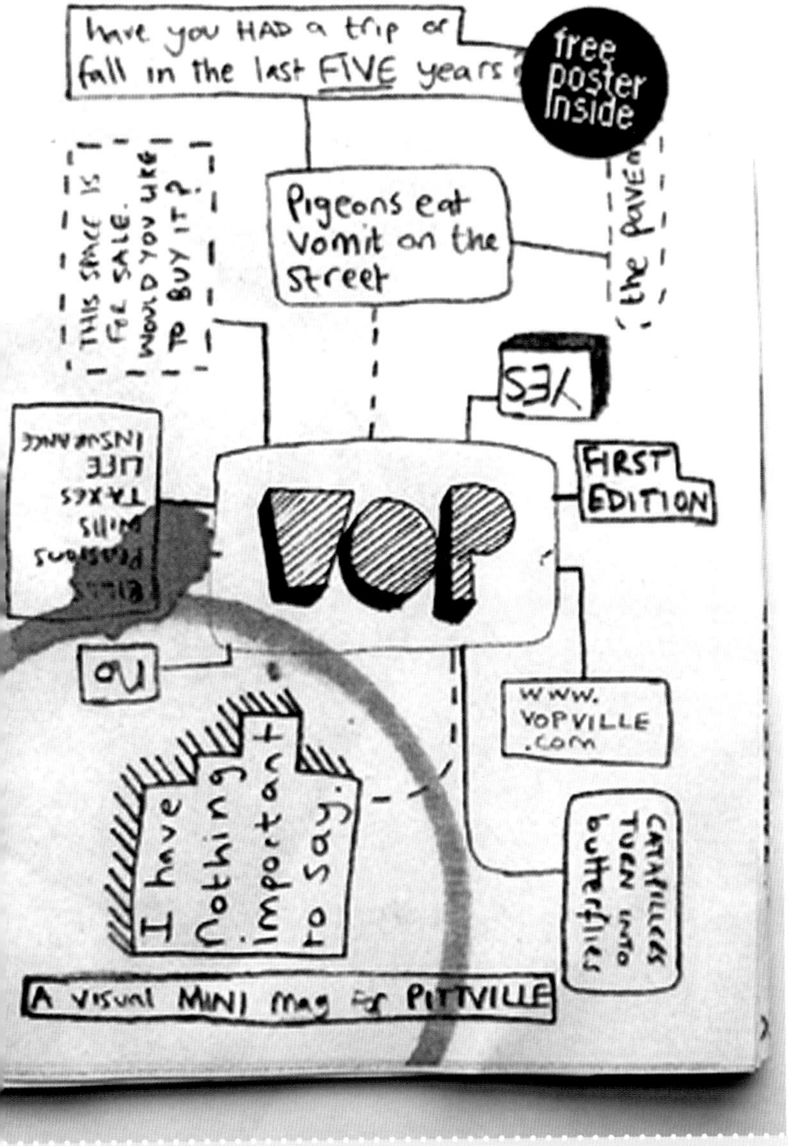

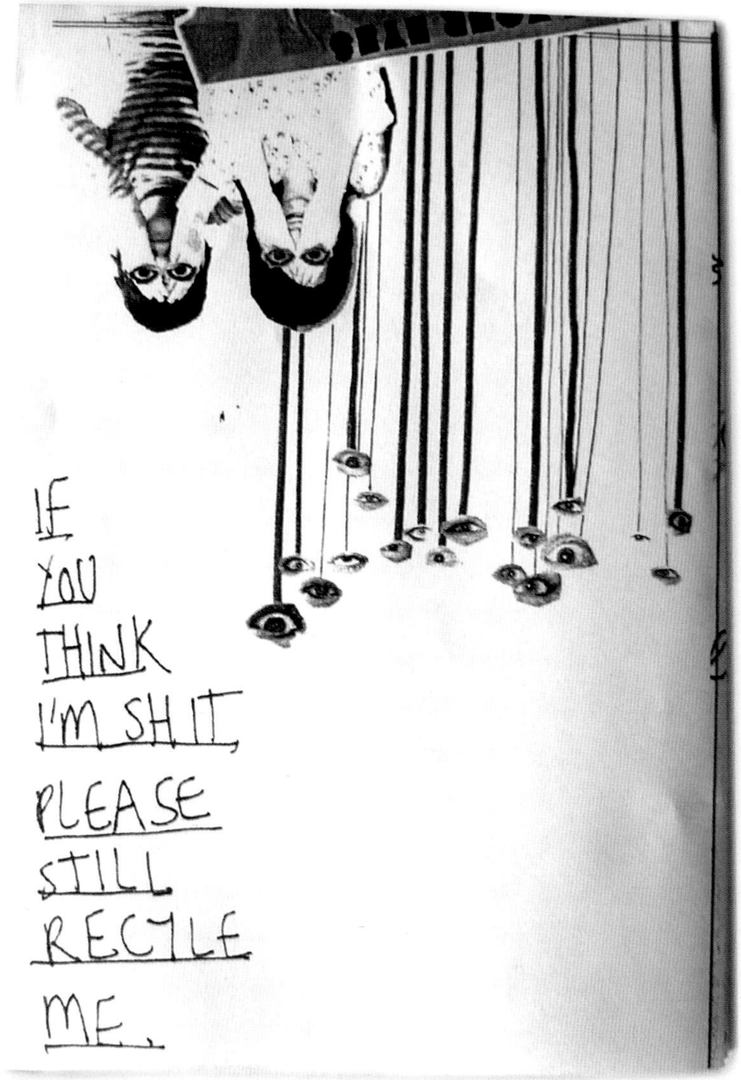

Simplicity is at the core of *VOP*, a monthly pocket-sized visual magazine for Pittville Campus at the University of Gloucestershire. A piece of A3 (297 × 420mm; 11¾ × 16½in) paper printed black and white and folded into a booklet, *VOP* is all about ideas, words, and images rather than glossy full-color pages and advertising. Its creators embraced the restrictions imposed by limited finances with the manifesto. "Content, bold and insightful, forget the fluff." The last thing they wanted was another "senseless wedge" of a magazine.

The magazine works to give art and design students a platform on which to showcase and air their ideas, hopes, fears, and—most importantly—their work. Students email their contributions via a website for inclusion. The work is diverse, and includes paintings, sketches, poems, and short stories. There are just two rules to *VOP*: keep it black and white, and keep it folded A3.

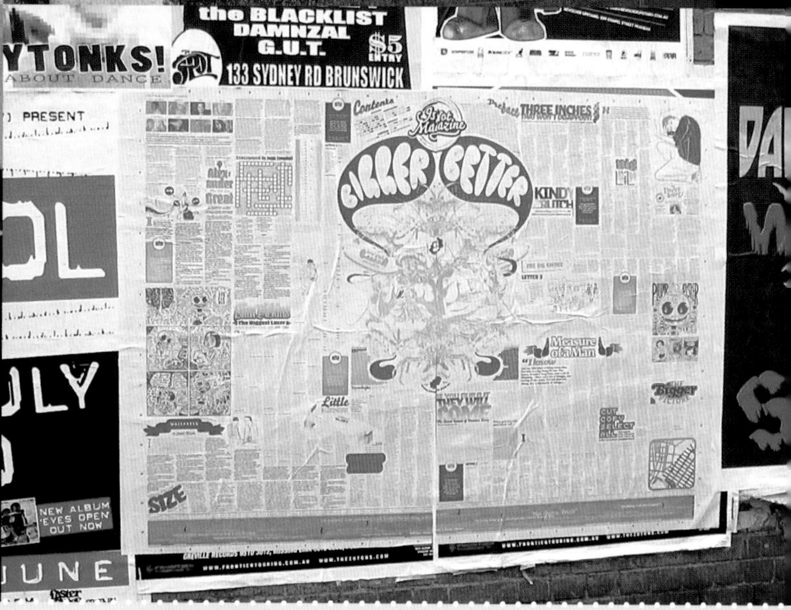

LIMITED BUDGETS

Is Not Magazine

PROJECT IS NOT MAGAZINE
DESIGNERS AND COFOUNDERS MEL CAMPBELL, STUART GEDDES, NATASHA LUDOWYK, PENNY MODRA, JEREMY WORTSMAN at IS NOT MAGAZINE
CLIENT SELF-INITIATED

PAPER FACTS:
STOCK MG LITHO 90gsm
SIZE 1.5 × 2m (59 × 78¾in)
PRINT TECHNIQUES ISSUES 1–3: SILKSCREEN; ISSUES 4–9: OFFSET LITHO
ADDITIONAL TECHNIQUE ISSUE 5: METALLIC INKS
PRINTER ROCK POSTERS

SPECIAL CONSIDERATIONS:
"Our first three issues were silkscreened. The black ink on Issue 1 smelled so badly no one wanted to stock it—but the overprinting was gorgeous. We changed to offset printing for Issue 4, and for Issue 5 we used a smoother stock. That looked too slick and sales dipped. We have since changed back to the rougher stock and continue to use offset. We still can't produce really nice glossy overprints like silkscreen, but type doesn't bleed, and we can produce higher-resolution artwork such as photographs."

Jeremy Wortsman, Australia

Is Not Magazine is a 1.5m × 2m (59 × 78¾in) billposter produced by five young Melburnians: Mel Campbell, Stuart Geddes, Natasha Ludowyk, Penny Modra, and Jeremy Wortsman. Conceived as a cross between a literary magazine and a street press, the format enabled the team to reach the largest audience with the smallest budget and without advertising. Melbourne already had an infrastructure for printing and distributing posters for concerts and events, and the magazine effectively harnesses this system. It is on display at outdoor poster sites in inner-city Melbourne and Sydney and is sold in some European venues.

As well as the production issues mentioned here, the biggest hurdle was to understand how to translate the design from a 15in (381mm) laptop screen to a four-sheeter. It took several issues to get it right. The esthetic, including the exclusive use of Underware typefaces, owes much to the culture of billposters and movie-theater posters. The team has built an international network of writers and artists and a community of passionate supporters who sustain the publication. It has attracted local and international press accolades, and won the Premier's 2006 Design Award for communication design.

CHAPTER 9

surface effects + the power of touch

ction of exceptional

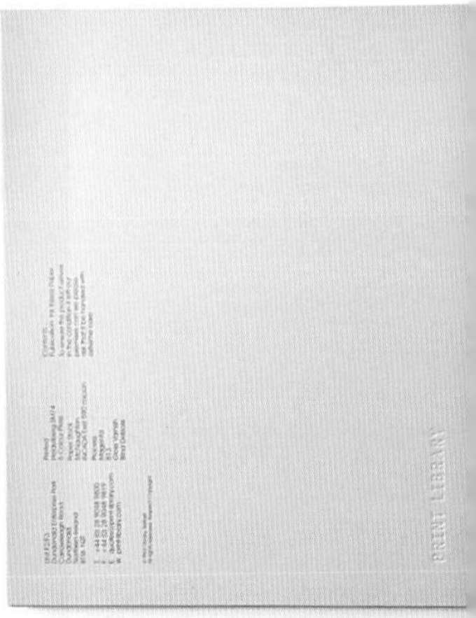

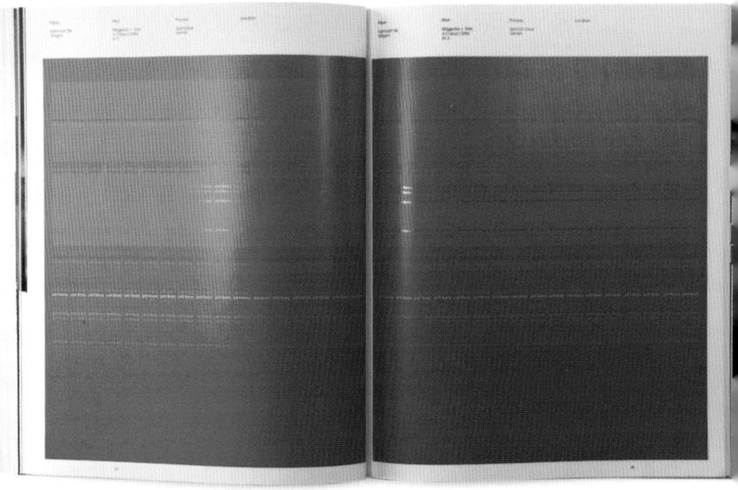

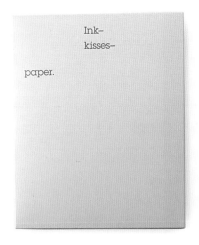

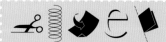

SURFACE EFFECTS +
THE POWER OF TOUCH

Nothing Diluted &c

PROJECT INK KISSES PAPER
DESIGNER NOTHINGDILUTED, HURSON
CLIENT PRINT LIBRARY

PAPER FACTS:
STOCK DUST JACKET: SKYE UNCOATED BRILLIANT WHITE 120gsm; COVER: SKYE UNCOATED BRILLIANT WHITE 300gsm; SECTIONS 1, 8: SKYE UNCOATED BRILLIANT WHITE 170gsm; SECTIONS 2, 4: HANNOART SILK 170gsm; SECTION 3: HANNOART GLOSS 170gsm; SECTION 5: HANNOART SILK 150gsm; SECTION 6: SKYE COATED EXTRA MATTE 150gsm; SECTION 7: SKYE COATED EXTRA MATTE 170gsm

PRINT TECHNIQUES DUST JACKET, PAGES 2–11, 22–25, 30–31, 38–43: FOUR COLOR; PAGES 12–13, 56–57, 60–64: FOUR COLOR + MAGENTA; PAGES 14–17, 28–29: FOUR COLOR + FLUORESCENT 806; PAGE 18–19: MAGENTA; PAGES 20–21: MAGENTA + TINTS; PAGES 26–27, 44–45: FOUR COLOR + PMS 813; PAGES 32–33: FOUR COLOR + MAGENTA + TINTS; PAGES 34–35: FOUR COLOR + MAGENTA + TINTS + PMS 813; PAGES 36–37: FOUR COLOR + BLACK + 7545 DUOTONE + MAGENTA; PAGES 46–47: FOUR COLOR + SPECIAL GRAY + PMS 813; PAGES 48–49: FOUR COLOR + METALLIC BLACK + BLACK + CYAN + MAGENTA; PAGES 50–51: FOUR COLOR + BLACK + CYAN; PAGES 52–55: FOUR COLOR + METALLIC 8200; PAGES 58–59: MAGENTA + TINTS + FLUORESCENT 806

ADDITIONAL TECHNIQUES COVER: FOIL BLOCKING, MAGENTA PIGMENT FOIL, BLIND DEBOSSING, MATTE VARNISH; PAGE 1: FOIL BLOCKING, WHITE-PIGMENT FOIL; PAGES 8–9, 12–13, 22–23, 26–27, 38–41, 46–47, 52–55: MATTE VARNISH; PAGES 10–11, 14–21, 28–31, 34–35, 44–45: GLOSS VARNISH; PAGES 58–59: GRADIENT VARNISH; PAGES 18–19, 40–41: EMBOSSING
SIZE 280 × 230mm (11 × 9in)
PRINTER PRINT LIBRARY
BINDING PERFECT BOUND

Conceived as a showcase for Print Library, Ink Kisses Paper was a year in the making. A host of printing and finishing techniques on a range of McNaughton paper stocks are galvanized by ambitious and engaging content, the result of collaboration between Grant Dickson and Ciaran Hurson. The imagery was captured by Dickson on a handheld Lomo Kompakt camera during a stay in San Francisco, with Belfast-based Hurson providing the words. The finished book—part travelogue, part artwork—beautifully merges the physical and ethereal.

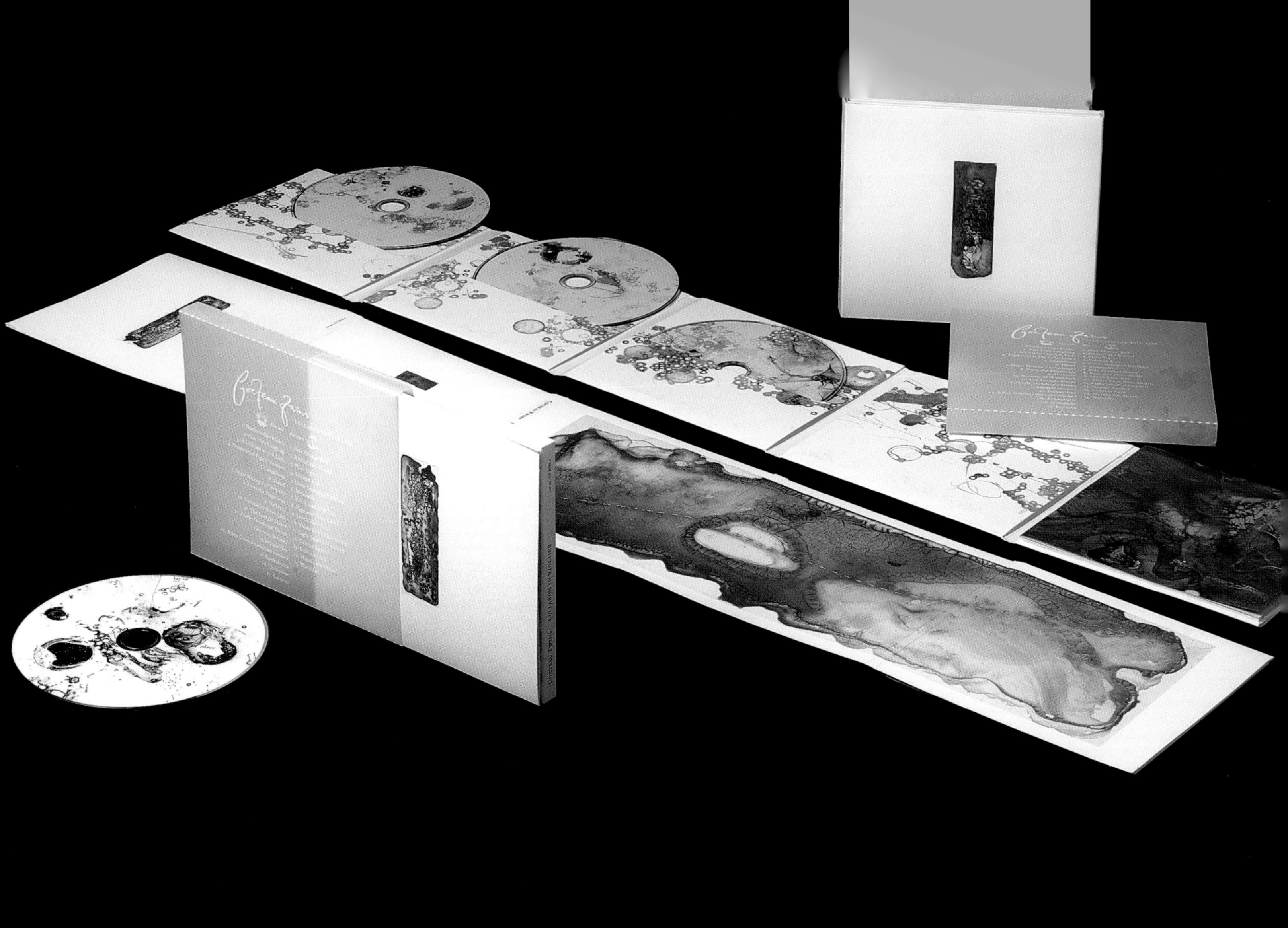

SURFACE EFFECTS +
THE POWER OF TOUCH

V23

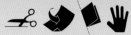

PROJECT COCTEAU TWINS: LULLABIES TO VIOLANE
DESIGNER VAUGHAN OLIVER, CHRIS BIGG at V23
CLIENT 4AD RECORDS, FONTANA

PAPER FACTS:
STOCK SLIPCASE: SIMULATOR 270gsm
CD PACK: CURIOUS TOUCH SOFT MILK 300gsm
SIZE 140 × 125mm (5½ × 4 15/16in) OPENING TO 725 × 125mm (28½ × 4 15/16in)
PRINT TECHNIQUE LITHO WITH UV INKS
PRINTER THINK TANK MEDIA

ADDITIONAL TECHNIQUES WHEN USING CURIOUS TOUCH THE INK NULLIFIES THE TEXTURE OF THE BOARD WHEN IT IS UV DRIED, SO MINIMAL COVERAGE WAS NEEDED TO ALLOW THE PACKAGE TO REMAIN TACTILE; HAND-GLUED PACK

Vaughan Oliver's long-standing relationship with the Cocteau Twins culminated in the design for this four-disk singles compilation. The band considered the choice of material perfect. "Curious Touch Soft Milk—it sounds like a Cocteau Twins track." The disks were hand-packed with antistatic gloves to avoid marking the packaging.

BAZOOKA
Call Allison and let the party begin. Cheers.
telephone 310 487 1210
asrobb@verizon.net
vocabulary to talk about it. One wine might remind you of oranges right off a neighbor's tree. Another may suggest thoughts of new leather, or of licorice ropes and tire tread on asphalt. Afterwards, you might find yourself recalling your unspoken past and be inspired to write your memoirs.
budding connoisseur. She holds a certification in vintage wine and custom-designs corporate and private tastings. Allison brings the party to you along with a unique palette of sensory materials, ranging from sliced grapefruit to slabs of concrete, to identify the aromas and sensations in wine while giving you the
The sheer essence of wine inspires memory and emotion. Ever taste wine that reminds you of newly mown grass in summer? Bread baking or bacon frying in a pan? Allison Robbins invites you to discover the impressions, tastes and smells conjured by wine. Her approach is equally instructive to the aficionado and the
scratch and sniff
allison robbins
WINE TASTINGS
YOU NEVER KNOW WHAT A GLASS OF WINE WILL CALL TO MIND.
YOUR FIRST FRENCH KISS ON THE FERRIS WHEEL AT THE STRAWBERRY FESTIVAL.
OR HOT CHERRY PIE AT THE TRUCKSTOP ON A MISGUIDED TRIP TO VEGAS.

konnectDesign

PROJECT ALLISON ROBBINS GIFT BAG BROCHURE
DESIGNER DAVID WHITCRAFT at konnectDESIGN
CREATIVE DIRECTOR KAREN KNECHT
PHOTOGRAPHER JODEAN BIFOSS
CLIENT ALLISON ROBBINS WINE

PAPER FACTS:
STOCK MOHAWK BRILLIANT WHITE 100lb COVER
SIZE CARDS: 3½ × 2¼in (89 × 57mm) FOLDED; HANGTAGS: 2 × 2in (51 × 51mm) TRIMMED
PRINT TECHNIQUES FOUR COLOR, SCRATCH'N'SNIFF
PRINTER TORAGRAFIX

A former television writer and producer of such shows as *Melrose Place*, Allison Robbins launched a new career hosting wine tastings. Her promotional material captures the interactivity of these seminars. A velveteen gift bag holds a series of cards, each containing a wine-inspired sensory payoff: a piece of bubblegum, a teabag, grass, and scratch'n'sniff pineapple. konnectDesign chose a quality paper that would feel rich to the touch and provide ample support for each sensory element. Traditional four-color printing methods were used along with the application of scratch'n'sniff scent.

SURFACE EFFECTS +
THE POWER OF TOUCH

konnectDesign

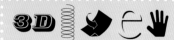

PROJECT NITIN: SNOW
DESIGNERS KAREN KNECHT, JOYCE PENNELL at konnectDESIGN
CREATIVE DIRECTOR KAREN KNECHT
CLIENT NITIN

PAPER FACTS:
STOCK BOOK: EPSON ENHANCED MATTE, CORVON IRIDESCENTS; COVER: NYTEK NOVASUEDE, LINEN; MAILER: TOPKOTE GLOSS COVER 130lb
SIZE BOOK: 13 × 9in (330 × 229mm); MAILER: 11¾ × 8½in (297 × 210mm)

PRINT TECHNIQUE FOUR COLOR WITH A GLOSS AQUEOUS COAT, ON EPSON PRINTER
ADDITIONAL TECHNIQUES BOOK: COVER FEATURES NITIN'S LOGO CONFIGURED AS A SNOWFLAKE, DEBOSSED ON NYTEK NOVASUEDE, WHICH IS REMINISCENT OF SNOW; MAILER: CLEAR MAILER POUCH DISPLAYS A SINGLE IMAGE FROM NITIN'S COLLECTION WITH HAND-ARRANGED SNOWFLAKES
BINDING CUSTOM-BOUND BY JOHN DEMERRITT OF DEMERRITT BOOKBINDING

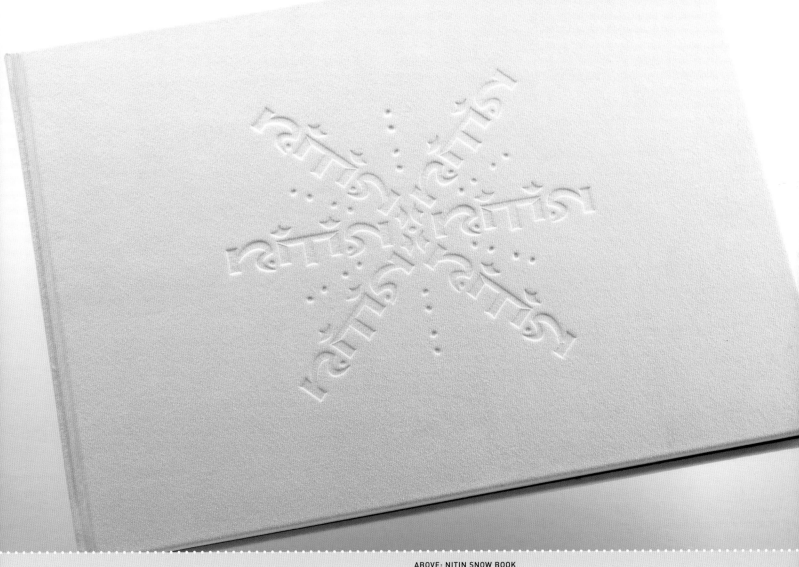

ABOVE: NITIN SNOW BOOK
Photography: JoDean Bifoss for konnectDesign

Photographer Nitin shot a series of images in snowy Vancouver for a new portfolio book. konnectDesign created a coffee-table volume and self-promo mailers with a wintry theme. The project's success relied on sensitivity to materials. Paper, binding, faux snowflakes, and see-through envelopes were chosen to evoke wintry characteristics: the state of being soft, crisp, and clear. The designers tested several papers to find the whitest sheet that would capture the luminous textural qualities of snow and light. For the endpapers, a Corvon Iridescents sheet was chosen in a shade reminiscent of a crisp night sky after snowfall.

The cover features Nitin's logo configured as a snowflake, so it was important to find a material that would read well and feel beautiful to the touch. The final selection, Nytek Novasuede, is reminiscent of soft snow, and it also debosses well. For the promo, konnektDesign selected a paper that would be sturdy enough to mail while accentuating the fine color and details of the prints. Each see-through mailer displays a single image from Nitin's collection and holds a clear pouch with hand-arranged snowflakes.

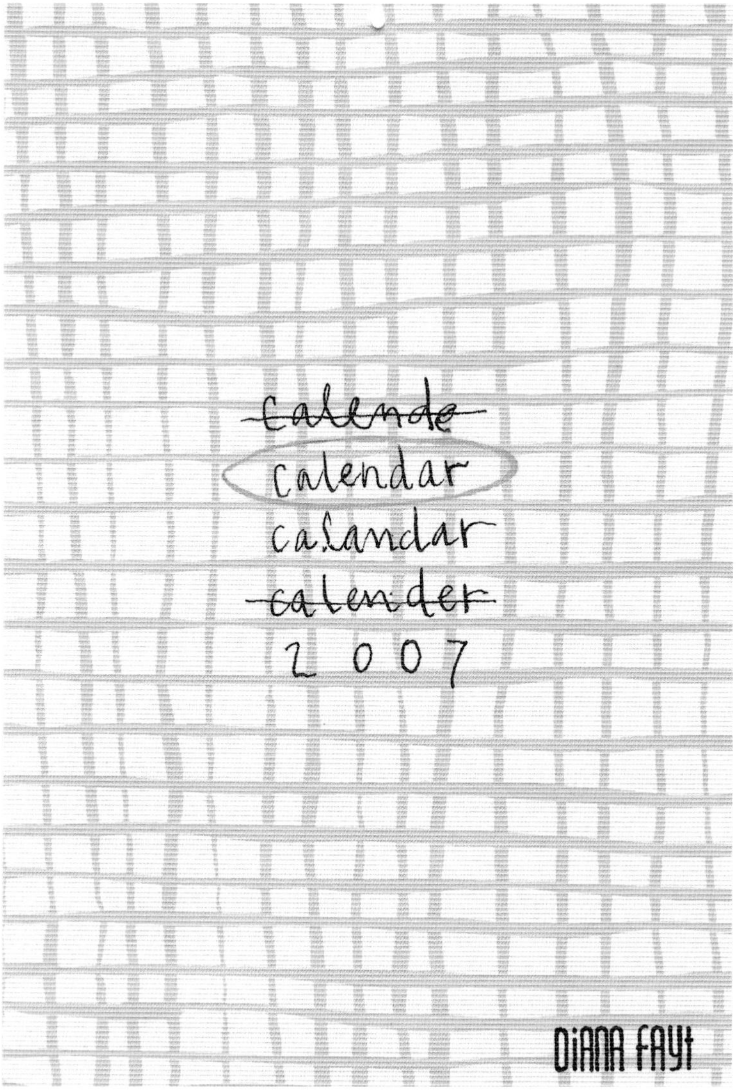

Diana Fayt

PROJECT CALENDAR
DESIGNER DIANA FAYT
CLIENT SELF-INITIATED

PAPER FACTS:
STOCK NT STRIPE GA SNOW WHITE 210lb
SIZE GIFT WRAP: 19½ × 27in (241 × 686mm)
PRINTER SANKYO PRINTING COMPANY

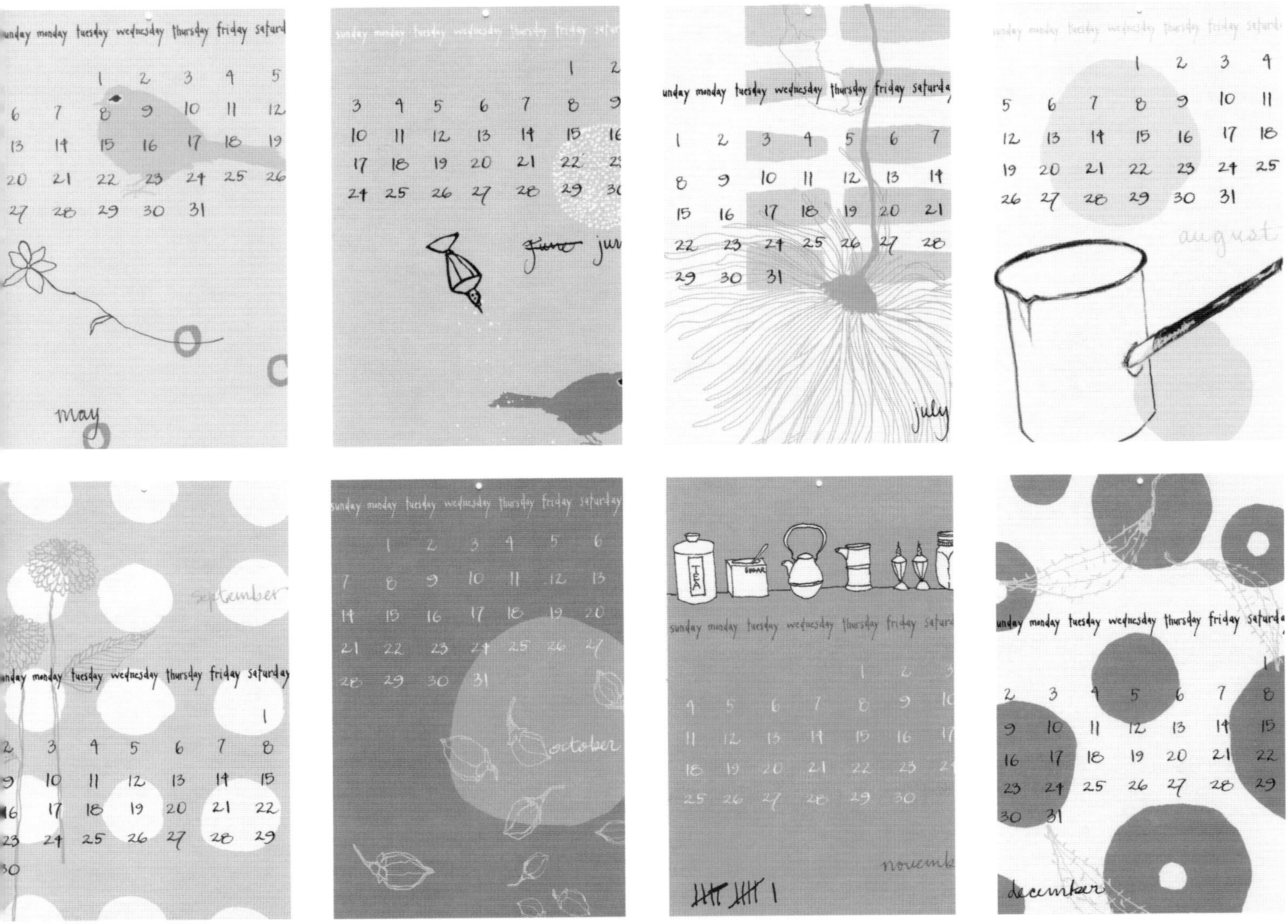

Diana Fayt is a ceramic artist with a distinctive personal style of surface design and illustration. "I have always loved handmade calendars," she explains, "and when visiting Japan I had seen a wide array of different styles and approaches in calendar design. I was inspired to incorporate some of the formats I saw along with my illustrations and hand-lettering to create a calendar that was attractive, functional, and simple." The hand-drawn images were scanned into Photoshop where the layout was then designed.

The textured paper stock that was chosen has a quality reminiscent of fabric, giving the graphics a softer look and the whole product a tactile feel, so emulating the traditional style of the Japanese calendars that had inspired her. Diana chose an open-page design, with each page left unattached so that the calendar can be displayed in a number of different formats. It's a simple solution that successfully emphasizes the handmade qualities of the piece.

Dalziel + Pow

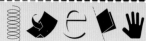

PROJECT CHA TANG TEA ROOM MENU
DESIGNER AKIKO SHISHIDO at DALZIEL + POW
CLIENT ILLUM DEPARTMENT STORE

PAPER FACTS:
STOCK GF SMITH TAPESTRY GLACE APPLIQUE 300gsm
SIZE 155 × 220mm (6⅛ × 8⅔in)

PRINT TECHNIQUE METALLIC FOIL ON EMBOSSED STOCK
ADDITIONAL TECHNIQUES HOLE-PUNCHED AND GATEFOLDED
PRINTER SOURCED BY CLIENT
BINDING BOUND WITH TIED MATCHING RIBBON

As part of their ongoing design program for Copenhagen department store Illum, London retail-design consultants Dalziel + Pow created an elegant tea room, located on the womenswear floor. The branding and collateral was designed to complement the "maximalist" chic interior, notably these touchy-feely menus, which go with the contemporary scheme while communicating the traditional connotations of a tea room.

The pearlescent and embossed floral pattern of the GF Smith Tapestry stock was chosen to reflect the elegance of the tea-room atmosphere and eliminated the need for an otherwise costly embossing process. Ornate script and serif graphics are lent a contemporary sharpness by foil blocking in a vibrant red. The hole-punched cover and menu insert are bound together with a ribbon chosen to echo the swirly typography, and to match the shade of the foil blocking.

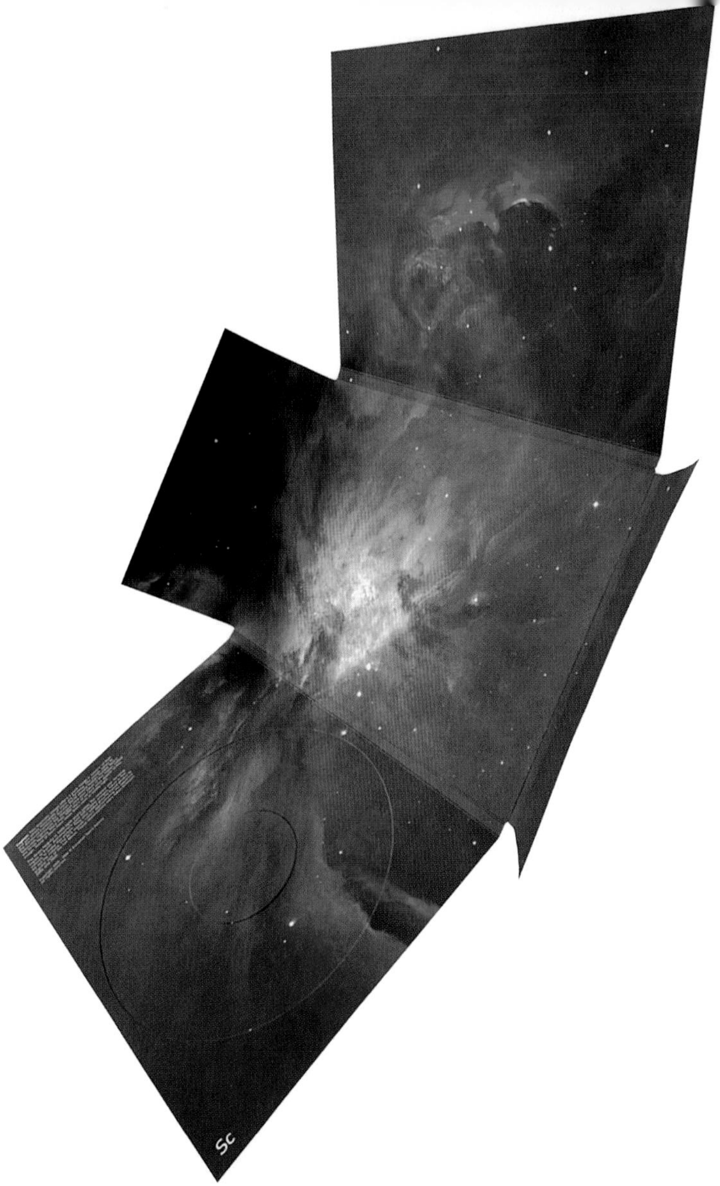

B&W Studio

PROJECT SPACE CONNECTIONS
DESIGNER LEE BRADLEY, STEVE WILLS at B&W STUDIO
CLIENT SPACE CONNECTIONS

PAPER FACTS:
STOCK CELLOGLAS MIRROR BOARD FLEETLINE SILVER 400gsm
SIZE FOLDER: A4 (210 × 297mm; 8¼ × 11¾in)
DIRECT MAIL: 210mm (8¼in)

PRINT TECHNIQUES FOLDER: SPECIAL SINGLE COLOR, FOUR-COLOR IMAGE ON REVERSE; DIRECT MAIL: SPECIAL SINGLE COLOR
ADDITIONAL TECHNIQUES FOLDER: EMBOSSING, FOLDING DIRECT MAIL: EMBOSSING
PRINTER HARROGATE PRINT LTD.

SPECIAL CONSIDERATIONS:
"When printing the Pantone blue onto the mirror board the drying time was days. They resorted to hanging the folders and using hair dryers!"

Lee Bradley, B&W Studio, UK

Space Connections is a UK government initiative to promote space education in schools and provide a link between education and the space industry. It is founded on the belief that the subject of space excites young people and that it can be used as a context for teaching a wide curriculum, from physics and math to music and drama. B&W Studio created its marketing collateral with the same enthusiasm for the space theme.

For the folder, Celloglas Mirror Board created an appropriately spacey feel, further enhanced by the prominently embossed brand icon: circles that represent the sun, moon, and earth. The inside features full-bleed imagery sourced from the NASA and ESA photo libraries. When unfolded it emulates a satellite opening its panels. For the direct-mail piece the same stock manifested itself as a circular flying saucer with a die-cut central hole.

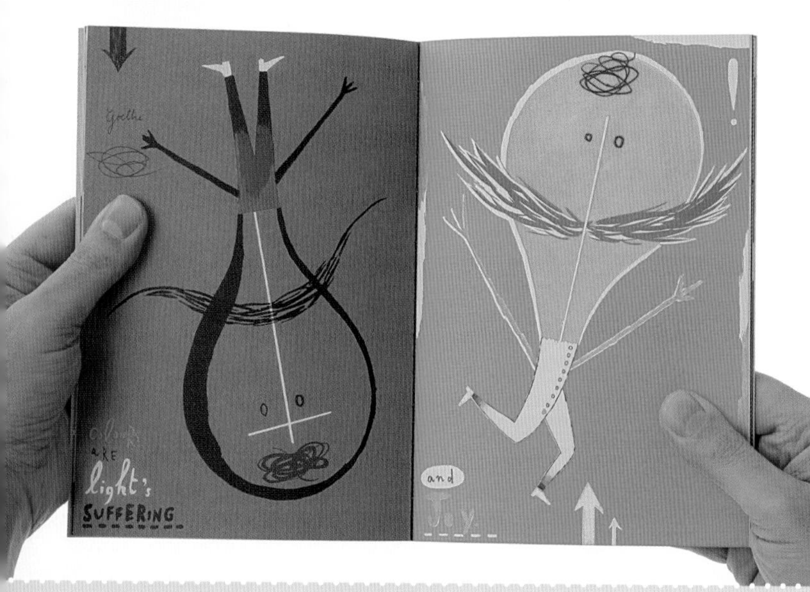

SURFACE EFFECTS +
THE POWER OF TOUCH

Kino Design

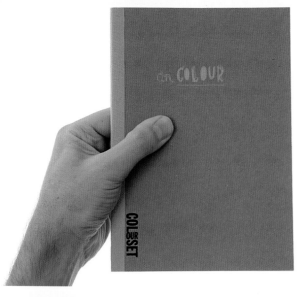

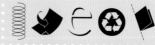

PROJECTS ON COLOUR, ON PRESS
DESIGNER KINO DESIGN
CREATIVE DIRECTOR ANDY STANFIELD
ILLUSTRATOR ON COLOUR: SARA FANELLI; ON PRESS: BRETT RYDER
CLIENT COLOURSET

PAPER FACTS:
STOCK ON COLOUR: FOUR-PAGE COVER: V.I.P. PAPERS SHOEBOX MOCCASIN 325gsm; 24-PAGE INSIDE: GF SMITH MONADNOCK ASTROLITE 176gsm; EIGHT-PAGE INSERT: MCNAUGHTON SKYE COATED EXTRA MATT 100gsm; ON PRESS: FOUR-PAGE COVER: V.I.P. PAPERS SHOEBOX MOCCASIN 325gsm; 28-PAGE INSIDE: MCNAUGHTON SKYE COATED SILK 150gsm; TWO-PAGE TIP-IN: V.I.P. PAPERS CRANE'S OLD MONEY REGULAR
SIZE BOTH: A5 (148 × 210mm; 5¹³⁄₁₆ × 8¼in)
PRINT TECHNIQUES ON COLOUR: FOUR COLOR, TWO SPOT COLORS (PANTONES 805 AND 872); ON PRESS: FOUR COLOR, FOUR SPOT COLORS (PANTONE RHODAMINE RED, 812, 1655, COOL GRAY 8)

ADDITIONAL TECHNIQUES ON COLOUR: GLOSS VARNISH, TWO FOIL-BLOCK COLORS (BLACK AND DAY-GLO ORANGE), REDUCED SIZE (110 × 160mm; $4\frac{11}{32} \times 6\frac{11}{32}$in) EIGHT-PAGE INSERT STITCHED INTO CENTER OF BOOK, OUTER COVER GLUED TO OUTER INSIDE PAGES; ON PRESS: UV GLOSS VARNISH, ONE FOIL-BLOCK COLOR (BLACK)
PRINTER COLOURSET
BINDING BOTH: SINGER-SEWN AND SPINE BOUND WITH TAPE

Printer Colourset approached Kino Design to create mailers that would speak to design agencies and act as inspiration for their own projects. Two booklets were produced: On Colour uses imaginative illustrations by Sara Fanelli to evoke quotes about color by a number of artists and philosophers; On Press depicts the history of print in illustrations by Brett Ryder. The toothy cover material makes the pieces a joy to hold as well as being very hard-wearing. Two tip-ins add further texture and interest: an eight-page insert on Skye Coated Extra Matt and a spoof Swedish banknote on Crane's Old Money, made from recycled US banknotes.

THE GLENLIVET ARCHIVE 21
COMING OF AGE
21 IS AN IMPORTANT YEAR IN SCOTLAND.
CELEBRATED AS THE YEAR ONE COMES OF AGE, 21 IS A RITE OF PASSAGE THAT'S WIDELY SYMBOLISED WITH A KEY TO UNLOCK THE POTENTIAL OF THE FUTURE. A LANDMARK YEAR, TOO, FOR FINE SINGLE MALT, WE ARE VERY PROUD TO INTRODUCE OUR MOST RECENT, AWARD WINNING, ARCHIVE COLLECTION 21 YEAR OLD – A SPIRIT THAT HAS REACHED ITS ELEGANT PRIME.

theFarm

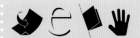

PROJECT THE GLENLIVET ARCHIVE AND CELLAR COLLECTION PRESS KITS
DESIGNER theFARM
CLIENT CHIVAS BROTHERS

PAPER FACTS:
STOCK PACKAGING: COMMISSIONED PAPER WRAPPED AROUND CHUNKY GRAYBOARD 2.5mm
INSERTS: UNCOATED PREMIUM CARD 300gsm
SIZE PACKAGING: 220 × 313mm (8 11/32 × 12 11/32in)
INSERTS: 215 × 302mm (8 1/2 × 11 7/8in)

PRINT TECHNIQUE FOUR-COLOR LITHO
ADDITIONAL TECHNIQUES PACKAGING IS EMBOSSED AND CLEAR-FOILED WITH ADDITIONAL GOLD-FOILED STICKER; INSERT TWO HAS A CD NIPPLE TO HOLD A CD; THE PAPER WAS DYED SPECIALLY FOR THIS PROJECT; PACKAGING BOXES WERE HANDMADE AND HAND-EMBOSSED
PRINTER 68 FRANK

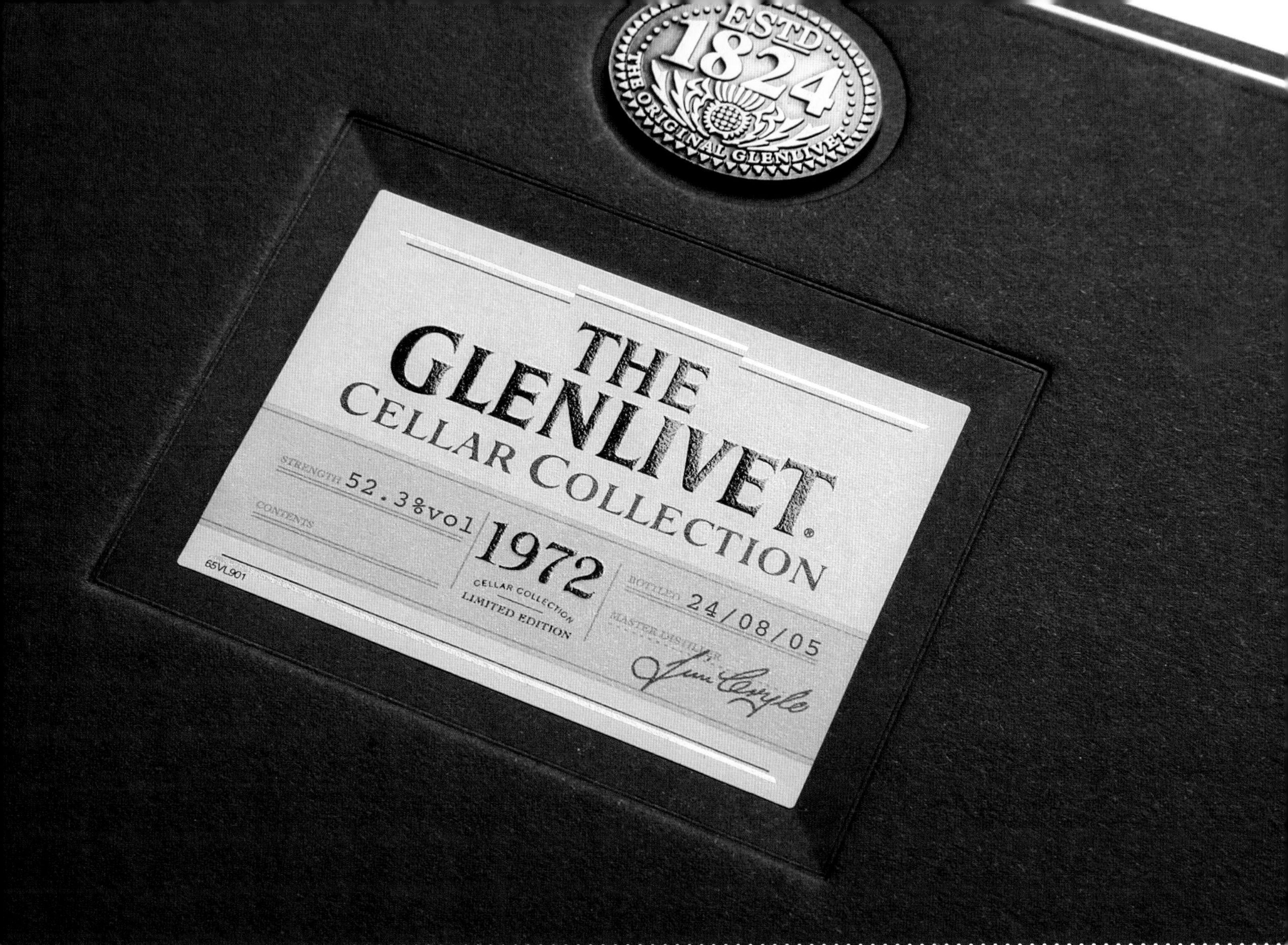

ABOVE: THE GLENLIVET ARCHIVE AND CELLAR COLLECTION PRESS KITS
Photography: Victoria Woolhead © theFarm

When Chivas release their limited-edition Glenlivet Archive and Cellar Collections they like to make a big noise in the press. theFarm were briefed to develop a promotional pack that would communicate The Glenlivet's brand values, its rich heritage, and the unique character of the product itself.

The specially dyed paper is totally unique to Chivas Glenlivet. There was a lengthy testing process of the cardboard and construction method to ensure all elements came together perfectly. The commissioned paper was wrapped around chunky grayboard to achieve the desired sturdiness.

Attention to detail was key to portraying the precious and premium look and feel of the bottles' packaging. The handmade boxes were hand-embossed and clear-foiled. A gold-foiled sticker was adhered to the front within the embossed frame. The inserts were printed on uncoated premium card, then foiled and folded. Insert 2 has a CD nipple to hold a CD containing press information.

CHAPTER 10

3D concepts

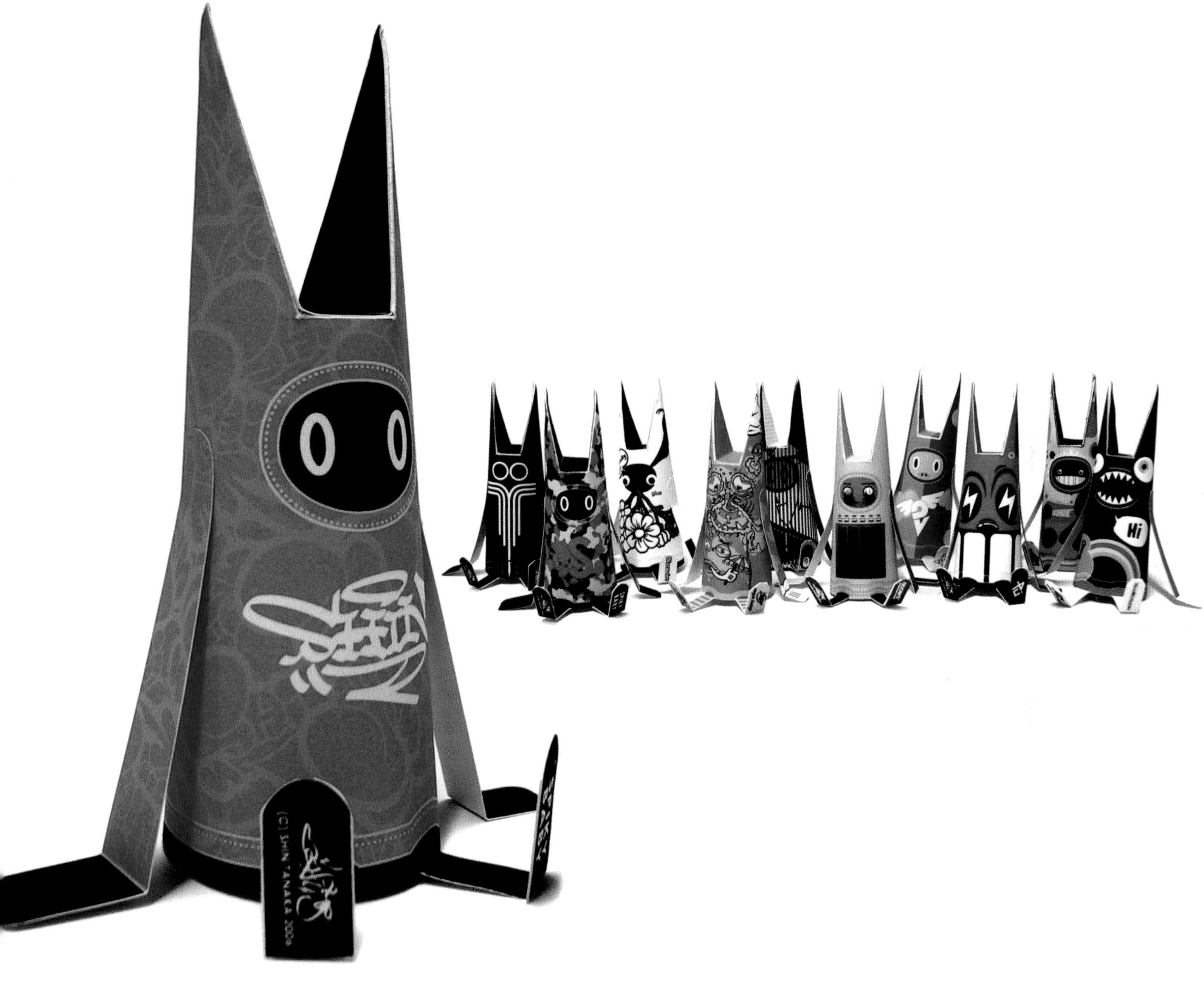
(C) SHIN TANAKA 2006
Hi

lo-tec

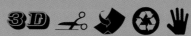

PROJECT LO-TEC SHOWCASE
DESIGNER LO-TEC
CLIENT SELF-INITIATED

PAPER FACTS:
STOCK SINGLE-WALLED CORRUGATED CARDBOARD BOXES
SIZE 450 × 300 × 380mm (18⅞ × 11¹³⁄₁₆ × 14³¹⁄₃₂)
APPROX. 120 BOXES
PRINT TECHNIQUE SCREENPRINT AND STICKERS
ADDITIONAL TECHNIQUES CUT OUTS, FIREPROOFING

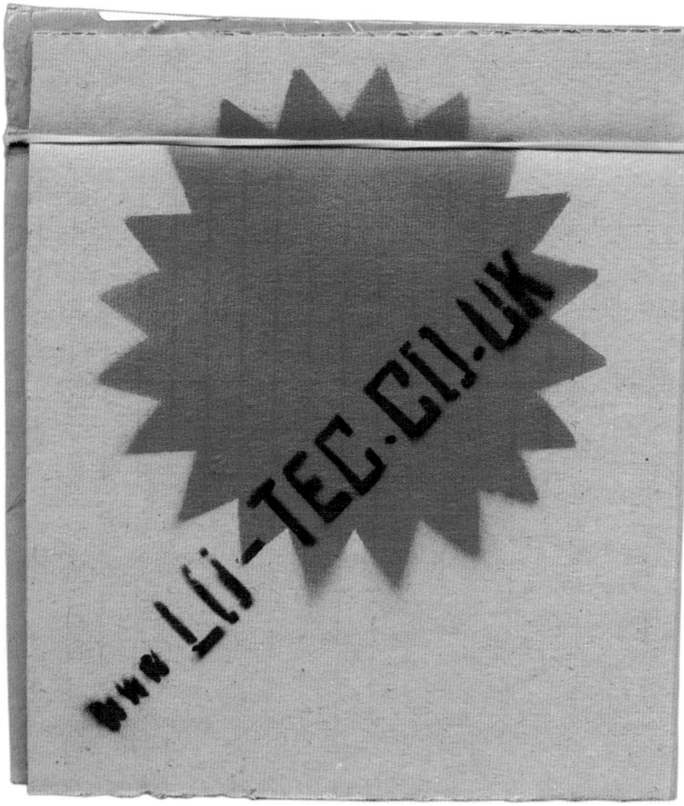

ABOVE: LO-TEC at 100% EAST
Photography: Keith Stephenson

Lo-tec is an up-and-coming design collective. For their first collective showcase their work was selected to be exhibited at 100% East, an event at the London Design Festival that focused on emerging design talent. The esthetic qualities of screened, stenciled, and stickered cardboard boxes perfectly communicated the Lo-tec ethos. The cost-effective display solution offered ease of transportation and set up and created the right tone for the exhibition. The flexible nature of the installation enabled them to make changes to the final design as it was built.

The brick formation turned out to be even stronger than expected, requiring no further support. The fireproofed boxes easily adapted as cut-out frames to house monitors and display work, and even as a mouse mat. As a follow-up piece, a CD was housed in complementary cardboard, secured with a simple elastic band. Both the displayed work and the box installation received a lot of interest from gallery curators and big-name department stores. Meanwhile, the boxes have found a new use: recycled as desks back at Lo-tec HQ.

Think Tank Media

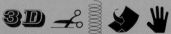

PROJECT MISFITS
DESIGNER AIRSIDE
CLIENT THINK TANK MEDIA

PAPER FACTS:
STOCK COVER: BROWN BRILLIANTA CLOTH ENDPAPERS; PAGES 1–8: STANDARD SILK PAPER 200gsm; PAGES 9–10: STANDARD SILK PAPER 200gsm, CHALLENGER OFFSET 170gsm; PAGES 11–16: CHALLENGER OFFSET 170gsm; PAGES 17–18: CHALLENGER OFFSET 170gsm, GLOSS ART 200gsm; PAGES 19–20, 23–26: GLOSS ART 200gsm

PRINT TECHNIQUES PAGES 1–2, 7–12, 23–26: FOUR-COLOR OFFSET LITHO; PAGES 3–4: SINGLE-COLOR CYAN; PAGES13–14: FOUR-COLOR OFFSET LITHO, DENSE BLACK + SPECIAL COLOR; PAGES 17–18: TWO-COLOR OFFSET LITHO, BLIND SILKSCREEN SPOT GLOSS; PAGES 21–22: FOUR-COLOR OFFSET LITHO, DENSE BLACK

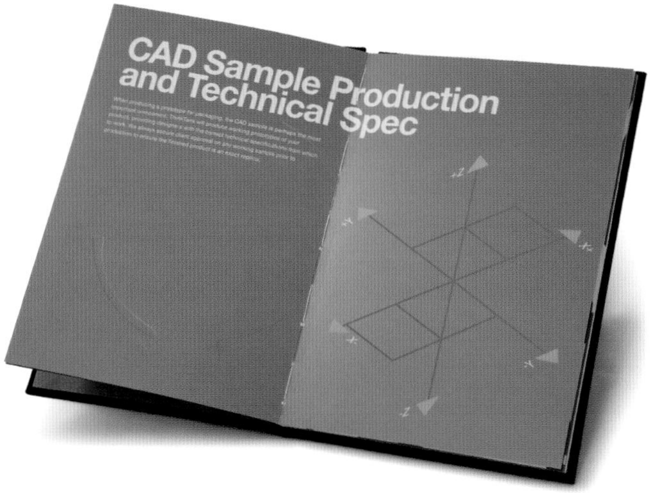

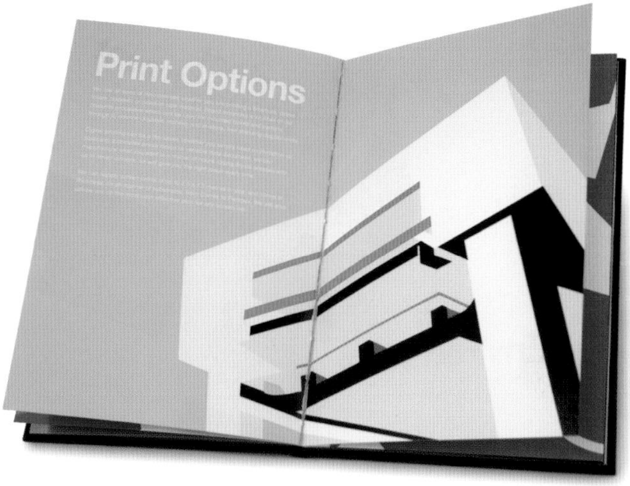

ADDITIONAL TECHNIQUES COVER: HEAT DEBOSSING; ENDPAPERS: METAL FX® TECHNOLOGY, SILK LAMINATION SPECIAL PACKAGING: EMBOSSING; PAGES 5–6: METAL FX® TECHNOLOGY; PAGES 7–8: SPOT GLOSS SILKSCREEN; PAGES 9–10: SHINY BLACK FOILED; PAGES 19–20: METAL FX® TECHNOLOGY, SPOT MATTE UV VARNISH; PAGES 21-22: SPOT MATTE UV VARNISH
PRINTER THINK TANK MEDIA

Not wanting to produce a standard mailer to promote their products and services, diverse media specialists Think Tank Media conceived an idea based on the children's game Misfits, and design agency Airside brought the idea to life. The pack is comprised of two parts: THINK, the game, representing the creative side of the company; and TANK, the book, representing the machinery that makes things happen. Using different printed substrates for the game and an array of different printing techniques for the book, the pack showcases their expertise and the diversity of their services.

Tango

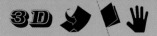

PROJECT NIKE SHOX 2:45
DESIGNER GARETH RUTTER at TANGO
CREATIVE DIRECTOR DANA ROBERTSON
CLIENT NIKE

PAPER FACTS:
STOCK CHALLENGER LASER MATT 170gsm
SIZE A4 (210 × 297mm; 8¼ × 11¾in) FLAT
PRINT TECHNIQUES THREE SOLID SPECIAL COLORS TO OUTER, FOUR-COLOR LITHO TO INTERIOR

ADDITIONAL TECHNIQUES MATTE-LAMINATED OUTER, GLOSS SPOT UV TO BOTH SIDES, FOUR-CREASE FOLDING, HAND-FINISHING
PRINTER BDL MANAGEMENT LTD.

For the launch of the Nike Shox 2:45, creative agency Tango designed a retail kit intended to provoke consumer interest and understanding, highlighting the key product benefit: columns of energy-efficient polyurethane foam that reduce the stress of injury-causing impact and offer extra spring. A shard-inspired graphic concept was developed to emphasize the properties of the sole, in hi-tech shades that reflect the shoe colors.

A4 (210 × 297mm; 8¼ × 11¾in) leaflets folded into aerodynamic shard shapes are housed in a die-cut, matte-laminated display box to create a simple, arresting 3D display. The four-crease sheets have various print finishes, including matte-laminated solid PMS in three vivid colors to the outer and spot UV to both sides. The strength of the piece comes from the vertical configuration. The folded leaflet must be picked out from the display and opened up to be read, ensuring that the consumer fully interacts with the information.

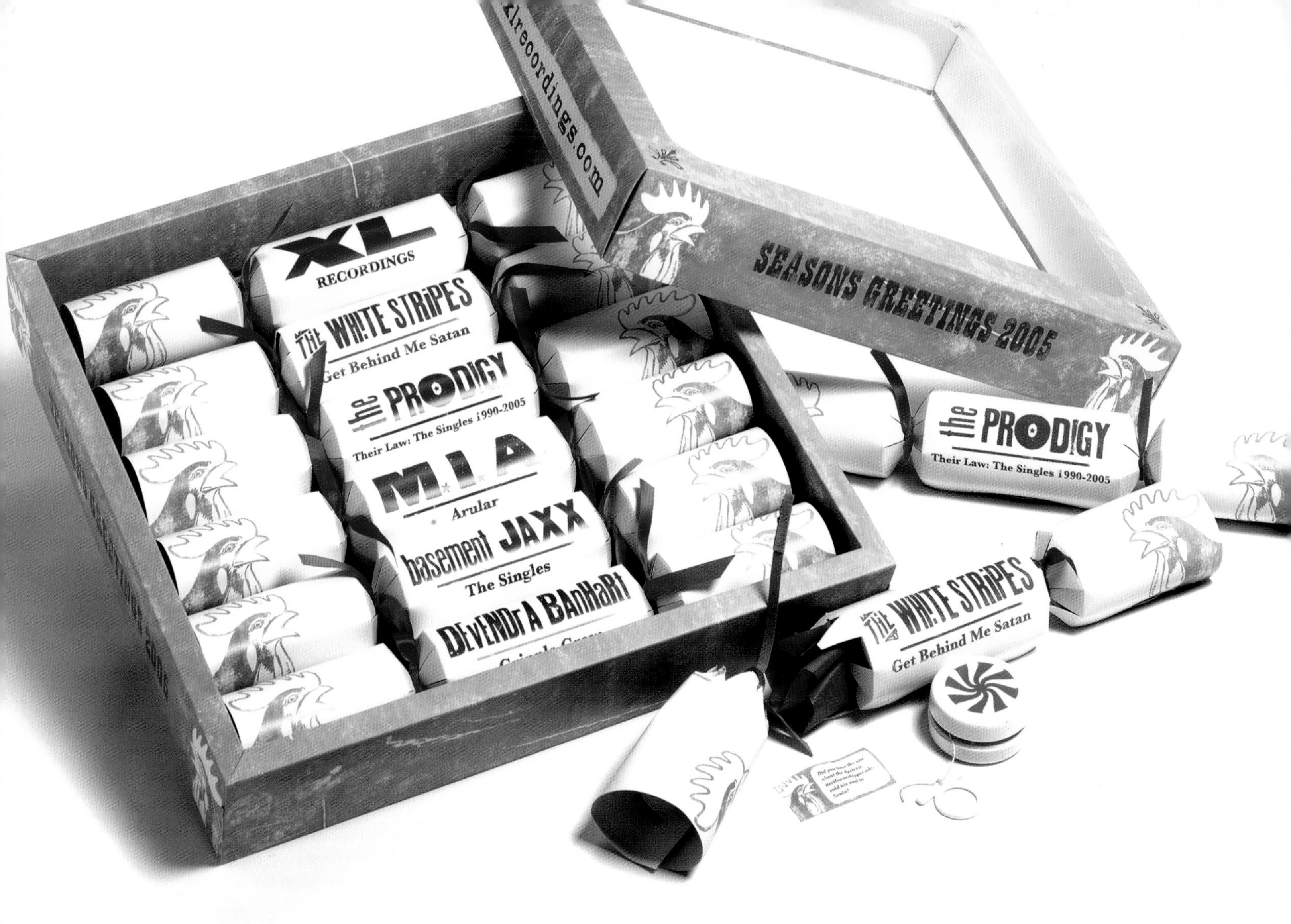

Think Tank Media

PROJECT BRANDED CRACKERS
DESIGNER THINK TANK MEDIA
CLIENT XL RECORDINGS

PAPER FACTS:
STOCK CRACKERS: 300gsm;
BOX: ONE-SIDED BOARD 375gsm
SIZE BOX: 400 × 400 × 65mm (15¾ × 15¾ × 2½in)
PRINT TECHNIQUES BOX: PRINTED REVERSE SIDE OF BOARD TO MAKE USE OF ROUGH TEXTURE
CRACKERS: PRINTED FACE SIDE WITH SILK SEALANT
PRINTER THINK TANK MEDIA

With a top roster of artists, record label XL Recordings wanted a stand-out promotional piece to tie in with the Christmas festivities. Always thinking in three dimensions, Think Tank Media delivered a boxed set of bespoke crackers, each one hand-filled with goodies to reflect the band it represents. The silk-sealed crackers tied with ribbon are seen through an acetate window glued to the lid. The bespoke box was printed on the rough reverse side for an added textural quality, while a cavity double-thickness base offered added strength.

Lucy Jane Batchelor

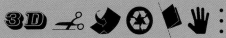

PROJECT SPECIAL OCCASION INVITATION
DESIGNER LUCY JANE BATCHELOR
CLIENT SELF-INITIATED

PAPER FACTS:
STOCK CURTIS FINE PAPERS ECO RANGE METAPHOR CREAM (100% RECYCLED: 51% POSTCONSUMER WASTE, 49% PRECONSUMER WASTE) 310gsm
SIZE 500 × 111mm (19¹¹⁄₁₆ × 4³⁄₈in) UNFOLDED
PRINT TECHNIQUE OFFSET LITHO WITH SOYA-OIL INKS
PRINTER ABBA LITHO (SALES) LTD.

ADDITIONAL TECHNIQUES HAND-FINISHED WITH PINK-GLITTERED BLOSSOM/BERRIES, CREASED, PERFORATED, AND DIE-CUT

SPECIAL CONSIDERATIONS:
"The stock is 100% recycled with a tactile finish and a distinctive flecked surface—the most expensive stock I ever use. Soya oil inks print the same as usual inks; the muted color is due to the soft paper finish."

Lucy Jane Batchelor, UK

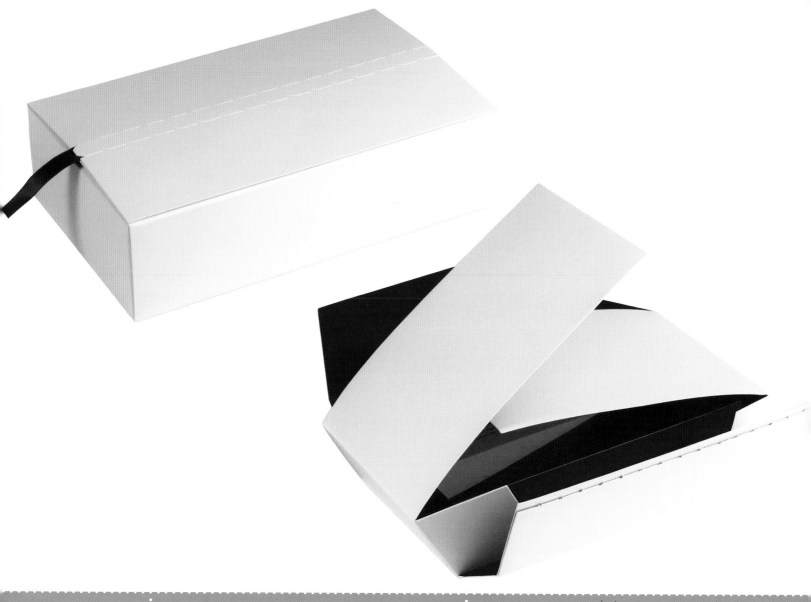

Egelnick and Webb

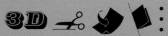

PROJECT EUPHORIA FRAGRANCE LAUNCH
DESIGNER EGELNICK AND WEBB
CLIENT CALVIN KLEIN

PAPER FACTS:
STOCK CELLOGLAS MIRRI WRAPPER BOARD 350gsm
SIZE 180 × 110 × 50mm ($7\frac{3}{32} \times 4\frac{11}{32} \times 1\frac{31}{32}$in)
PRINT TECHNIQUES SILKSCREENED CELLOGLAS MIRRI, DIGITAL-PRINT ORCHID, SINGLE-COLOR SPECIAL

ADDITIONAL TECHNIQUES PERFORATED STRIP AND RIBBON PULL
PRINTER BEP SILKSCREEN, G&B PRINTERS

For the launch of Calvin Klein's new fragrance Euphoria, Egelnick and Webb were asked to develop a series of exclusive invitations. The bottle design was based on an opening orchid, so the designers developed a graphic style that combined orchid imagery with a feeling of "euphoric" sensuality. The objective was to ensure A-list celebrities and influential fashion editors turned up. A tiered system of invitations was decided upon: a simple retail one of clear-foiled Colorplan; the main invitation of silver foil on silver mirri foil card; and an exclusive 3D invitation, of which only ten were made.

The latter arrived as an intriguing white box that opened with a ribbon-pull, perforated strip to present a rich solid-cassis inner, containing an iconic glasslike block. Viewing it from different angles revealed the event information, screenprinted in cassis text on silver mirri foil, and glued to the base. A digital print of the orchid abstract was glued to the rear face, and the logo was silk screened to the front face. The event attracted the biggest turnout to date to any Calvin Klein launch, according to the brand PR manager.

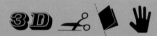

Shin Tanaka

PROJECTS T-BOY, HOODY, SPIKY BABY
ARTIST SHIN TANAKA
CLIENT SELF-INITIATED

PAPER FACTS:
PRINT TECHNIQUE INK-JET
ADDITIONAL TECHNIQUES HAND-CUTTING, HAND-FOLDING

SPECIAL CONSIDERATIONS:
Shin has created a new design and colorway of Mask Hoody exclusively for this book. Reproduced here at around 50%, it's ready to scan, size up, print out, and make.

Acclaimed Japanese artist Shin Tanaka first attracted international attention with his range of miniature paper sneakers. His blend of street art and fashion culture has manifested itself more recently in a fusion of paper toys and art. "Many artists have designed vinyl toys, but only famous artists get invited for such projects," explains Shin. "Other artists have been looking for a canvas to express their artworks, so I made a paper toy for them. Paper is much easier to customize than a vinyl toy."

The toys are designed to be made using a regular ink-jet printer and paper—though Shin admits his recent acquisition of a high-performance printer "makes my toy more brilliant." Over 150 designers and artists have downloaded and built the little street-styled alien characters—including T-Boy, Hoody, and Spiky Baby—and the community is growing by word of mouth.

Legalizer

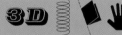

PROJECT GOPINGPONG CATALOG
DESIGNERS LEO SCHERFIG, LAURA JOHANNE, GRUE DANIELSSEN at LEGALIZER
CLIENT GOPINGPONG

PAPER FACTS:
STOCK PAPYRUS MULTI OFFSET 130gsm
SIZE COVER: 400 × 210mm ($15^3/_4$ × $8^1/_4$in);
FULL SPREAD: 420 × 200mm ($16^1/_2$ × $7^7/_8$in)

PRINT TECHNIQUE FOUR-COLOR OFFSET LITHO
ADDITIONAL TECHNIQUE HAND-FOLDING
BINDING COVER: DOUBLE-FOLDED; SPREADS: PART FOLDOUT BINDING
PRINTER VIBENHUS BOGTRYK

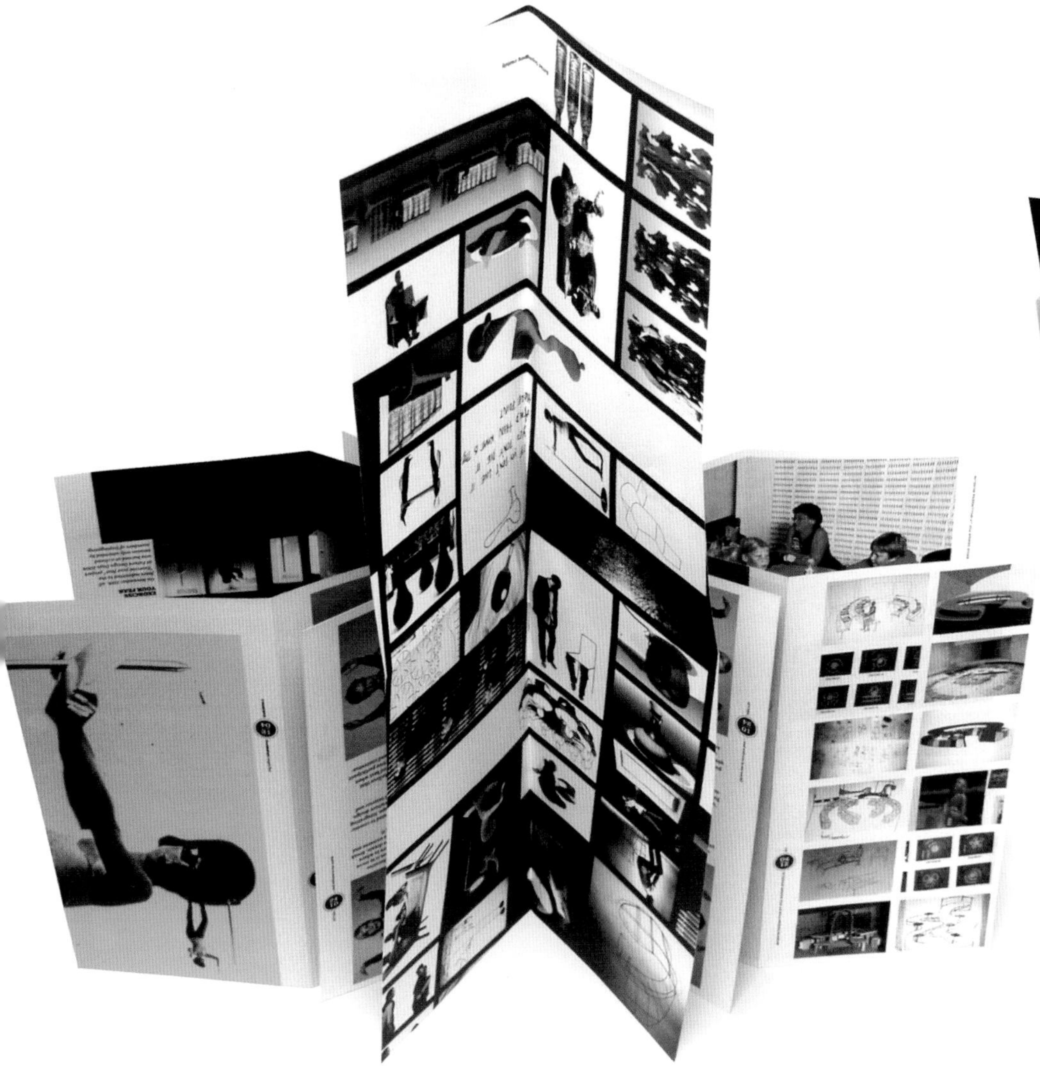

Perhaps Denmark's most experimental furniture-design group, Gopingpong required a brochure to present their work with wit and intelligence. Danish design consultants Legalizer felt that, as everything Gopingpong do is surprising, any brochure presenting their work should be no less surprising. They had the idea of the reading-flow starting in many different places, with no defined beginning or end to the information.

As well as the onscreen design process, the development of the brochure required much paper folding to test the flow. The final brochure employs hand-finishing techniques and uses foldout binding, with the cover double-folded. The brochure is, therefore, as experimental as the furniture and products it presents. The printed material opens out into different planes to create many 3D configurations, and recipients consider the brochure part of the Gopingpong back catalog an integral part of their work.

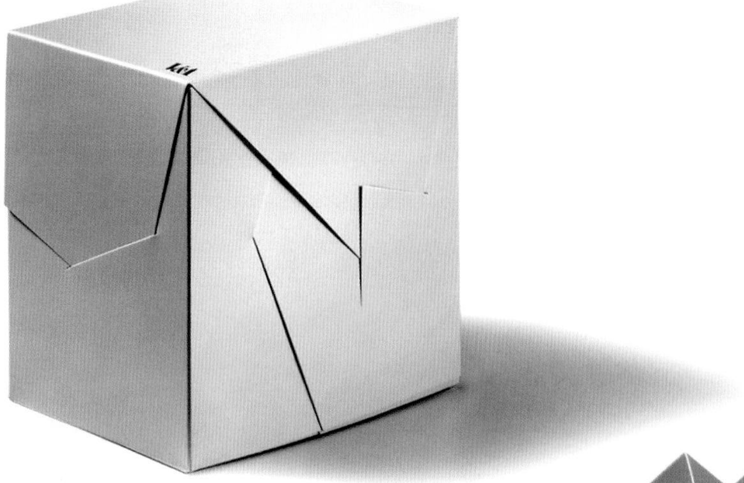

johnson banks

PROJECT THE SPIRAL
DESIGNER JOHNSON BANKS
CLIENT VICTORIA AND ALBERT MUSEUM

PAPER FACTS:
STOCK MATTE-COATED ART 400gsm
PRINT TECHNIQUE FOUR-COLOR OFFSET LITHO
ADDITIONAL TECHNIQUES DIE-CUTTING, HAND-FOLDING
PRINTER FERNEDGE

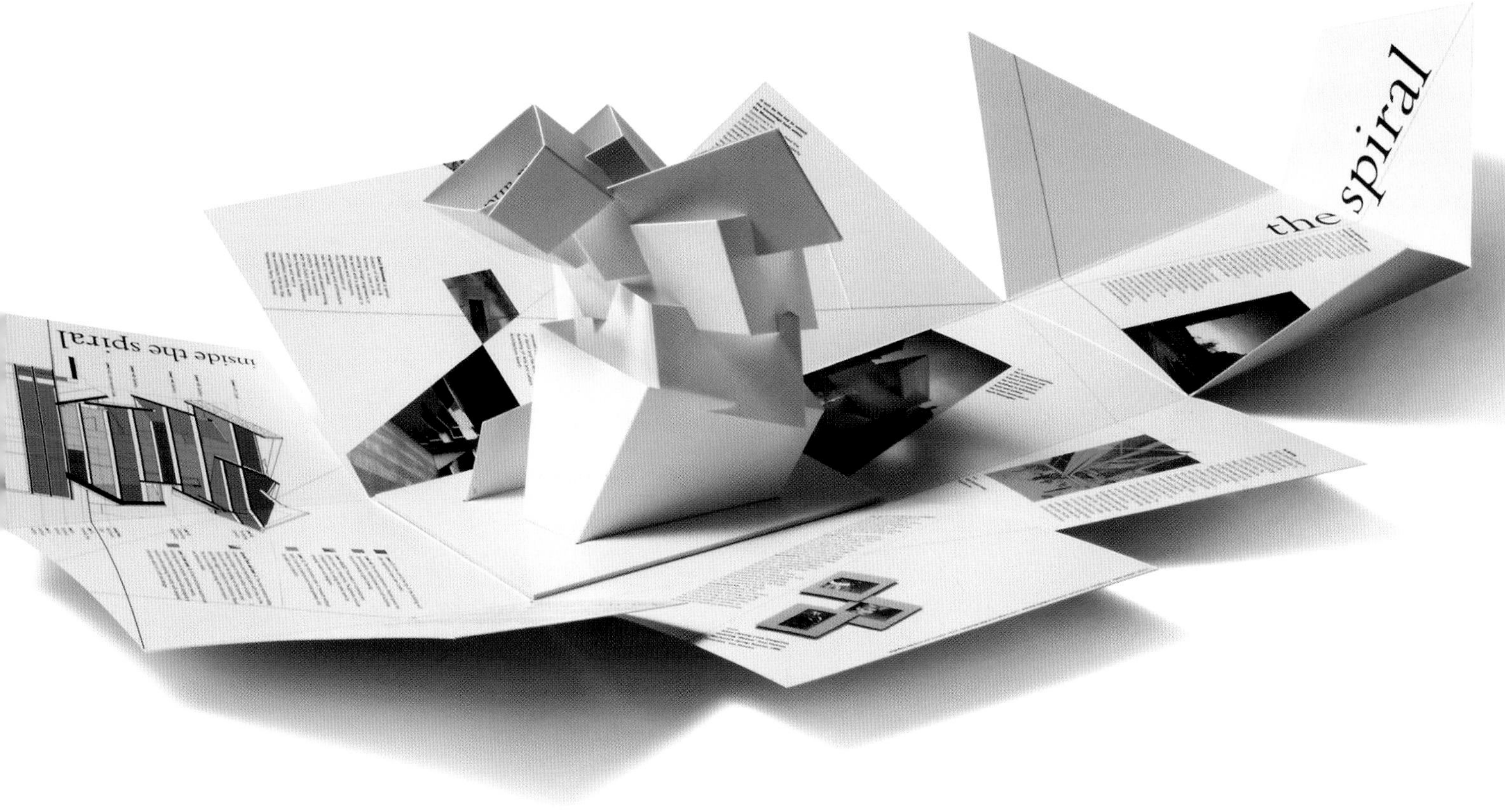

Michael Johnson of design agency johnson banks recalls the challenge of designing a brochure for The Spiral, architect Daniel Liebeskind's proposed extension to London's Victoria and Albert Museum. "We were struggling. Then we stopped designing brochures and produced a three-dimensional collapsing box enclosing a paper sculpture instead."

This is one of those great design epiphany stories, and it demonstrates perfectly the potential of paper in the right hands.

Targeted donors and opinion formers were sent what appeared to be a plain white box. When prised open, the box fell away to reveal a brochure printed on the inside and a model of the architect's 24-plane spiral proposal for the extension. The whole project relied on both the die-cut box and model being meticulously hand-assembled.

B&W Studio

PROJECT SWEENEY TODD
DESIGNERS LEE BRADLEY, STEVE WILLS at B&W STUDIO
PHOTOGRAPHER MIKE FEATHER
CLIENT LEEDS YOUTH OPERA

PAPER FACTS:
STOCK ESSENTIAL SILK PREMIER PAPER 200gsm
SIZE A3 (297 × 420mm; 11¾ × 16½in)
PRINT TECHNIQUE FOUR-COLOR OFFSET LITHO, SPECIAL RED ON BOTH SIDES
PRINTER HARROGATE PRINT LTD.

Leeds Youth Opera has a reputation for staging rare works and experimental productions. Briefed to design a promotional poster for their production of Stephen Sondheim's *Sweeney Todd*, B&W Studio wanted to create something multifunctional—a promotion and a free gift. In the end, they designed something multidimensional too. Inspired by the occupation of the musical's central character, the reversible poster could be rolled up to create a traditional red-and-white barber's pole.

The choice of paper was essential to the piece. The designers wanted a clean, crisp white for maximum contrast with the red-printed stripes and gruesome photography. Texturally, the glossy stock helped the piece resemble the plastic finish of the barber's pole. Six hundred posters were hand-rolled, secured with a gloss circular sticker, and given to each person who attended the opening night. For their efforts, B&W Studio won a Roses Design Award.

Tin Tab
A unique design and manufacturing company with a highly considered approach to detail and an in-depth understanding of materials.
Disciplines include:
Staircases
Furniture
Kitchens
Buildings
Multi-Ply specialist materials

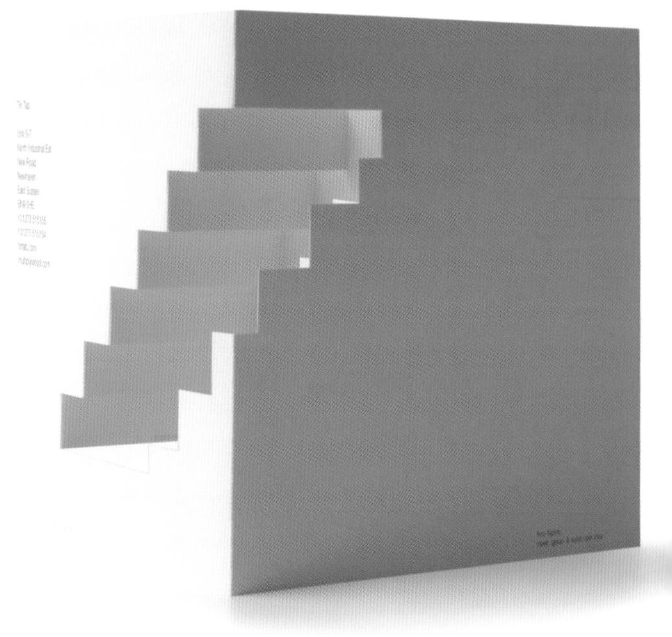

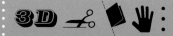

Aloof Design

PROJECT STAIRCASE MAILER
DESIGNER LEIGH SIMPSON at ALOOF DESIGN
CLIENT TIN TAB

PAPER FACTS:
STOCK ZEN 300gsm
SIZE 165 × 165mm (6½ × 6½in) FOLDED
PRINT TECHNIQUE FOUR-COLOR OFFSET LITHO
ADDITIONAL TECHNIQUES HAND-FOLDING, DIE-CUTTING, CREASING, PERFORATION
PRINTER LONGRIDGE PRINT

SPECIAL CONSIDERATIONS:
"We wanted to use an uncoated board, but our client was insistent that the final design included images as well as the pop-up feature. In print, to ensure we retained the image definition, an uncoated 'surface-enhanced' board was specified offering tactility, image quality, and structural integrity."

Michelle Kostyrka, Aloof Design, UK

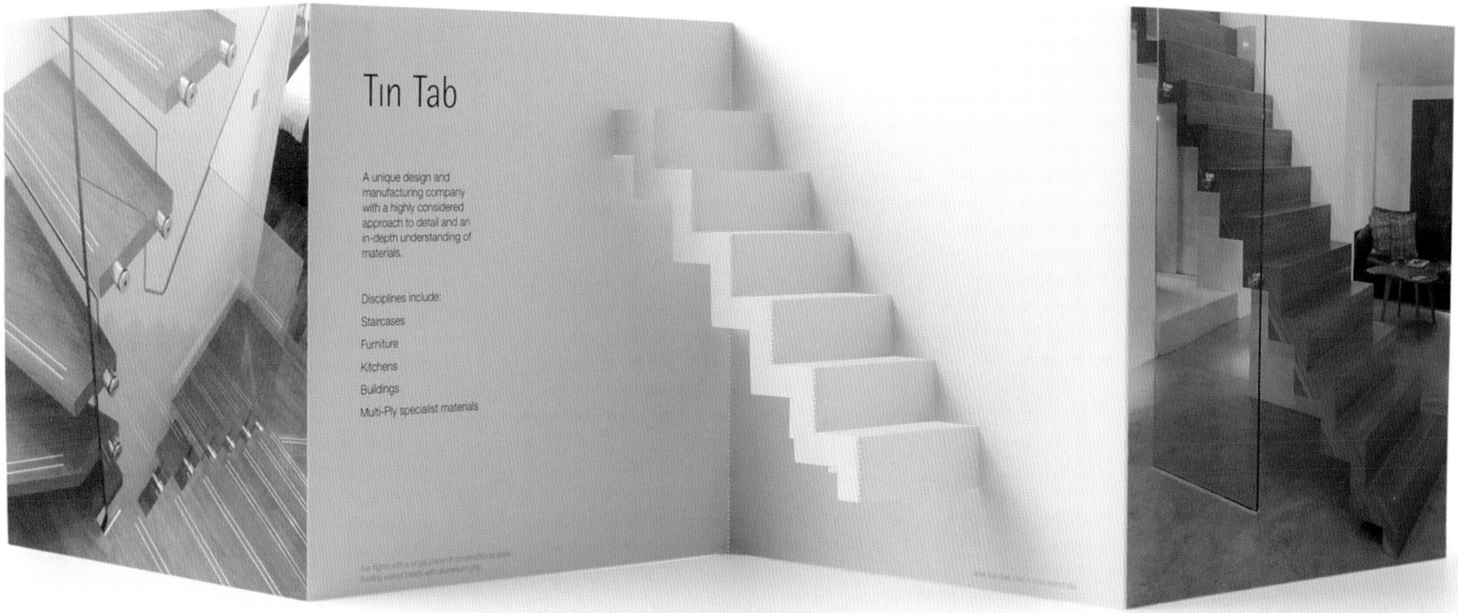

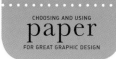

Tin Tab design and manufacture contemporary furniture and public and commercial interiors, including the design and production of complex, bespoke staircases. Aloof Design were approached to create a brochure that could be distributed at a trade fair and be used as a future mailout to promote Tin Tab's expertise. Within an eight-page format, they engineered a paper pop-up staircase that becomes 3D as the brochure opens. There are no glue tabs or extra fastenings to achieve this; the staircase is simply die-cut and perforated from the flat sheet.

Handmade mock-ups were created in the studio with artworking taking place on the computer only once the team were happy that the pop-up mechanism would work in practice. Each card was litho-printed flat and then die-cut, creased, and perforated in one hit before being expertly folded by hand. Over a year on, Tin Tab continue to use the staircase mailer, and the design plays a significant part in helping them secure new business with architects and private clients.

Aloof Design

PROJECT EUREKA 2005 INVITATION
DESIGNER LEIGH SIMPSON at ALOOF DESIGN
CLIENTS DESIGN NATION, LAURENT PERRIER

PAPER FACTS:
STOCK SPLENDORLUX BIANCO 250gsm
SIZE 105 × 105mm (4⅛ × 4⅛in) FOLDED
PRINT TECHNIQUE SINGLE-COLOR OFFSET LITHO
ADDITIONAL TECHNIQUES HAND-FOLDING, CREASING, PERFORATION, DIE-CUTTING
PRINTER BENWELL SEBARD

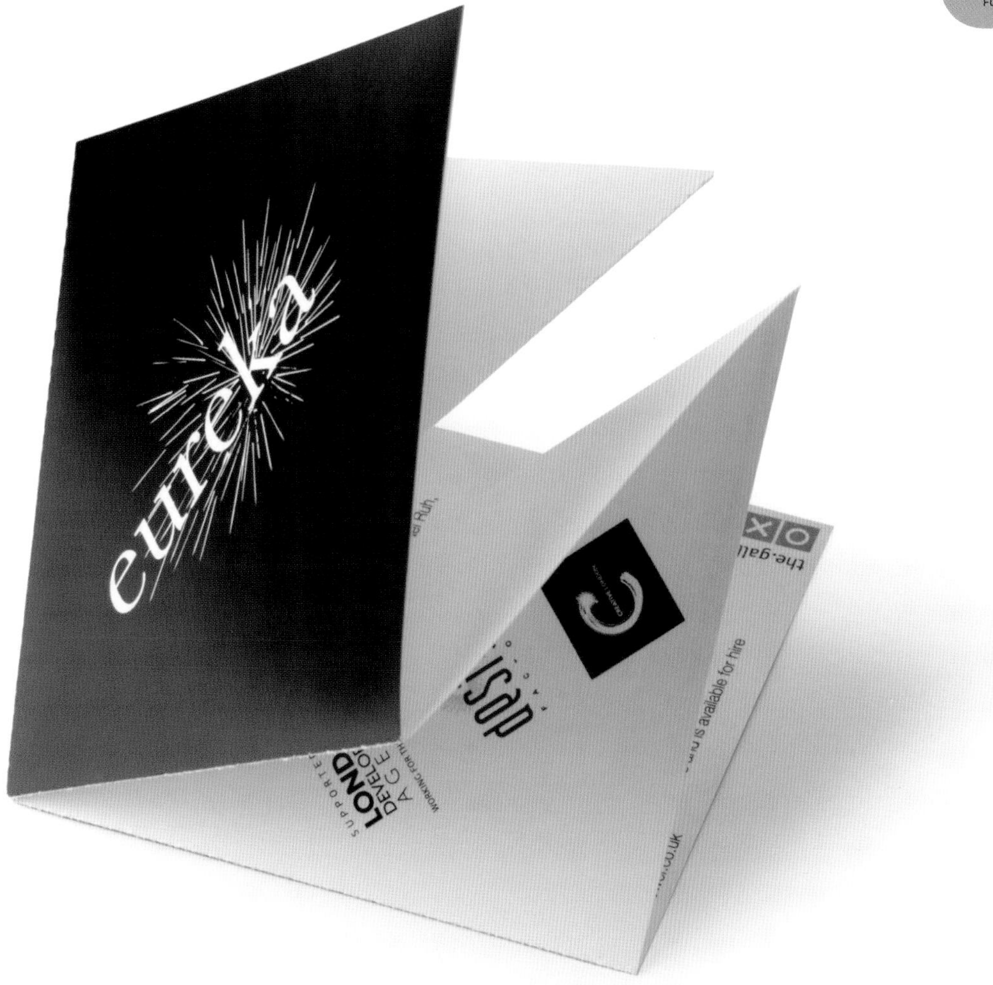

Eureka is a British initiative bringing new design to the consumer. Aloof Design were commissioned to develop a relatively low-cost invitation and brochure for the Eureka show. In keeping with the energy and anticipation that exemplifies the Eureka project, Aloof designed an eight-page invitation with a unique folding mechanism that would be memorable as well as functional. The inventive format, sensitive use of type, and specification of quality materials contributed to the success of the piece.

Budget constraints dictated they could print in only one color so, to add to the contrast between front and back, the team wanted a two-sided board with a different finish on each side that would be able to hold the ink on the solid areas. Fedrigoni's Splendorlux Bianco was specified, as this one-sided high-gloss material offered the best contrast between two surfaces. The cast-coated side of the board forms the front and back cover, displaying the brand marks for Eureka, Laurent Perrier, and other sponsoring organizations.

CHAPTER 11

materials, techniques + suppliers

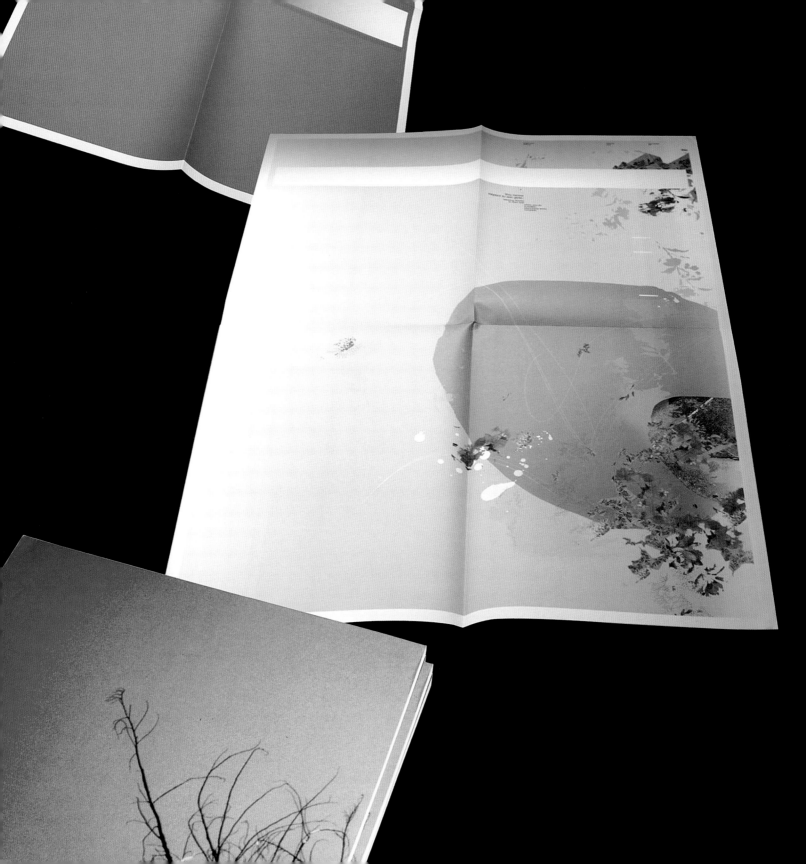

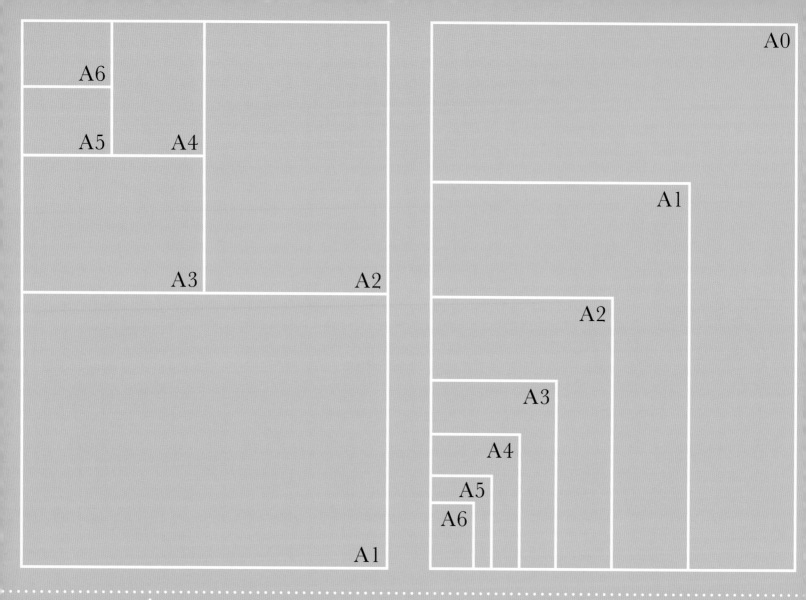

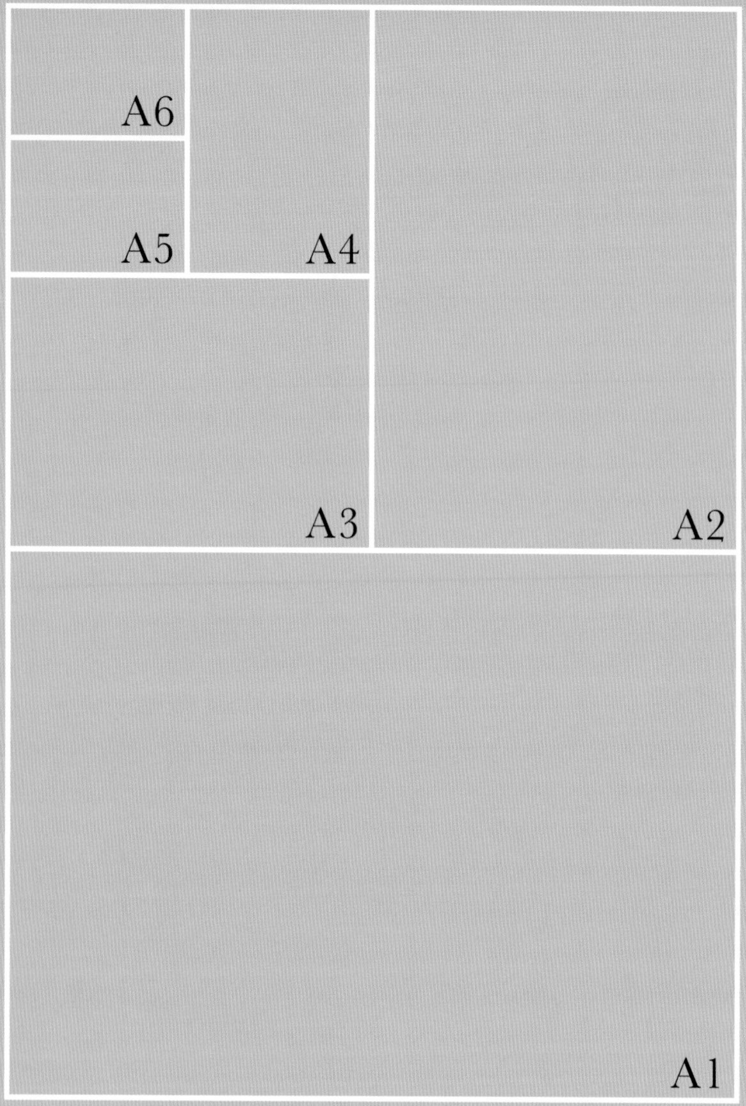

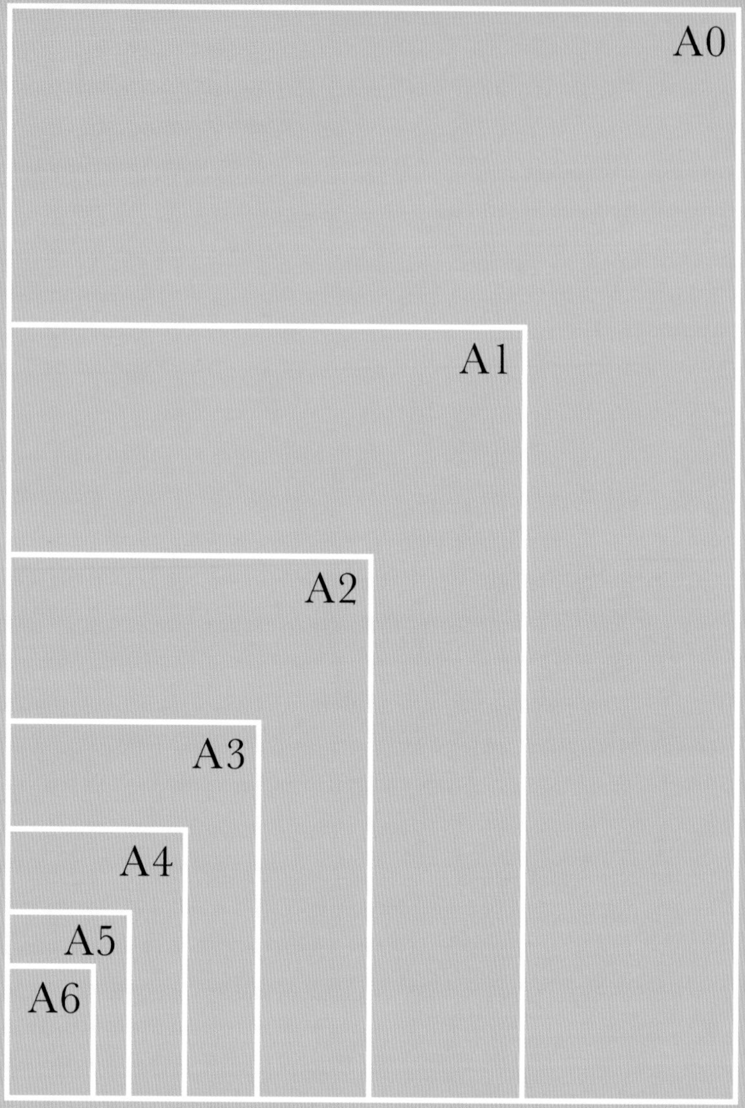

iso paper sizes

A series

The International Standards Organization (ISO) system of paper sizes is based on the metric system, with the base format being a sheet of paper measuring 1m² in area. It applies to all grades of paper and board manufactured and sold outside of North America, and has five series of sizes: A, B, C, RA, and SRA.

	A	B	C	RA	SRA
Sheet Size 0	841 × 1,189mm	1,000 × 1,414mm	917 × 1,296mm	860 × 1,220mm	900 × 1,280mm
Sheet Size 1	594 × 841mm	707 × 1,000mm	648 × 917mm	610 × 860mm	640 × 900mm
Sheet Size 2	420 × 594mm	500 × 707mm	458 × 648mm	430 × 610mm	450 × 640mm
Sheet Size 3	297 × 420mm	353 × 500mm	324 × 458mm	305 × 430mm	320 × 450mm
Sheet Size 4	210 × 297mm	250 × 353mm	229 × 324mm	215 × 305mm	225 × 320mm
Sheet Size 5	148 × 210mm	176 × 250mm	162 × 229mm	152 × 215mm	160 × 225mm
Sheet Size 6	105 × 148mm	125 × 176mm	114 × 162mm	107 × 152mm	112 × 160mm
Sheet Size 7	74 × 105mm	88 × 125mm	81 × 114mm	76 × 107mm	80 × 112mm
Sheet Size 8	52 × 74mm	62 × 88mm	57 × 81mm	53 × 76mm	56 × 80mm

ISO PAPER SIZE CHART

The A series is the most recognized, and includes A4 (highlighted on the chart), the standard European letterhead size.

The RA and SRA series specify the sizes of untrimmed paper used by printers. They are slightly larger than the A series to allow for grip, trim, and bleed.

The C series is mainly used for folders, postcards, and envelopes. A C4 envelope is ideal for holding a nonfolded A4 sheet.

The B series, though rarely used, provides intermediate sizes for the A series.

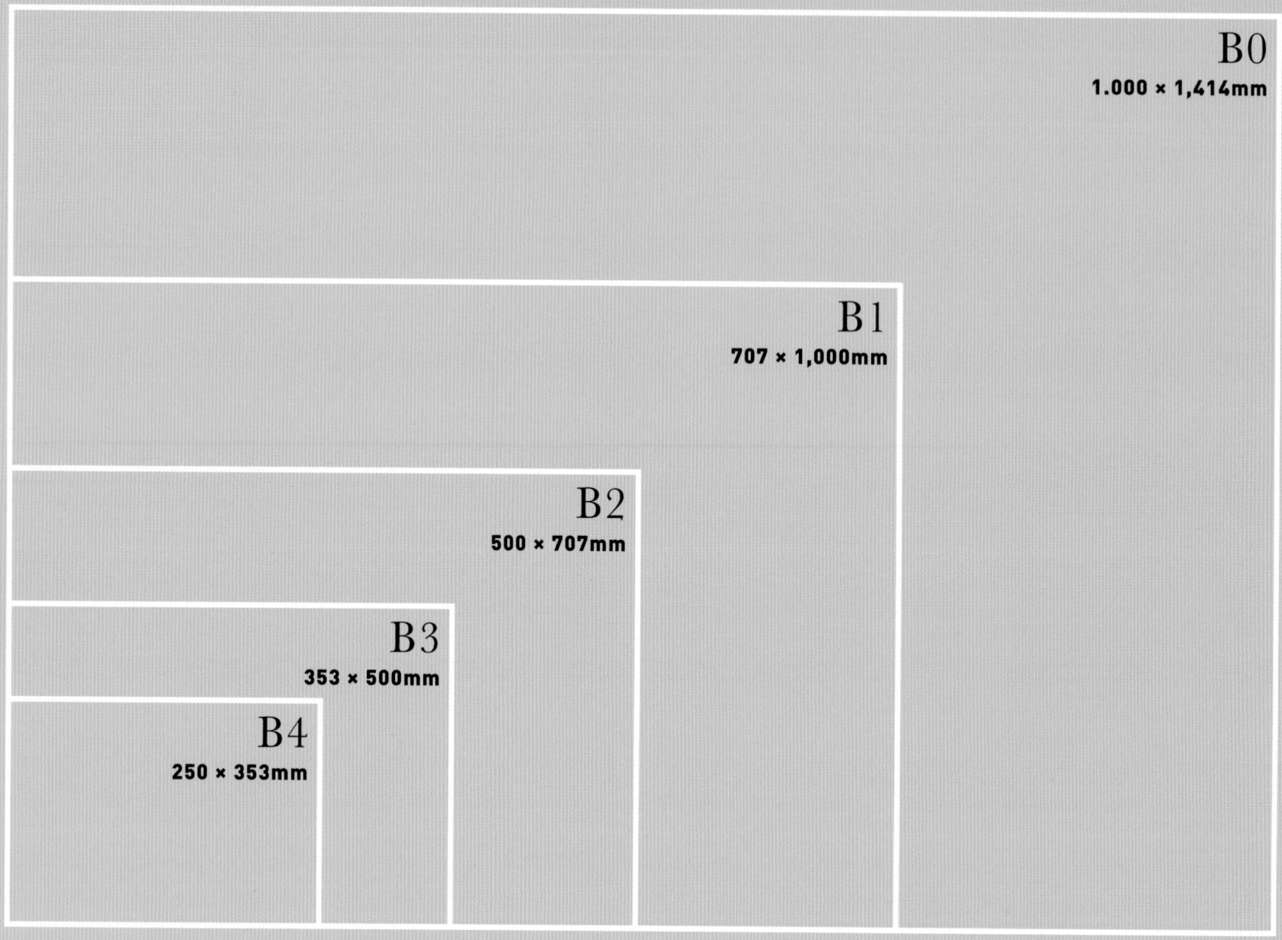
B0
1.000 × 1,414mm
B1
707 × 1,000mm
B2
500 × 707mm
B3
353 × 500mm
B4
250 × 353mm

B series

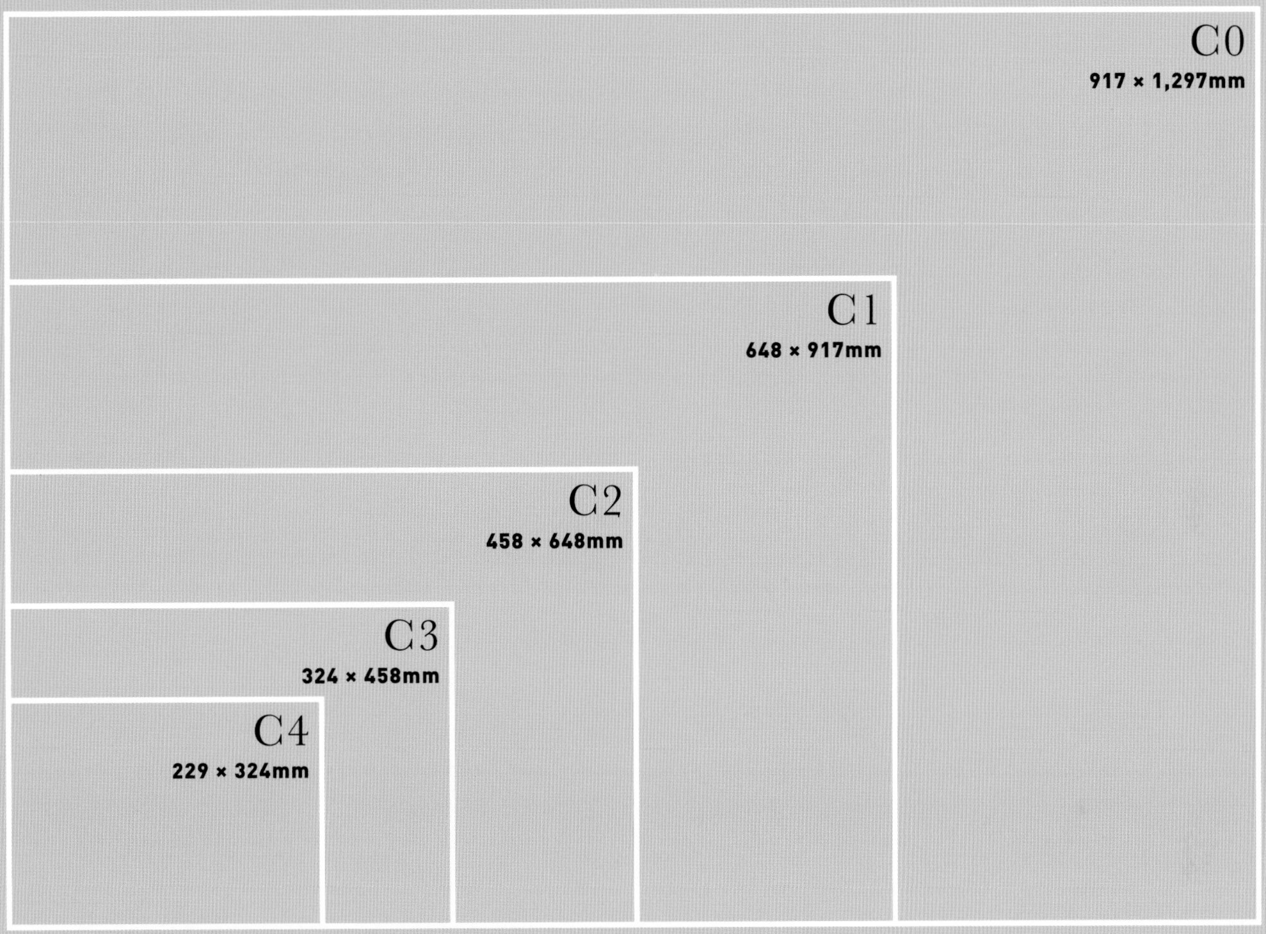
C0
917 × 1,297mm
C1
648 × 917mm
C2
458 × 648mm
C3
324 × 458mm
C4
229 × 324mm

C series

MATERIALS, TECHNIQUES + SUPPLIERS

north-american sheet size

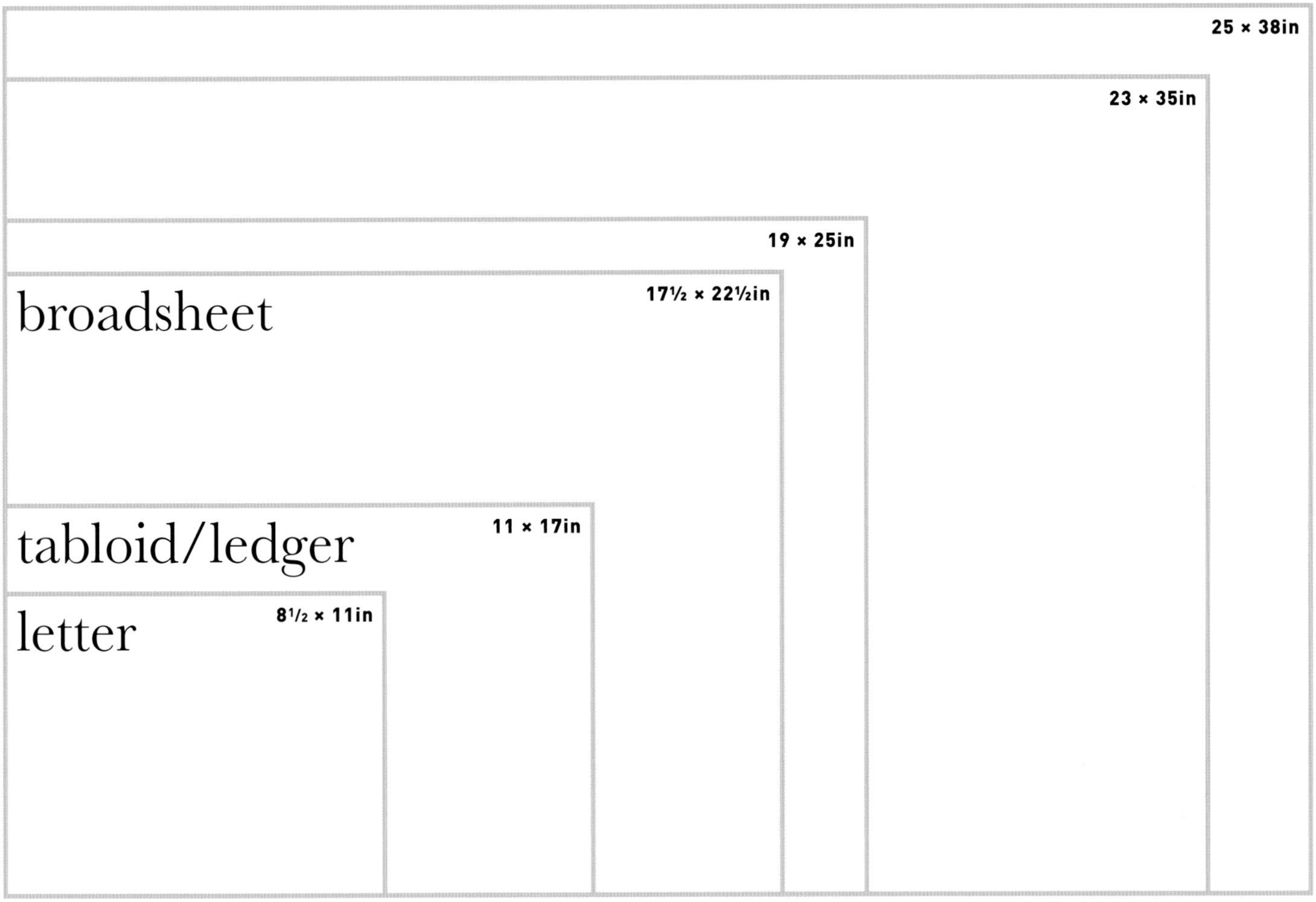

North-American sheet sizes are based on multiples of 8½ × 11in. Some sheet sizes, such as 11 × 17in, are exact multiples of this standard, whereas others, though based on this standard, are slightly oversized to accommodate bleed margins and grip while on press.

A

A Series
International ISO paper size referring to papers used for general printing matter.

ABCD scheme
A UK initiative that classifies type and amount of recycled fiber in paper.

Abrasion resistance
The level at which paper can withstand continuous scuffing or rubbing.

Acid-free paper
Paper produced to have a neutral pH reading, making it more durable and less prone to yellowing.

Against the grain
At right angles to the paper's fiber direction. It's best to fold with, not against, the grain.

Air dried
Paper-drying process using hot air circulating around it to give the paper a hard cockle finish.

Aluminum plate
A metal press plate used to carry the image for moderate-to-long runs in offset lithography.

Antique finish
Paper with a rough finish, but a good print surface, used mainly in book printing.

Apron
Extra space at the binding edge of a foldout, which allows folding and tipping without interfering with the copy.

Aqueous coating
A water-based coating applied on the printing press to protect the print on paper.

Archival paper
A paper with longevity (approx. 100 years). Has good color retention and is acid- and lignin-free.

Art paper
Highly calendered papers with a chalk or china-clay coating.

B

B Series
International ISO paper size referring to large papers used for posters and wall charts.

Backbone
Also called a spine, the back of a bound book along which the sheets are fastened.

Backing up
Printing the reverse side of a sheet already printed on one side.

Band
A strip of paper that wraps around loose sheets or assembled pieces as an alternative to binding with a cover.

Bank
Lightweight, wood-free paper used for correspondence and copy typing—sometimes tinted.

Base paper
Unprocessed and precoated paper.

Basis weight (North America)
The weight in pounds per ream of paper cut to its basic size in inches.

Bible paper
An opaque printing paper, used for bibles and dictionaries, with maximum weight of 50gsm.

Binding
Attaching sheets together by adhesives, sewing, stitching, metal prongs, snaps, etc. See pages 54–59.

Blanket
The rubber-coated fabric clamped around the blanket cylinder, which transfers the image from plate to paper in offset lithography.

Bleed
A printed image that runs off the edges of a page. The migration of ink into unwanted areas.

Blind embossing
A bas-relief design that is pushed forward without foil or ink.

Blistering
Problem caused by overheating when drying the ink on a heavy coated stock.

Blotting paper
Highly absorbent paper used to soak up excess ink.

Blueprint
A type of photoprint used as a proof. It can be folded to show how the finished printed product will look.

Board
Heavy paper over 220gsm.

Bond paper
A grade of writing or printing paper generally manufactured for letterheads or forms.

Glossary

Book paper
Papers most suitable for book manufacture.

Brightness
The reflections of paper when measured under a specially calibrated blue light.

Bristol
Paper 6pt. or thicker with basis weight between 90lb and 200lb. Used for products such as index cards, file folders, and displays.

Bulk
Paper thickness. Sometimes used as the number of pages per inch (ppi).

Bulking dummy
Unprinted sheets of actual paper folded in the signature size and number of a given job to determine bulk.

Butted joint
Joining two webs of paper, placing them end-to-end and pasting a strip over and under to make a continuous sheet without overlapping.

C

C Series
International ISO paper size referring specifically to envelopes.

Calendered
Paper that has been smoothed and polished between sets of rollers called a calender, usually done at the dry end of a papermaking machine.

Caliper
Thickness of paper measured in microns (1000 microns = 1mm).

Carbon paper
A lightweight-grade paper used to make copies, coated on one side with a mixture of carbon black and a chemical carrier substance.

Carbonless paper
Paper coated on one or two sides with an emulsion of colorless dyes and oils to chemically transfer images from one sheet to another without carbon paper.

Casebound
A book bound with a hard cover.

Cast coated
Paper coated and dried against a polished cylinder for a high-gloss finish.

Chain lines
The lines on laid paper parallel with the grain.

Chalking
When the ink vehicle has been absorbed too rapidly into the paper leaving a weak and dusty pigment layer.

Chemical ghosting
A light duplication of a printed image on the other side of the same sheet.

Chemical pulp
Pulp made by cooking the wood in the presence of chemical agents, which eliminates most of the nonfibrous material.

Chiyogami
A type of Japanese paper decorated with brightly colored, woodblock-printed patterns, first produced in the late 18th century.

Coated paper
Paper or board with a coating of minerals held together by a binder, applied to one or both sides to produce a smooth, ink-receptive finish that will enhance the sharpness and gloss of the printed image.

Cold pressed
A paper surface with slight texture produced by pressing the finished sheet between cold cylinders.

Cold-set inks
Inks that are in solid form originally, but are melted in a hot press and then solidified when they contact paper.

Color-process printing
Printing process using cyan, magenta, yellow, and black inks, each requiring its own negative and plate. Also called process color or four-color process.

Comb binding
A type of binding where the teeth of a flexible comb are inserted through holes punched along the side of a document.

Concertina fold
A method of folding a sheet of paper, first to the right and then to the left, so that the sheet opens and closes in the manner of a concertina.

Conditioning
Allowing paper to adjust itself to the temperature and humidity of the printing plant prior to use.

Cotton-content paper
Papers utilizing cotton fabrics and cotton linters, usually for letterhead applications.

Corrugated board
Corrugated board is made from a combination of two sheets of paper, called liners, glued to a corrugated inner medium called the fluting. These three layers of paper are assembled in a way that gives the overall structure greater strength than that of each particular layer.

Cover paper
Heavyweight stock used for covers of catalogs, brochures, books, or business cards.

Cromalin proofs
A proofing process in printing that uses photosensitized clear plastic, which is exposed to the image and processed in layers of color to simulate the final printed image.

Cross direction
The direction across the grain. Paper is weaker and more sensitive to changes in relative humidity in the cross direction than in the grain direction.

D

Dandy roll
In papermaking, the cylinder that creates a laid, wove, or watermark effect.

Deboss
The process in which an image is recessed into the paper.

Deckle edge
The feathered edge of paper, created by an air jet or a stream of water as it is being manufactured.

Density
Ratio of the weight of paper to the volume. High-density paper has a high weight-to-volume ratio.

Die
A design cut in metal for stamping, embossing, or die-cutting.

Die-cutting
Male and female dies are used to cut out paper or board in desired shapes.

Dimensional stability
A paper's resistance to dimensional change during production or with changes in humidity.

Dished
Concave rather than flat pile of paper.

Dividers
Tabbed sheets used to identify and separate specific sections of a book.

Dot
Individual element of a halftone-printing plate.

Dot gain
A printing problem where dots print larger than desired, creating darker tones or color imbalances.

Dots per inch (dpi)
A reference for the resolution of a printed or screened image. Higher numbers mean higher resolution, or more dots, composing an image.

Drilling
Precise piercing of stacks of papers with round hollow drills at high speeds.

Dry-end
The part of the paper machine where the paper is dried, calendered, and reeled.

DT cover
Stands for "Double Thick." A sheet of paper made by bonding two thicknesses of paper together resulting in an extra-stiff sheet.

Dummy
An exact, handmade format sample created with blank paper to show the desired size, shape, weight, and general appearance of a project prior to production.

Duotone
Two-color halftone reproduction from black-and-white original.

E

ECF
Elemental Chlorine Free. Paper pulp bleached without the use of elemental chlorine.

Embossed finish
The overall design or pattern impressed in paper when passed between metal rolls engraved with the desired pattern.

End-leaf paper
Strong, fine-quality papers, either plain or coated, and sometimes colored or marbled, used at both ends of a book.

Engraving
Printing by the intaglio process. Ink is applied to the paper under extreme pressure resulting in a printed surface being raised. Used for fine letterheads, wedding invitations, etc.

F

Fanfold
Continuous multiple-ply form manufactured from a single wide web that is folded longitudinally.

Fanout
In printing, distortion of paper on the press because of waviness in the paper.

Feathering
Tendency of an ink image to spread with a fuzzy, featherlike edge.

Felt finish
Uncoated, uncalendered surface texture produced by using patterned felt belts and pressure in forming paper on the paper machine.

Felt side
The side of the paper that does not touch the wire on the paper machine. The felt, or top, side is preferred for printing because it retains more fillers.

Filler
A material such as china clay or calcium carbonate that is added to make paper smoother and increase opacity.

Filling in
A condition in offset lithography where ink fills the area between the halftone dots or plugs up the type.

Film coat
Also called wash coat. Any thinly coated paper stock.

Finish
Term describing the characteristics of a paper's surface.

Flat color
Printing two or more colors without overlaying color dots. This differs from process color, which is a blending of four colors to produce a broad range of colors.

Flatbed press
A press on which plates are positioned along a flat metal bed against which the paper is pressed by the impression cylinder—unlike a rotary press, which prints from curved plates.

Flush binding
A binding where the cover is trimmed to the same dimensions as the text papers.

Foil stamping/blocking
The application of foil to paper where a heated die is stamped onto the foil, leaving the design of the die on the paper. Foil stamping can be combined with embossing to create a more striking 3D image.

Folding endurance
Test made on paper to measure the number of double folds that can be given to a strip of paper clamped between two jaws before it will break.

Folds
See pages 80–81.

Folio
A sheet of paper, folded once to form two leaves (four pages) of a book. Also, page numbers.

Forest certification
See FSC and PEFC.

Formation
Degree of fiber distribution uniformity in a sheet of paper. Uniform distribution is described as close formation, while an irregular one is said to be wild formation. Affects ink absorption and thus the printed image.

Fourdrinier
A paper machine developed by Louis Robert and financed by Henry and Sealy Fourdrinier that produces a continuous web of paper.

Free sheet
Paper that contains little or no mechanical wood pulp (groundwood). Also called wood-free.

French fold
Individual sheets of paper folded in half and bound together at the open, rather than the creased, edge. Sheets folded this way can either be glued together or bound with a coil, posts, or stitches. Often used to avoid double-sided printing.

FSC
Forest Stewardship Council. A worldwide organization that certifies sustainable forestry practices and encourages the use of FSC-certified paper.

G

Gatefold
A four-page insert with foldouts on either side of the center spread.

Ghosting
Unwanted images that develop during the delivery of the printed sheet and are traceable to onpress conditions, ink starvation, form layout, and even to the blanket itself.

Glassine
A glossy transparent paper used for envelope windows and photo bags.

Gloss
A coating on paper that provides a higher reflection of light and results in a shiny appearance. Gloss coatings reduce ink absorption, which allows excellent contrast and color definition.

Gloss ink
An ink containing an extra quantity of varnish, which gives a glossy appearance when dry.

Glossy paper
Paper that has undergone advanced calendering on a supercalender. Steam and pressure are applied to burnish the paper and improve uniform reflection of light.

Grade
The classification given to paper based on its characteristics, including brightness, opacity, cotton content, etc.

Grain direction
The direction of the fibers in paper.

Grain long
The grain of paper is parallel to the long dimension of a sheet of paper—e.g. "45 × 64cm long grain" indicates that the grain is traveling in the 64cm direction.

Grain short
The grain of the paper is parallel to the short dimension of a sheet of paper—e.g. "64 × 45cm short grain" indicates that the grain is traveling in the 45cm direction.

Grammage
The metric term used to denote the weight of paper or board; the measurement used is the weight of a single sheet of one square metre, expressed as grams per square metre (gsm). A good comparative measure because it does not vary with sheet size.

Gravure
An intaglio or recessed printing process. The recessed areas are like wells that form the image as paper passes through.

Gripper
A row of clips that holds a sheet of paper as it speeds through the press.

Gripper edge
Leading edge of a sheet of paper as it passes through the printing press.

Groundwood pulp
A mechanically prepared wood pulp used in the manufacturing newsprint and publication papers.

Guard book
A binding that uses a bulked-out spine to allow for the addition of extra inserts.

Guide edge
The edge of a printed sheet at right angles to the gripper edge, which travels along a guide on the press or folder.

Guide marks
A method of using crossline marks on the offset press plate to indicate trim, centering of the sheet, centering of the plate, etc.

Gutter
The blank space or inner margin on a press sheet from printing area to binding.

H

Half bound
Bound in material of two qualities with the material of better quality on the spine and corners.

Half-title
The title of a book printed on the first page of the text or on a full page preceding the main title page.

Hansetushi
Japanese calligraphy and drawing paper.

Hard-sized
Paper treated with a large amount of size to increase its moisture resistance.

Hardwood pulp
Pulp obtained from deciduous trees (short fibers), which gives good printing quality and imparts high bulk, compressibility, and good opacity to the paper.

Headband
A small strip of cotton or silk used to decorate the top of a book between the sheets and the cover.

Heat sealed
An adhesive paper coating that is activated by the application of heat.

Hickeys
Imperfections in the printed image because of dirt on the press, dried ink skin, paper particles, dust, etc.

High-bulk paper
Paper stock that is comparatively thick in relation to its weight.

Hinges
The flexible joint where the covers of a hardbound book meet the spine.

Hogogami
Ancient Japanese term for recycling.

I

Ikkanbari
Japanese process similar to papier-mâché, used to make tableware and boxes.

Imperial
Premetric British paper sizes based on three core sizes: foolscap, imperial, and crown, which derive their names from the watermarks given by the mills that produced each size.

Index
Bristol paper made for products such as index cards and file folders.

Ink holdout
The degree to which a paper surface resists penetration of ink. An inked image printed on paper with a high degree of ink holdout will dry by oxidation rather than absorption. Higher ink holdout means higher print gloss.

Ink-jet print paper
Printing paper manufactured to produce best results with an ink-jet printer.

Intaglio
Type or design etched into a metal plate as opposed to raised letters as in letterpress.

Internal bond strength
Measure of internal strength of paper and paperboard. Low internal bond strength could lead to picking the clay from the paper when tacky inks are used.

Interscrew
Metal or plastic screw and threaded tube used to bind loose leaves in a portfolio.

ISO
International Standards Organization paper and board sizes. See pages 234–237.

J

Jacket
The paper cover of a hardbound book. Sometimes called the dust cover.

Japanese stab binding
This technique is ideal for binding single sheets of paper. The thread passes through each hole a number of times to complete the pattern. The front and back covers are attached to the text block by decorative stitching at the spine.

Jog
To align sheets of paper into a compact pile.

K

Kaolin
White clay used as an additive and filler in paper and coating.

Key plate
In color printing, the plate used as a guide for the register of other colors. It normally contains the most detail.

Kirigami
Japanese paper art where the paper is cut rather than simply folded.

Kiss impression
Printing performed with only slight pressure. The normal procedure for quality printing.

Kraft
A kind of strong, smooth manila paper used for wrapping.

L

Label paper
Paper coated on one side, used for labeling applications.

Laid finish
The paper surface made by a dandy roll covered with evenly spaced parallel lines. (The ribbed impressions are actually watermarks.)

Laminated
Paper created by fusing one or more layers of paper together to create the desired thickness and quality.

Laser cutting
Using a laser ray to evaporate the paper to create a very precise cut.

Letterpress printing
Print technique that uses type or designs cast or engraved in relief on a variety of surfaces, including metal, rubber, and wood. The ink is applied to the raised printing surface. Nonprinting areas or spaces are recessed.

Lignin
Noncellulose material found in wood and other cellulose plants; lignin in paper makes it weaker and more inclined to discolor when exposed to light.

Linen finish
A paper surface design made by embossing the paper with a linen-cloth pattern.

Lip
The allowance for overlap of one half of the open side edge of a folded section, needed for sewn and saddlestitch binding, for feeding the sections.

Lithography
The process of printing that utilizes flat inked surfaces to create the printed images.

M

M weight
The weight of one thousand sheets of paper of a specific grade and size, or double the ream weight.

Machine coating
Applying coating to paper on the paper machine on which the paper is made.

Machine dried
Process of drying paper on the paper machine as opposed to air drying the paper after removal from the machine.

Machine finished
Paper that is calendered on the paper machines, but is not supercalendered to give a very smooth finish or gloss. Has good bulk and is often used for book manufacturing.

Margin
The unprinted area around the edges of a page.

Matte finish
A dull, clay-coated paper without gloss or luster.

Mechanical pulp
Same as groundwood pulp. Pulp produced by grinding logs and wood chips into pulp.

Micrometer
Instrument used to measure the thickness (caliper) of paper.

Mill brand
Paper which is brandnamed by the manufacturer as opposed to the merchant house, which is known as a private brand.

Millpack
A quantity of between 100 and 125 sheets of paper.

Moiré
Geometric pattern caused when two screened images are superimposed at certain angles. Occurs when making a halftone from a halftone image.

Moisture content
The amount of moisture in paper, normally ranging between 5 and 8%.

Mold made
An imitation handmade paper manufactured on a cylinder-mold machine.

Mottle
A spotty or uneven printed surface, which is most apparent in solid areas.

Mullen tester
Device that measures the bursting strength of paper.

N

NAPM recycled mark
The National Association of Paper Merchants' scheme for designating a paper as recycled. To qualify, a grade must contain at least 75% recycled fibre.

Natural
A term to describe papers that have a color similar to that of wood. Also called cream, off-white, and ivory.

Nested
Signatures assembled inside one another for binding as opposed to gathered.

Newsprint
The relatively low-grade paper on which newspapers are printed; it is mainly produced from mechanical pulp and recycled fibres.

Nordic Swan
An environmental label promoted by the Scandinavian governments as an international standard, awarded to products meeting appropriate criteria to reduce environmental impact.

O

Octavo
A book size resulting from the use of standard size sheets of paper folded three times to make eight leaves or 16 pages.

Offcut
Paper of usable size obtained as a by-product when larger sheets or reels are cut down to the size of the order.

Offset lithography
The most commonly used lithographic printing method, whereby the printed material does not receive the ink directly from the printing plate, but from an intermediary cylinder called a blanket that receives the ink from the plate and transfers it to the paper.

Offset paper
An uncoated sheet specially suited for offset printing.

Onionskin
A lightweight, cockle-finish paper used for making copies of correspondence.

Opacity
Property of paper that minimizes the showthrough of printing from the back side or the next sheet. A paper with low opacity is more transparent.

Optical whitener
A dye that is added to the fiber stock or applied to the paper surface at the size press to enhance its brightness.

Orange peel
A granular surface on coated or printed paper that looks like orange peel.

Origami
The Japanese art of folding paper.

Out of register
Descriptive of pages on both sides of the sheet that do not back up accurately. Also, two or more colors that are not printed in the proper position, so where the register does not match.

Out of square
Paper trimmed improperly so that the corners are not a true 90°.

Overhang cover
A cover larger in size than the pages it encloses.

P

PAA
Paper Agents Association.

Pagination
In computerized typesetting, the process of performing page makeup automatically.

Paperbound
A paper-covered book. Also called paperback or softcover.

Paper grades
Paper is classified into different grades according to the end use, the pulp used, and the treatment of the paper.

Paper master
A paper printing plate used on an offset duplicator.

Paper surface efficiency
Measure of the printability of a sheet of paper, dependent on the amount of ink the paper absorbs, the smoothness of its surface, and the evenness of its caliper.

Papeterie
A special watermarked or embossed paper used for stationery.

Papier-mâché
French for chewed paper, a construction material that consists of pieces of paper, sometimes reinforced with textiles, stuck together using a wet paste of glue or starch. The object hardens when dry and is light yet strong.

Papyrus
An early form of paper made from the pith of the papyrus plant. First known to have been used in ancient Egypt, it was also widely used throughout the Mediterranean region as well as inland parts of Europe and southwest Asia. The origin of the word paper.

Parchment
A thin material made from calf, sheep, or goat skin. It differs from leather in that it is not tanned, but stretched, scraped, and dried under tension.

Parent sheet
Any sheet larger than A3.

Pasted
Grades of paperboard or paper made up of layers pasted together.

PCF
Process Chlorine Free. Indicates that fiber is recycled and is unbleached or bleached with nonchlorine compounds. PCF papers cannot be considered totally chlorine-free because of the unknown bleaching process of its recycled content.

PCW
Postconsumer Waste. Indicates material that is collected from end users and recycled. The preferred form of recycled material because it reduces pressure on forests, saves water and energy, and diverts waste from landfills.

PEFC
Program for the Endorsement of Forest Certification. A scheme for auditing forestry operations, taking into account the effects on the environment.

Perfect binding
Method of binding books in which all the pages are converted to single sheets. They are then held in a clamp and attached to a cover with an adhesive.

Perfecting press
Commonly referred to as a perfector. Press that prints both sides of the sheet of paper at the same point.

Perforate
Punching a series of holes or slits in a line in the paper to weaken it so tearing will occur easily along that line. Also the making of slits in paper during folding, at the fold, to prevent wrinkles and to allow air to escape.

PH value
Degree of acidity or alkalinity measured on a scale from 0 to 14 with 7 the neutral point.

Piling
A buildup of pigment or paper coatings onto the plate, blankets, or rollers.

Pin holes
Tiny holes in paper caused by fine particles of foreign matter on the paper surface during manufacture. When paper is calendered, the particles are crushed and fall out leaving a hole.

PMS®
Pantone Matching System®. The most widely used ink color system. The color number and formula for each color are shown beneath the color swatch.

Pocket
Paper or other material made into a pocket, with or without gussets, affixed inside the front or back cover of a book. May be made separately and glued in after binding or made over the lining sheet in a case.

Point
A measurement unit equal to 1/72in. There are 12 points to a pica, 72 points to an inch.

Porosity
The property of paper that allows the permeation of air, an important factor in ink penetration.

PPI
Pages per inch, a measure of bulk.

Press
During manufacture, the paper web passes through sets of rolls called the press, either to remove water from the web at the wet press, to smooth and level the sheet's surface at the smoothing press, or to apply surface treatments to the sheet at the size press.

Proofs
Samples of copy and layout produced at various stages of production.

Pulp (chemical)
Pulp obtained through the elimination of a large proportion of noncellulose matter through a chemical treatment.

Pulp (mechanical)
Pulp obtained from various raw materials, mostly wood, entirely through mechanical means.

Pulp (semi-chemical)
Pulp obtained when eliminating the noncellulose components from the raw material by means of a chemical treatment.

Q

Quarter bound
Bound in material of two qualities with the material of better quality on the spine only.

Quarto
A book size resulting from the use of standard-size sheets of paper folded to make four leaves or eight pages.

Quire
A specific quantity—24 sheets of handmade, or 25 sheets of machine-made paper.

R

Rag
Often meaning cotton rags, formerly the principal raw material used in the papermaking process.

Rag content
The amount of rag fibers in a sheet, between 25 and 100%.

Ream
A specific quantity—480 sheets of handmade or 500 sheets of machine-made paper.

Recto
A right-hand page of an open book or front of a loose document.

Recycled paper
Paper made from old paper pulp. Used paper is cooked in chemicals and reduced back to pulp after it is de-inked.

Reel
A continuous length of paper wound on a core.

Refining
The mechanical treatment of pulp fibers to develop their papermaking properties.

Register mark
Mark placed on a form to assist in proper positioning of after-printing operations.

Registration
Alignment of printed images upon the same sheet of paper.

Right side
The felt side of a sheet, also the side on which the watermark, if any, may be read.

Roll size
The width of a roll of paper.

Rosin size
A size added to paper to make it water resistant.

Rotary press
Printing press in which the plate is wrapped around a cylinder.

Rub-off
Ink on printed sheets, which smears when handled after sufficient drying.

Runnability
Paper properties that affect the ability of the paper to run on the printing press.

S

Saddlestitch
The binding of booklets or other printed materials by stapling the pages on the folded spine. Also called saddle wire.

Satin finish
A smooth, delicately embossed finished paper with sheen. Also called silk.

SBS
Solid Bleached Sulphate. A type of heavyweight board that is a single thickness run on a Fourdrinier paper machine using sulphate-produced pulp.

Scoring
Impressing paper with a rule to make folding easier.

Screen angles
Technique used in four-color printing, which sets halftone screens at various angles to avoid moiré patterns.

Section
Folded signatures.

Self-cover
A cover made out of the same paper stock as the internal sheets.

Sewn book
A style of bookbinding in which the signatures are gathered in sequence and then sewn individually in 8s, 16s, or 32s. The sewing threads are visible at the center of each signature.

Sheetfed printing
Printing onto flat sheets as opposed to a web, offering greater control of register.

Sheridan saddle stitcher-trimmer
A machine used to gather, cover, stitch, and trim saddlestitch books.

Showthrough
The condition in which the printing on the reverse side of a sheet can be seen through the sheet under normal lighting conditions.

Side stitch
Stapling sheets or signatures on the side closest to the spine. Pages cannot be fully opened to a flat position.

Signature
Section of book obtained by folding a single sheet of printed paper in 8, 12, 16, or 32 pages.

Silkscreen printing
Print from a stencil imagemaker where the ink is applied by squeegee through a meshed fabric screen.

Silverprint
A proof print made from single negatives that are used to produce the final proof prior to printing.

Singer-sewn
A method of side or fold sewing printed matter, such as brochures, with thread. Despite the fact that the term implies the use of a particular machine, it has come to be a generic term for the sewing of publications that would ordinarily be stitched.

Size/sizing
The process by which gelatin, rosin, starch, or any other synthetic substance is added to paper to provide resistance to the absorption of moisture or eliminating ink feathering and bleed through. Sizing added to the vat of pulp is known as internal sizing. After a sheet is formed, it may be either surface sized (painted or brushed on the surface) or tub sized (immersed in a bath).

Size press
Section of paper machine where surface treatments are applied to the sheet of paper to give it special qualities.

Smoothness
Texture of the surface of paper. Also called its finish. Measured by the time required for a given volume of air to flow between the surfaces of the paper sample and a piece of optically flat glass under standard loading conditions.

Smyth sewing
A method of fastening signatures side-by-side so that each is linked with thread to its neighbor, as well as saddle-sewn through its own centerfold. Smyth-sewn books open flat.

Soy-based inks
Environmentally friendly inks that use vegetable oils rather than petroleum products as pigments.

Spiral binding
Wires in a spiral form inserted through specially punched holes along the binding edge.

Spot color/varnish
Ink or varnish applied to only a portion of the sheet as opposed to an overall application.

Spread
Two adjacent pages opened out flat.

Stab binding/stitching
Binding a large number of sheets by driving metal staples over halfway through the back margins from both sides.

Stability
The quality of paper to maintain its original size when it undergoes pressure and moisture changes.

Stamping
Pressing a design onto a book cover using foil or ink, applied with metal dies.

Starch
Material used as a surface or internal additive to provide strength.

Stochastic screening
A digital screening process that converts images into very small dots (between 14 and 40 microns) of equal size and variable spacing. Second-order screened images have variable-size dots and variable spacing.

Stock
In papermaking, refers to the wet pulp before it is fed onto a papermaking machine or during the papermaking processes before it becomes a sheet of paper; contains around 99% water and 1% fiber. In graphic arts, stock means paper.

Stretch
The give of a sheet of paper as it undergoes tensile pressure.

Strikethrough
Penetration of printing ink through a sheet of paper.

Sulfate pulp
Alkaline process. Paper pulp from wood chips and pressure-cooked in a solution of caustic soda and sodium sulfide. Also known as kraft.

Sulfite pulp
Acid process. Paper pulp made from wood chips cooked under pressure in a solution of bisulfite of lime.

Supercalender
Machine for giving paper a very smooth surface by passing it through a series of alternate metal and composition rolls, revolving with high speed and pressure.

Swiss binding
Binding where cloth is adhered to the spine and hinge, with the cover glued to the back hinge.

Synthetic papers
Papers made from synthetic rather than natural material, Tyvek®, for example.

T

Tabbing
During binding, the cutting or adhering of tabs on the edges of pages.

Tag
A dense, strong paper stock.

TCF
Totally Chlorine Free. Paper pulp that is bleached without using chlorine in any form.

Tear strength
Force parallel to the plane of the specimen required to produce failure in a specimen of given width and length under specified conditions of loading.

Tensile strength
The ability of a sheet to withstand tension. Paper possesses greater tensile strength in its grain direction.

Text papers
High-quality book papers, manufactured in a wide variety of designer finishes and colors. Many mills feature matching cover-grade papers.

Thermochromatic ink
Ink that changes color with changes in temperature.

Thickness caliper
Thickness of paper in millimeters or thousandths of an inch.

Tip in
A sheet or section incorporated into a book by means of a strip of adhesive.

Titanium dioxide
Pigment made from titanium ores, which is of minute particle size and has great opacifying and brightening properties when added to papermaking furnish.

TMP
Thermomechanical Pulp. Pulp made by steaming wood chips prior to and during refining, producing a higher yield and stronger pulp than regular groundwood.

Tooth
A characteristic of paper, a slightly rough finish, which permits it to take ink readily.

Translucency
Ability to transmit light without being transparent.

Twin-wire machine
Fourdrinier papermaking machines with two wires instead of a wire and felt side. This assures higher quality when two sides are used for printing.

Two-sidedness
The property denoting a difference in appearance and printability between its top (felt) and wire sides.

Tyvek®
Manufactured by Dupont from very fine, high-density polyethylene fibers, Tyvek® offers all the best characteristics of paper, film, and fabric in one material. Often used for envelopes.

U

Unbleached
Paper not treated with bleaching. It has a light-brown hue.

Uncoated
Paper that has not been coated.

Underrun
An order produced or delivered that is less than the quantity specified by the customer.

UV coating
A very slick, glossy coating applied to the printed paper surface and dried on press with ultraviolet (UV) light.

V

Varnish
Thin, protective coating applied to a printed sheet of paper for protection or improved appearance.

Vellum
A toothy surface, relatively absorbent for good ink penetration.

Vellum paper
Very strong, good-quality, cream-colored or natural paper made to impersonate calfskin parchment.

Verso
A left-hand page of an open book or the back of a loose document.

Virgin pulp
Pulp manufactured and used for the first time.

W

Washi
Traditional Japanese papers made from the long inner fibres of three plants, *wa* meaning Japanese and *shi* meaning paper.

Water finish
High finish produced on paper or board as it passes through the calender stack by moistening one or both sides with water.

Watermark
The image impressed into the formation of paper by the dandy roll on the wet end of the paper machine. Can be seen by holding the watermarked sheet up to the light. Can be either a wire mark or a shaded image.

Waviness
A form of paper curl resulting when the sheet edges in the pile absorb moisture that the center of the pile cannot absorb or the sheet edges surrendering moisture while the center remains moist.

Web
The roll of paper that is used in web or rotary printing.

Web break
A tear in a web roll during the printing process.

Web press
A printing press that prints on rolls of paper passed through the press in one continuous piece, as opposed to sheets of paper. Pages are separated and cut to size after they have been printed.

Weight
Weight or grammage of a sheet of paper (usually in gsm).

Wet strength
Papers made by the addition of a resin to the stock during paper manufacture. They retain an appreciable percentage of their mechanical strength after soaking in water.

White lined board
A multi-ply construction made predominantly from selected waste paper.

Whiteness
The paper is perceived to be white because of high clarity, elevated diffusion, and minimum perception of hues.

Wire side
The side of a sheet next to the wire in manufacturing; the opposite of the felt or top side. Usually not as smooth as the felt side.

With the grain
Folding or feeding paper into a press parallel to the grain.

Wood-free
Pulp and paper that contains little or no mechanically ground fibers. Implies that fibers are chemically treated, thereby eliminating lignin (which binds wood fibers in the tree) and making the product purer, whiter, and stronger. Woodfree is a historical papermaking term shortened from groundwood-free, and does not denote a paper or pulp made from materials other than wood.

Wood pulp
Wood reduced to a pulp for subsequent papermaking processes. Can be mechanical, chemical, or a combination.

Wove finish
A sheet with impressions in it formed by a dandy roll covered with woven wire.

Wraparound cover
A cover that is not attached to the pages beneath, simply wrapped around them.

Wrong-read image
A mirror image such as that appearing on the blanket in offset printing.

X

Xerographic paper
Papers made to reproduce well in copy machines and laser printers.

Y

Yellowing
A transformation caused by aging, inherent to all vegetable fibers. Yellowing is very evident in groundwood papers and only a few hours in direct sunlight is enough to yellow newspaper.

Z

Zig-zag folding
The fanfolding used on continuous forms to convert roll paper to a continuous flat stack of forms.

ABSOLUTE ZERO°
www.absolutezerodegrees.com

ALOOF DESIGN
www.aloofdesign.com

ART MEETS MATTER
www.artmeetsmatter.com

B&W STUDIO
www.bandwstudio.co.uk

BRUKETA&ŽINIĆ
www.bruketa-zinic.com

CARTER WONG TOMLIN
www.carterwongtomlin.com

CAT CHOW
www.cat-chow.com

CHARLES S. ANDERSON DESIGN
www.csadesign.com

CRAIG KIRK
www.craigkirk.net

CURIOUS
www.curiousdesign.com

DALZIEL + POW
www.dalziel-pow.co.uk

DESIGN PROJECT
www.designproject.co.uk

DIANA FAYT
www.dianafayt.com

DOSHI LEVIEN
www.doshilevien.com

DYNOMIGHTY
www.dynomighty.com

EGELNICK AND WEBB
www.egelnickandwebb.com

EGG
www.eggusa.net

FACTOR DESIGN
www.factordesign.com

FELTRON
www.feltron.com

GUM
www.gumworld.com

HENRY HOBSON
www.henryhobson.co.uk

HYPERKIT
www.hyperkit.co.uk

IS NOT MAGAZINE
www.isnotmagazine.org

JENNIFER COLLIER
www.jennifercollier.co.uk

featured designers

JENNY OREL
www.roteprinzessin.de

JHI
http://jhigoodidea.com

JOHNSON BANKS
www.johnsonbanks.co.uk

KINO DESIGN
www.kinodesign.co.uk

KNOCK KNOCK
www.knockknock.biz

konnectDESIGN
www.konnectdesign.com

LAURA COOPERMAN
www.lauracooperman.com

LEGALIZER
www.legalizer.dk

LO-TEC
www.lo-tec.co.uk

LUCY JANE BATCHELOR
www.lucyjanebatchelor.me.uk

MARK BOLITHO
www.creaselightning.co.uk

MILK, TWO SUGARS
www.milktwosugars.org

NEXTBIGTHING
www.nextbigthingcreative.com

NOTHINGDILUTED
www.nothingdiluted.com

PAPERPOD
www.paperpod.co.uk

PAUL COCKEN
www.paulcocken.co.uk

PEARLFISHER
www.pearlfisher.com

POP INK
www.mrfrench.com/popink.asp

ROUNDEL
www.roundel.com

SHIN TANAKA
http://shin.co.nr

SQUIRES & COMPANY
www.squirescompany.com

TANGO
www.tangodesign.com

theFARM
www.the-farm.co.uk

THINK TANK MEDIA
www.thinktankmedia.co.uk

TREVOR PITT
trevorpittuk@aol.com

V23
www.v23.biz

VOLUME INC.
www.volumesf.com

WINK
www.wink-mpls.com

YANG RUTHERFORD
www.yangrutherford.com

3M RADIANT FILM
www.3m.com

ACCENT®
www.internationalpaper.com

AGRIPINA
www.igepagroup.com

ALEZAN CULT GAZELLE
www.gmund.com

ARCHES WATERCOLOR PAPER
www.arches-papers.com

ASTROBRIGHTS
www.wausaupapers.com

CARNIVAL
www.smartpapers.com

CELLOGLAS
www.celloglas.co.uk

CHALLENGER OFFSET
www.mcnaughtonpaper.com

CHIYOGAMI PAPER
www.paper-source.com

CHROMOLUX
www.zanders.com

CHROMOMAT
www.arjowigginsfinepapers.co.uk

CLASSIC CREST
www.neenahpaper.com

COLORPLAN
www.gfsmith.com

CORONADO BRIGHT WHITE
www.foxriverpaper.com

CORVON IRIDESCENTS
www.fibermark.com

COUGAR OPAQUE SMOOTH TEXT
www.weyerhaeuser.com

CRANE & CO, NATURAL WHITE
www.crane.com

CURIOUS COLLECTION
www.arjowigginsfinepapers.co.uk

CYCLUS
www.mcnaughtonpaper.com

ERA SILK
www.mcnaughtonpaper.com

ESSENTIAL SILK
www.paper.co.uk

FINCH FINE
www.finchpaper.com

FRENCH CONSTRUCTION
www.mrfrench.com

FRENCH SMART WHITE
www.mrfrench.com

GO! SILK
www.roberthorne.co.uk

featured papers

HELLO SILK
www.roberthorne.co.uk

IKONO SILK, IKONO SILK IVORY, IKONO GLOSS, IKONO MATT
www.zanders.com

IMPRESSIONS TEXTURES
www.arjowigginsfinepapers.co.uk

INCADA SILK
www.mcnaughtonpaper.com

KASKAD
www.roberthorne.co.uk

MAINE CLUB GLOSS
www.paperco.co.uk

MATRISSE COTTON
www.fennerpaper.co.uk

METAPHOR
www.curtisfinepapers.com

MODO
www.m-real.com

MOHAWK BRILLIANT WHITE
www.mohawkpaper.com

MOHAWK TEXTURES
www.mohawkpaper.com

MONADNOCK ASTROLITE SMOOTH
www.mpm.com

NYTEK NOVASUEDE
www.nytek-usa.com

OKI BANNER PAPER
www.oki.co.uk

PARILUX
www.roberthorne.co.uk

POP'SET
www.arjowigginsfinepapers.co.uk

PRINT SPEED
www.antalis.co.uk

REINCARNATION MATTE
www.newleafpaper.com

REVIVE UNCOATED
www.roberthorne.co.uk

SAPPI HANNOART, SAPPI MAGNO SATIN, SAPPI ROYAL XPRESS
www.sappi.com

SCHNEIDERSÖHNE LUXOSATIN
www.schneidersoehne.com

SKYE UNCOATED
www.mcnaughtonpaper.com

SPECKLETONE, DUR-O-TONE, PARCHTONE, MOD-TONE
www.mrfrench.com

SPLENDORLUX BIANCO
www.fedrigonicartiere.com

SPRINGHILL®
www.internationalpaper.com

TAPESTRY RANGE
www.gfsmith.com

TOPKOTE
www.topkotepapers.com

TRANSPARENCE FLEUR
www.gmund.com

TRIPLEX
www.roberthorne.co.uk

TYVEK®
www.tyvek.com

UPM FINE
www.upm-kymmene.com

UTOPIA ONE X
www.appletoncoated.com

VERUS OMAR
www.gfsmith.com

WAUSAU PAPERS EXACT OPAQUE
www.wausaupapers.com

ZANDERS EFALIN FEINLEINEN
www.zanders.de

ZANDERS SPECTRAL
www.zanders.com

ZEN
www.gfsmith.com

ZETA AND ZETA RECYCLED
www.zanders.com

index

ACKNOWLEDGMENTS
First, we would like to thank all the designers who generously devoted their work and spent valuable time giving us information for the book. Many thanks for their support to Lindy Dunlop, Tony Seddon, and April Sankey at RotoVision. As always, many thanks to Spike. Finally, special thanks to Shin Tanaka, who offered to create a special colorway of one of his Mask Hoody characters exclusively for the book.

ABOUT THE AUTHORS
Keith Stephenson is the founding director of London-based branding and design agency Absolute Zero°, whose work encompasses corporate identity, packaging, and retail design. The studio's diverse output includes a range of interior-design products, comprising wallpaper, fabrics, and ceramics.

Mark Hampshire is a brand consultant and head of strategy at Absolute Zero°. Prior to his branding career he worked as a television researcher and was one half of furniture-design partnership Hampshire and Dillon.

Together they have also written *Communicating With Pattern: Stripes* and *Communicating With Pattern: Circles and Dots*, both for RotoVision.

acknowledgments